AMERICA THE BEAUTIFUL OR AMERICA THE CAPUT?

AMERICA THE BEAUTIFUL OR AMERICA THE CAPUT?

RAYMOND W. CONVERSE

Algora Publishing
New York

Library of Congress Cataloging-in-Publication Data

Converse, Raymond W.
   America the beautiful or America the caput? / Raymond W. Converse.
      pages cm
   Includes bibliographical references and index.
      ISBN 978-1-62894-156-2 (soft cover: alk. paper) — ISBN 978-1-62894-157-9 (hard
cover: alk. paper), ISBN 978-1-62894-158-6 (eBook). 1. United States—Politics and
government—2001- I. Title.
   JK275.C665 2015
   320.973—dc23
                              2015027252

Printed in the United States

Table of Contents

PREFACE

This book was written with everyone in mind who is tired of the constant slamming of America; the constant mudslinging rhetoric of professional politicians and the blame game. A steady diet over the last five years consisting of TV talk shows, cable and mainstream news programs, newspaper op-eds, magazine articles and scholarly books brought me to the point of mental bankruptcy. Regardless of where I looked, all I could find is opinions of gloom and doom, upcoming crisis and the blame game.

I decided to attempt to sift through the information to determine for myself whether it contained even a kernel of truth. It quickly became apparent that one of two positions was true: either America is still the beautiful or it is on the verge of becoming caput. My conclusion is that America is still beautiful — but is in need of some tender loving care.

I am not a sociologist, economist or scientist, let alone a talk show host, journalist, professional politician or renowned scholar. I am what I think my reader is: educated, informed and a concerned voter. As such I have relied mainly on common sense and everyday experience to draw a picture of what I see as the real America. I expect that my readers will draw their own conclusions, but I hope this book will goad into action the people who matter most.

Chapter 1. American Foreign Policy

The United States was founded when the Constitution was ratified 226 years ago (in 1789). The Constitution, the contract between the American people and their government regarding how liberty, individual freedom and equality would be protected from tyranny, announced three major political principles. First, all the major offices of the federal government were to be filled either through direct election by the people (the House of Representatives) or appointed by individuals who had been elected directly by the people (President and Vice-President through the Electoral system and Senators by the state legislatures).

This system was a stark repudiation of direct democracy. The men who wrote the constitution did not trust either professional politicians or the passions of the people. The first principle, therefore, was that the new nation should be a Republic based upon representative democracy. The second principle expressed in the constitution was that of federalism. Under this concept the US was to consist of three levels of relatively sovereign governments, i.e., the federal government, the various state governments, and the local governments. This principle again represented the lack of trust held by the founding fathers in the nation states that had appeared in Europe. They did not want a truly national government in which the federal level held all the sovereign power and delegated whatever power it wished the state and local governments to have. At the same time, they also had experienced the Articles of Confederation and knew that the federal government needed to have substantial sovereign power. The constitution was to delegate the powers that were to be held by federal government; and also to deny certain powers to the states. The local governments (the people) were to retain all sovereign power not delegated to the federal government or denied to the states. In short, the intent was that the power of the federal government would be strictly limited to the powers delegated, and that the States would hold a majority of the sovereign power while the local governments would execute all the laws of the land. The latter provision was to keep the power of government close to the people to insure that it was justly enforced and that it could be properly controlled.

American society was to be governed by the rule of law rather than the caprice of government. This clearly indicated a distrust of any form of tyranny, whether it be individual or the majority of voters. The Constitution was to be the supreme law of the land, with the states holding a secondary position, and the laws being enforced at the local level where government was personal. It is in this division of government, under the principle of federalism, that was to be the main guarantee of liberty, individual freedom and justice or democracy as it was then understood. The Constitution as ratified also contained the first ten amendments (the bill of rights) which guaranteed certain rights both to the states and to the people that weren't mentioned directly in the Constitution. The clear intention was that the majority of sovereign power would lie with the state and local governments. The local governments, it was felt, would be the most informed concerning the needs of the people, and most likely be best placed to justly apply the actions taken to resolve those needs. This would also allow the people the most direct access to having whatever grievances they had to be heard by their political representatives. The third principle was found in the Constitutional provisions that set up the three divisions of the federal government. There were to be checks and balances that would prevent one branch of government from tyrannizing over the other two, as well as specific Articles setting forth the powers and duties of each branch. It was expected that government service would be a burden borne by the people most qualified (substantial property holders, businessmen, and the educated) rather than by professional politicians. The terms of service would be short enough to not become too large a burden and give the people an opportunity to replace those they no longer wanted to serve. Although this was not explicitly mentioned in the Constitution, the founding fathers clearly set forth their negative feelings regarding political parties.

It is these relatively few political principles that are being questioned today in terms of how the US system operates. A growing number of voices are screaming as loud as possible in warning that these political principles no longer hold sway in the society. Some are even claiming that the US is no longer a democracy, but rather, something akin to either an oligarchy or an aristocracy of professionals. It is evident that those making these claims are indicating that they don't believe that the US represents a republic based upon representative democracy. This will be one of the major sources of investigation to be followed here in attempting to determine if the US is in fact still operating under its traditional political principles. If not, then an attempt will be made to determine whether anything should or could be done to reinstate these political principles; as well as, to determine what might have replaced them. This segment of the investigation will be done in connection with the investigation of the traditional economic principles that were found in the early US.

Once again there are relatively few traditional economic principles that need to be taken into consideration. First, the main line of economic thought found in the early US was the concept of the importance of private property. This concept included the equally important concept of the need to protect the right of contract and the importance of the rule of law in protecting both principles. Second, the US was founded on the belief that the only way a democracy could survive was if it operated under the free market system economy. The main intent under this concept is that the "invisible hand" of the market would be given as free a play as possible to determine how the economy would operate, that is, the market was to operate with as little governmental intervention as possible. This was, of course, the basis upon which the economic system of capitalism was based. Included within the basic economic principles were the individual principles, or concepts, of individualism and self-reliance.

There are many voices again being raised today in warning that the US has lost its reliance on the free market system, individualism and self-reliance. The fear is that government intervention has reached a point at which capitalism is no longer sustainable and that it will be replaced with a socialist-type economic system (controlled economy); or that it will collapse completely within the near term.

In most scenarios the traditional political and economic principles operate together to produce a viable democratic system. The aim of this book is to investigate the claims to see whether there is any truth to them and, if so, to assess whether anything should or could be done about it if, in fact, they are no longer operating in this fashion.

In the attempt to investigate these claims two major areas will be concentrated on: first, whether or not the US system is still operating as a federal republican representative democracy; and two, whether or not the US is still operating in the economic sphere as a free market capitalistic system. Although the founding fathers did not use the term capitalism they were aware of the principles set forth by Adam Smith concerning the free market system and its supposed connection with the political concepts of liberty, freedom and justice. The concept is somewhat more complicated today; but democracy as we know it is still seen as dependent upon the operation of the free market system. Three, a look must be taken at how the US involvement in international affairs affects the two principles set forth above and whether this policy adds to or detracts from the ability to maintain them. There are in addition demographic changes that have taken place within the US domestic scene that must be investigated to see what, if any, effect they have had on the above principles. Societies are constantly subjected to changes that effect the perception of the people and these also must be taken into consideration. The answer to this investigation should determine whether it is still America the Beautiful or America the Caput.

It would seem reasonable to assume that the area that would have the least effect on the principles set forth above would be international affairs, or foreign policy decisions. This being said this area will be the first to be looked at in detail.

The reason for this relatively lengthy look at the foreign policy of the US is to show what effect, if any, this policy has on the traditional principles set forth above. The early US, indeed for the first 120 years of its existence, i.e., until roughly 1918, approached foreign policy with an attitude of laissez faire. George Washington set the tone for US foreign policy at his farewell address by warning the political leaders of the time to avoid all overseas entanglement, especially in relation to the wars of Europe. This advice was largely heeded until the First World War. There was international contact between the US and the rest of the world but it was not seen as capable of interfering with the flow of American domestic life. The US was largely involved in foreign affairs along two major lines, that is, some local military actions and in the area of trade. The military actions were largely involved with the expansion of the US across the continent and involved mostly Indian nations. The War of 1812, for example, was fought over a perceived interference by Great Britain with US expansion into the Ohio Valley through exciting Indians nations to raid settlements in the area. The US was successful on the Great Lakes against the British navy, but the US capital was invaded, occupied and burnt. The end result, however, was the establishment of a firm border with Canada and the US in sole control of the Ohio Valley. The same result came about in the short war against Spain in 1819 when Andrew Jackson invaded Florida to stop Indian raids into Georgia. Here the US ended up using the invasion as a bargaining chip to buy Florida from the Spanish government. In the short war with Mexico in 1846 the war was fought to protect US citizens from Indian deprivations and Mexican governmental regulations; it ended up with the US taking control of the whole of the now American Southwest. It was not until the second war with Spain in 1898 that the US began to extend its concerns beyond the expansion of the US at home. The military action took place in Cuba as a result of the bombing of the warship

Maine. The result was again the taking of additional territory, that is, Puerto Rico, the Philippines and other small islands. The consequences of this war were determined by the fact that the US had already become one of the major global trading partners, especially in Asia, making the territorial acquisitions a national interest.

As stated, the second major area in which American foreign policy was found is the trade arena. This began with the purchase of Louisiana in 1805 giving the US control of the Mississippi and the port of New Orleans. This was followed up in 1823 with the Monroe Doctrine that essentially attempted to set all of Latin America aside as an American free trade zone. The doctrine was set forth when it became apparent that the leading European colonial powers were eyeing a reestablishment of colonies in Latin America. Although the US did not have the legal status to justify this doctrine, nor the military power to enforce it, it did effectively stop all new colonial action in Latin America. By 1900 the US had become a major player in the manufacturing, financial and trade carrying sectors of global trade. This had involved the US in various treaty arrangements both formal and informal. This in turn altered the effect that international affairs had on the domestic scene. The US, however, up until at least 1900 can be seen as essentially isolated from world affairs. As a result the foreign policy of the US had very little effect on the domestic scene of the US, that is to say, foreign policy had little effect on the traditional principles set forth above prior to 1900. All societies, however, are subject to constant change and the US was no exception. We will see later the effect of these changes on the traditional principles under consideration later.

The first real departure from the early laissez-faire policy (isolation) came with the US entry into the First World War in 1917. In response to the needs of the war the Wilson administration set up the National War Labor Board and the War Industries Board which were given the power to set prices, set wages, ration products needed for the war effort, and generally to control the economy of the US. The war also removed some 4 million men out of the work force. The First World War represented the first major intervention into domestic US affairs directly caused by foreign policy decisions. The powers that were assumed by the federal government during the war seem in retrospect to be authorized by the earlier progressive actions of Theodore Roosevelt in reaction to the development of domestic business monopolies and the practices related to them. In this instance there had been legislation passed to deal with this phenomena. Roosevelt, as President, decided to ignore the statutes and to handle the problem through executive action with the creation of the Bureau of Corporations and the new Department of Commerce. This was the first real departure from the former laissez faire policy in regard to the domestic economy. More will said about this aspect when attention is turned to domestic processes affecting the traditional economic principles. The precedent had been set by the Wilson administration actions taken during the First World War; however the American public, through its representatives, made it clear that they wanted a return to a foreign policy based on isolation (laissez faire). The vigorous attempt by the Wilson administration to involve the US in the League of Nations failed to pass congress, and the US entered into what has become known as the "roaring twenties".

The two decades between World War I and World War II was to prove to be the last hurrah of the old isolation policy. During this period, however, the US involvement in global trade, manufacturing and finance continued to grow. The Second World War brought even greater government control of the economy. In this case, however, the American public did not ask for a return to isolation after the war, but rather, accepted the fact that the US was a major player in international affairs.

It is, therefore, only after 1940 that it is reasonable to ask the question of how foreign policy affects the traditional principles in question. The US is today heavily entangled in international affairs. This is a fact that no one can seriously deny. The US military budget is larger than that of all other nations combined and represents 25% of the total GDP of the US. The loss of human and material assets since 1940 has been enormous by any calculation. The question is what effect has this had on the traditional political and economic principles under review. First, the three major post war conflicts, that is, Korea, Vietnam and the War on Terrorism resulted in a change in how the US treats its domestic population. The Patriot Act, for example, gave the US government powers to open private banking records and to tap into private phone conversations (among other things) to detect domestic terror activities. There seems to be little doubt that the Patriot Act impinges on individual rights that are clearly protected under the Constitution. The only way that this could be justified is through the issuance of a court order overriding the constitutional protection on the basis of imminent danger to the public. This was, however, specifically waived within the wording of the act, that is to say, the government was given the power to act without a search warrant or a court order of any type. The Homeland Security Agency was given the power to arrest people and hold them as prisoners without the benefit of the rule of law, as was the National Security Agency. American citizens could be, and were, arrested for suspected terrorist activities without the benefit of civil rights as they could be held in military prisons and put under military law. These actions followed the early use of Alien and Sedition Acts to bar public criticism of actions taken during World War I, the imprisonment of Japanese-Americans in holding camps during World War II, and federal actions to prohibit protests during the Vietnam War. The cost of the military, including the arms race, the race into space, and the race for clients (foreign aid), coupled with the cost of the various wars has been at least partially responsible for the large budget deficits, national debt, and stagnant economy that has come to the forefront of today's domestic issues. In addition, the US has become very active in global solutions to problems such as environmental pollution, global warming, and the defense of whole regions, such as Europe, Japan, and Latin America. The US has also been drawn back into its role as the world's policemen in the Middle East and the Ukraine. It is argued by one side that the US foreign policy decisions have limited the freedoms and legal rights of citizens at home. It is also claimed that the drag on the economy from international affairs is at least as large as that of domestic policies. The conclusion, however, in reference to this inquiry, is that foreign policy decisions have directly affected the operation of the traditional political and economic principles within the US. The most serious effect is arguably to be found in the effect of foreign policy on the traditional economic principles. This aspect will be looked at in relation to the domestic scene later in the book.

Chapter 2. Domestic Issues: Political and Economic

There appear to be two main ways in which the two sides to the argument see the picture being presented. The one side wants proactive foreign policy to continue while allowing the domestic affairs to take care of themselves as has always been the case in the past. The Other side wants a more proactive approach to domestic affairs while letting international affairs to take care of themselves (a policy of at least modified isolation)

It is certainly true that all the administrations that have held office for the last four or five decades have entered into power with the intention of concentrating on domestic issues. It is equally true that all of them for one reason or another have ended up focusing most of their attention on international issues rather than domestic issues. George H. W. Bush entered office with a campaign promise to concentrate on domestic issues but spent most of his time handling the Gulf War that removed Iraq from Kuwait. Bill Clinton entered into office with the intention of creating a national health care system and other equally important domestic programs. He also became bogged down in international affairs including the break-up of the former nation of Yugoslavia, and the Israeli–Palestinian conflict, among others. He was, however, able beyond all others who have served since 1989 to deal with domestic issues. For example, he was able to negotiate a compromise within congress providing for a balanced budget for four years before running out of time in office. George W. Bush spent five years on efforts to battle terrorism leading to unilateral decisions to invade Iraq, to avoid a UN settlement in Afghanistan, and to deal with the destruction of the financial and investment communities. Barack Obama has been unable, due to the deadlock in congress, among other reasons to accomplish much in either the international or domestic arenas. He was successful in passing the first comprehensive national health care act in US history at the beginning of his first term but has been unable to follow this up with any type of success in the domestic arena. He still has three years left on his second term in office but is faced with a hostile congress. He has begun an initiative that includes diplomatic activity on the international front consisting of an implementation of a new foreign policy initiative. He has been successful in opening negotiations for the destruction of Syria's chemical weapons, mainly through the assistance of Russia's leading politician Vladimir Putin; and has also opened up negotiations with Iran over their nuclear power program. Either of these, if successful, could easily be his signature accomplishments as President. The negotiations, it is important to remember, are in lieu of strong demands both at home, and from allies abroad, for military action in both Syria and Iran. The only real competition for the spotlight during this rather long period on the domestic front came from the bursting of the high tech bubble; the failure of the iconic manufacturing corporations and financial institutions; the bursting of the housing bubble and the onset of the so-called "Great Recession." All of these important domestic issues deserve to share the spotlight with developing international affairs; however, these domestic issues so far have not been approached with any positive solutions. All of this has brought on nostalgia for the "do-nothing" days of the Eisenhower administration and the relative peace and quiet of the Reagan through the Clinton administrations. Whether this nostalgia is for something real or not is highly debatable. The "glorious fifties" may not have been so glorious and the balanced budgets of the Clinton years may be nothing more than a temporary aberration.

The end result—regardless of how one believes the US got to where it is today; or how the US should react in the future to its current conditions—is the following. First, the US economy is expected, depending on whose predictions one is using, to grow at no more than 1 or 2% of national GDP over the next few years (read 3 to 10 years). Second, the expected growth rate of the economy is universally seen as incapable of reducing the accumulating rate of permanent unemployment among American workers. Third, because of the growing level of permanently unemployed citizens, temporarily unemployed citizens, and retired citizens, there will be no substantial reduction in the cost of the welfare state in the near term future. This means that over the near term the size of budget deficits and sovereign debt will continue to grow. The real question appears to be not which one of these scenarios is the correct one but whether or not these predictions are based upon what is in reality occurring within the United States and globally.

It might be best to start from a less technical point of view. A position can be taken where the domestic political system is set forth in terms of how it is operating today (what is the status quo). When a large picture is drawn the main feature that stands out is the ideological stalemate that has appeared. US politics has throughout its history been very contentious to say the least. In the past it was argued that, although contentious, the political disagreements never reached a stage at which it became impossible to compromise. Indeed, it is fair to say that when push came to shove and the people's interest came to the forefront, a compromise solution was always attained to solve the problem. Since at least 2010 the disagreement in political positions has not only been contentious but ideologically frozen in nature. In terms of political positions ideology is used here to describe a general set of operating principles that are beyond the ability to compromise. In the broadest terms the ideological positions are a demand for limited government and a delegation of power back to the state and local governments, on the one hand; and on the other hand, a demand for bigger government in terms of its activism into every area of life; and the continued growth of the bureaucracy to support this position. All issues that have come before congress, and the administration, have been cast in the light of this ideological dialog. There are for all practical purposes only two positions being taken.

On the one hand, in the case of the twin problems of a very sluggish, if not negative, rate of economic growth and large scale unemployment the solution is either to deal with them by increasing the amount of money spent on infrastructure projects, technological research and investment projects and the development of a more effective educational program (this is what has come to be known as economic stimulus per se. Also included in this spending program are the various QE programs consisting of billions of dollars of bond purchases per month by the Federal Reserve). The intent is to stimulate the economy into a level of economic growth that will sustain current consumer spending levels and also create enough jobs to eliminate the unemployment problem. It is expected under the tenets of this position that the various spending programs will boost the economic growth rate into the range of 3.5% of national GDP over the next two or three years. The year 2013 ended with a nominal growth rate of less than 2%. This means that 2013 showed no additional growth in tax revenue; or more likely an actual decrease in tax revenue. Should the economy over the next two or three years attain a 3.5% growth rate or more, then the increase in tax revenue would, of course, be substantial, and it would be achieved without a tax rate increase on the middle class; but it does include increasing the tax rate to be applied to the wealthiest tax payers and corporations. This is expected to increase revenues over the next ten years in amounts that would allow for a balanced federal budget, or at least a substantial decrease in annual budget deficits. The only cut in spending envisioned by this plan is focused on the military budget. The beginning of 2013, in fact, saw the beginning of the sequester cuts mandated by congress in 2012, with a large share of these cuts being applied to the military budget. Lastly, this position is calling for a general reform of both the taxation system and the welfare system. The former would consist in establishing, or reinstating, a truly progressive tax rate. Currently half the tax payers making less than $75,000 a year pay no taxes at all. At the other end, the top one percent of tax payers are currently paying a lower percentage than those who make under $150,000 per year. The loss of revenue to the various governments in total is staggering. The reform of the welfare system is based upon the need to maintain the benefit level for those now drawing the benefits or expected to start drawing them within the next ten years (Social Security). Those beyond this exemption will face a later retirement age (68); and a reduction in benefits earned. This plan is one that most people find compatible with the Democratic Party and the current Obama administration.

The other position takes the stance that the sluggish economy and unemployment problems can only be overcome by reducing federal spending as well as spending at the lower levels of government, especially in relation to what they claim to be the major driver of budget deficits and sovereign debt, that is, the welfare system. Within the welfare system this position is particularly focused on the reduction of spending on the part of the federal government in relation to Social Security, Medicare and Medicaid, although they propose in addition that all federal and state entitlement programs receive serious attention. This reduction in welfare spending would be accompanied by a reduction in the tax rate applied to the income on corporations (the business community generally, but in particular the taxes on small to medium sized businesses). The result of both the spending reductions and the lowering of corporate taxes would be an economic stimulation through the increased creation of good paying permanent jobs. In the view of this position it is small and medium sized businesses that drive both the growth rate of the economy and the production of jobs. In addition, it is the innovative processes used, or developed, by these businesses that will allow the US to be competitive both domestically and internationally. Regardless of how the economy is brought back to robust growth rates the result is the same, that is, a large increase in available revenue to the various governments. The most important aspect for the position currently being studied, at least as it relates to the federal government, is the creation of an environment in which these businesses will be comfortable in making the needed investments over time. The federal government can accomplish this by reducing the level of taxation on these businesses and by reducing the level of regulation that is applied to them. The federal government can also aid these companies in their investment projects by reducing the cost of providing health care and other non-wage benefits required via federal regulations. This position also takes a stand on the need for reform of both the taxation and welfare systems but for totally different reasons. While the former position seeks reform of these systems in order to keep them in place, the latter would use the reforms to reduce the programs to the lowest level of benefits feasible, if not total elimination of the programs where possible (such as the creation of private retirement accounts to replace SSI). This is the position most often applied to the Republican Party and most loudly proclaimed by its tea party wing.

These two positions have been locked in a vigorous stand off from at least the mid-term elections of 2010. The standoff is where the ideological issue becomes truly apparent. Reduced to its lowest possible denominator the democrats are seen as desiring more government in terms of spending and the growth of the bureaucracy; while the republicans are seen as demanding a limited government in terms of spending and personnel. Any attempt by either party to present legislation that would advance either ideological program is immediately opposed in total by the opposite party. The standoff has produced several serious self-inflicted wounds in the eyes of the American public. The first wound resulted from the standoff between the congressional members over raising the federal debt ceiling so that the bills already contracted by the federal government could be paid. If the federal government was denied an increase in the debt ceiling the result would be an eventual default by the government on its existing debt. Up until this point the debt ceiling issue has always been a non-issue, that is to say, the increase in the debt ceiling had been granted without much debate. This time, however, the issue could not, or was not, allowed to come to a vote until the so-called 11th hour. The authorization to increase the debt ceiling was finally given only for a period of a few months. The result of this standoff was the reduction of the US credit rating from AAA to AA+.

Second, and even more noticeable, was the uneasiness brought to the business and financial communities as a result of this tempting of financial fate. This uneasiness brought about a call to come to a longer term solution through the obtaining of a "grand deal" between the administration and congress. The Administration, for its part, called for the creation of a committee, which became known as the Simpson-Bowles Commission. This commission was charged with coming up with recommendations for spending reductions amounting to $1.5 trillion over three years; and revenue recommendations of an equal amount that would bring down the current budget deficits. As an incentive for congress to seriously consider these recommendations it was written into the legislation that created the commission that if the commission failed to come up with these recommendations, or the recommendations were not made law, that an automatic level of spending reductions would go into force beginning March 1, 2013. This has since been labeled the process of sequester and over three years will amount to some 1.5 trillion in spending reductions.

March 1 was soon dubbed the "fiscal cliff" by those who foresaw the occurrence of terrible fiscal consequences if these automatic spending reductions were put in action. It is now obvious that the administration and congress were unable to come to a grand deal and the US has, at least partially, gone over the fiscal cliff. Part of the peril of the fiscal cliff, however, was avoided, that is, the provisions calling for the elimination of the Bush Era Tax cuts were reduced in effect to elimination only in the case of those in the top 5% of income. The two-year moratorium on withholding taxes for Medicare were allowed to expire and hit those at the lowest level of income directly. This had little effect on the wealthy as they are not subject to withholding taxes.

Lastly, the debt ceiling and "doc fix" legislation were kicked a little further down the road. The original legislation, as it applies to spending, was left in place and will over the next three years force a congressional debate over additional spending reductions on a regular basis. Already another standoff over raising the debt ceiling came to the front burner. It was again kicked a little further down the road, but will reappear in the short term.

The wounds also include a severe drop in the credibility ratings of both the administration and the congress on the part of the American public. The worst ratings, however, seem to belong to the Republican Party, which the public appears to blame most for the standoff overall. In fact, the Republicans did very well in the mid-term elections giving truth to the statement that Americans have a short memory. The focus of the standoff is found in the question of how the US federal government will react to the problems facing it, that is, a sluggish economy, high rates of unemployment, increased levels of budget deficits and increasing levels of sovereign debt, among many other problems.

This same ideological standoff can be found when one considers some of the social issues involved in the overall picture of problems facing the US. These are essentially all bound up in the issue of whether the federal government should be proactive, or passive, in relation to regulating the issues involved. There are several issues that have over the last few years been brought in front of the American public. The earliest may have been the initial round of corporate failures, including such iconic names as General Motors, Chrysler and others. The decision was made to bail out these companies by loaning them money through the federal government. The theory was that these companies were too large to fail without causing serious damage to the overall economy. It was expected when the bailouts were made that the companies involved would over a relatively short period of time pay back the money. This, in fact, over the last few years has proven to be a valid expectation; the money (except for roughly 40 billion) has in fact been paid back and the tax payers have even seen a small profit on this money. The second round came with the bursting of the housing market which caused the near meltdown of the financial and investment community. Once again the approach was to bailout the institutions affected. The most evident issue was the collapse of Lehman Brothers prior to the time that financing could be arranged to save it (the repercussions of this failure were global in scale). Although the housing market failure is thought to have resulted in the onset of the Great Recession, it was much milder than expected. In this case the bailout was not as favorable to tax payers, as there was no provision for the money to be repaid (most of the 700 billion set aside was used for other purposes), and there was no serious attempt to prevent repetition of the behavior that led to the melt down in the first place. Many feel that the banking and investment industry is once again putting itself in the position where another round of failures is inevitable.

The last great social issue is the manner in which both the business community and private citizens are being regulated in their daily activities by the federal government. Once again the dichotomy of solutions is to be found; first, the Democratic Party is calling for a more proactive reaction by the federal government; while the Republican Party is calling for a removal of the federal government from a large portion of its regulatory responsibilities; and calling for this activity to be delegated to the state and local level. Once again, whether the specific issue is immigration reform, environmental regulation, business regulation, or the regulation of banks and investment corporations no agreement can be expected on the federal congressional level until after the 2014 mid-term election, and more likely until after the 2016 Presidential election. Therefore, while both sides of the debate are attempting to reach the same goal, that is, robust economic growth; a full employment environment; the return of the long term unemployed to the labor market; a rational amount of regulation leading to an environment that is comfortable to both the business and financial communities; to promote investment in long term productive endeavors, among others, they cannot agree on how to accomplish these goals. As a result they cannot find enough agreement between them to even determine the parameters of the debate. The result is that very little, if anything, of substance has been accomplished by either the administration or congress over the last five years. A break in the standoff also seems very unlikely, at least, in the short term. The

Republicans won control of congress in the midterm election of 2014 and great changes are being promised. Time will tell whether these promises, or predictions, will be converted into real action. The pundits are already predicting continued deadlock due to intraparty disputes over policies and the reluctance of the President to accept the mandate of the election as they see it. At any rate there is little expectation of progress in resolving the issues in the short term. In the meantime the American people, or at least the majority of them, continue to see a steady decline in the real value of their income and a real decline in the value of their assets.

The latest two issues to fall prey to the stalemate, and which tends to show the depth of the stalemate, were the recent gun and immigration reform legislation. The first was legislation presented as a result of the massacre in Newtown, CT. This tragedy, for a short period of time, brought the issue of gun control to a full boil. It was clear that the overwhelming desire of the American Public was that some form of gun control, in particular, control of certain weapons (the so-called assault weapons), should be passed. The congress, however, could not set aside its ideological debate to pass even a watered down version of the original legislation. The last issue was made equally clear during the congressional recess, that is, the American people overwhelmingly were in favor of the passage of comprehensive immigration reform legislation to deal with the 11 million illegal residents now residing in the United States; and the increase in unescorted juveniles coming over the border. Once again the congress could not lay aside ideological positions long enough to even generate a vote on the legislation offered before recessing for its five week summer break. In essence the desires of the American people do not seem to make a difference in the positions taken by their elected representatives. The same is not true, however, in the case of the various interest groups. These interest groups are well organized, and well financed, giving them the political clout to make their desires known to congress. The National Rifle Association was certainly heard in the debate over the fate of the gun legislation; and the business interest groups were clearly heard in their opposition to the immigration legislation. In relation to this issue many experts are claiming that a majority of those now serving in congress have over the years been able to redefine their districts in such a way as to create "safe seats." This is to say, that regardless of the position they take; or any position that might be taken by any minority within their district, their reelection is guaranteed. This has led to some members of congress serving for decade after decade up to a half century. The net result is not that individual members may not be reelected but that it is getting more difficult to change the overall makeup of the congressional houses. The Republicans, as noted above, now control the congress with a surprisingly sound defeat of the Democrats. It is, however, already being questioned whether they will be able to hold onto these gains through the 2016 election. If deadlock continues they may not be able to repeat in 2016. Even in the case of issues which are not constantly in front of the American Public, and are therefore rather tangential to the ideological battle, there appears to be no desire on the part of the members of congress to seek compromise. What is evident, on both sides, however, is the desire to place the blame squarely on the back of the other party, or under some circumstances on the back of the administration, especially the personal policies of Barrack Obama. Should this deadlock continue, for whatever reason, it would seem unlikely that any of the problems facing the US will receive attention even if the economy should enter into a robust period of growth. In that case, however, the pain felt by the American public would not be great even though the problems remained.

Chapter 3. Specific Domestic Issues: Political and Economic

The political and economic arena is not the only area in which significant issues are facing the US. In addition to our economic and political woes there are a series of technical problems that are in need of resolution. For example, the investment community for the first time in two hundred years is faced with a situation in which there are no safe havens for money. Essentially this boils down to the fact that there are no forms of investment that carry a zero, or near zero, risk. Prior to the 2008 crisis the purchase of sovereign bonds, which give a relatively small return on the money invested, carried a near zero risk of non-payment. These sovereign bonds where in fact a safe haven for money in times of financial distress. The same was for a long time true of the purchase of gold, at least, during the period that gold was used to expedite currency exchange, as a similar safe haven. The latter became untrue with the demise of the Breton Woods Treaty by which all currencies became valued in relation to the dollar. Gold is now more or less a commodity traded in today's markets as another form of investment, although for some it still represents a sort of insurance against devaluation of currency. The result, according to some experts, is that the federal government now has the power to print whatever amounts of money it might need, as is evidenced by the QE program. These economists are claiming that the near default and haircut taken by investors in the case of Greece exemplifies the risk now associated with sovereign debt. The claimed lack of sustainability of much of the industrialized world's sovereign debt has changed the nature of the risk in buying these bonds. The bonds still retain their low rates of return, while at the same time seeing an increase in the amount needed to service this debt, adding to the perceived risk of owning them. This has resulted in an environment that has forced investors into the stock market for a reasonable chance for profit.

The massive influx of money into the stock market, on the other hand, has led to the over-evaluation of stocks resulting in the creation of a stock market bubble as unstable as that of the housing market in 2008. Economists expect that the bursting of the stock market bubble to have repercussions that will dwarf even the effects of the housing market bubble collapse.

A second technical problem is found within the economy overall. This problem involves the conversion of the economy from one based on manufacturing to one based on the providing of services. The effect of this conversion, according to the experts studying these phenomena, could be as wide spread economically as the conversion of the economy from an agricultural base to an industrial base during the industrial revolution. The manufacturing base was highlighted by its creation of vast numbers of good paying, permanent, low skilled jobs; indeed, it is credited with the creation of the middle class as it is known in the United States. On the other hand, the service based economy is highlighted by the creation of temporary, low-paying, unskilled jobs. This conversion is seen as the reason for the decline in the real value of middle class income and assets. It is being claimed that the end result of this conversion will be an increasing gap between those who are gainfully employed and those who are not. In short, the middle class, according to this view, is expected to disappear over time unless the middle class can reeducate to obtain the skills necessary to enter the high technology fields. Such alterations within society take a relatively long time to become evident, maybe as long as a generation or two. In the meantime more and more people who are losing the long term good paying manufacturing jobs will be forced to take the less well paying temporary or part time employment offered by the service sector.

There is at least one consideration outside the control of the American system that may change this environment. The areas of the world that saw an influx of American manufacturing operations due to low labor costs, low rates of non-wage benefits, and favorable regulatory environments are altering their systems. The workers are beginning to demand higher wages, higher levels of benefits, regulations controlling the destruction of the local environment, and other provisions that raise costs. Over time this could indeed produce a situation where domestic American manufacturing operations will once again become competitive in the international arena. However, this also will take time; and will in addition require the wherewithal to update, or rebuild, the manufacturing plants and equipment, as well as, to expand and repair the existing infrastructure to support a rebirth of manufacturing. These requirements for the rebirth of manufacturing are the basis of the claim that once manufacturing jobs are lost to an economy they never return in great numbers. Even the experts that are claiming that overall American competitiveness is increasing are concerned that this spike may just be a temporary event. Agreement among the experts seems to be relatively universal that the most likely way in which a new American middle class will be constituted is by the creation of new industries not now known; but which will become known through the advance of new technological breakthroughs. This will result in the creation of more high paying, stable jobs as was true of the earlier manufacturing base; and decrease the number of lower paying less stable jobs. This over time will result in the reconstitution of the American middle class.

The other side of the argument is claiming that the continued destruction of the middle classes will result in the lower and middle classes merging into one large class. The lower class of this two class system will represent about 80% of the income producers and the upper class will consist of roughly the remaining 20%. The lowest segment of the lower class will represent about 25% of the lower class and will be living at or below the poverty level; while the upper reaches of the upper class will represent about 1% of the upper class and be made up of those who are wealthy beyond measure. Many of the jobs held by those making up the lower upper class will require high levels of skill and/or a relatively long apprenticeship while getting the needed education and the flexibility that allows for changes brought about by rapidly evolving technology. The top 1% essentially will be composed of the very wealthy and will constitute what can reasonably be seen as a sort of new aristocracy. As a result the experts holding this view are predicting that the "new normal" will consist of an economy that rarely, if ever, exceeds 2% per year of national GDP in terms of growth and unemployment levels that rarely fall below 10% overall (and will exceed 40 or 50% in some specific areas such as the inner urban and very rural communities).

Although it is never really talked about, but is to be expected nevertheless, there will be a significant increase in black market activities, crime, immigration and discontent (some see this as already apparent in the inner urban areas). There can be little question that the real value of assets among the majority of U.S. households will continue to decline over the relative long term. The housing bubble left millions of people upside down in relation to their largest asset, that is, their home. This not only caused millions of mortgage foreclosures, but also put so many houses on the market that they could not be sold. Even those who were not upside down in relation to this asset did not escape the result of the housing bubble. They saw the value of their homes decrease by 30 to 50% in most areas — and more, in the rest. In some rare cases, such as the City of Detroit, houses were on the market for as little as five dollars. In addition, the effect of the collapse of the housing market occurred in such a way that the investment community as a whole appeared poised to collapse. The losses sustained by the investment community, in particular those holding retirement packages, such as 401Ks, saw a reduction in their cash value of up to 70%. This was a direct reduction in the value of the assets held by the middle class in particular. Much of the loss of value that early on was seen in the stock market has been replaced by the movement of investors from the bond market back into the stock market. This has resulted in the recoupment of most of the losses to retirement packages such as 401Ks, with the exception of those that were being drawn upon for retirement income. The recoupment of the losses represented by the value of houses, however, has not yet been fully repaired. Experts in this field are confident that the full value of the housing assets will never be recouped. The same is true of those accounts which were being used as high risk investments (401Ks) during the downturn.

In addition to the private sector one need also to take into consideration the debts found at the state and local governmental levels. Recently several cities, including the City of Detroit, have filed for and received bankruptcy protection. The step into bankruptcy has forced the unions, the workers, and existing public pension beneficiaries to take a considerable reduction in wages, income benefits and pension benefits; while the people of these bankrupt units have been forced to accept reduced services, including infrastructure repair. Many of these cities, including Detroit, are poised to survive these changes and once again become viable cities, but on a reduced scale. At the state level the problem seems to revolve around the lack of funding in the governmental pension plans, Welfare benefits, or a combination of both. Illinois, for example, has a public pension fund that is underfunded by nearly $110 billion. Although some legislation has been recently passed to correct this shortfall over time (30 years), the state public service employees union is instituting a lawsuit attempting to get this legislation set aside as unconstitutional. The Illinois problem is the largest in the nation, but others are not far behind. This type of problem has caused the various state and local governments to be listed as undesirable credit risks which means, of course, that they cannot borrow money (sell their bonds) at a reasonable interest rate. Should Illinois, or even a medium-sized state, go bankrupt, there would seem to be no way that they could be bailed out and they would end up going the same direction as Detroit. For the employees currently drawing benefits from these pension plans, and for those who are close to retirement, the real value of these funds has been diminished to near zero should the state go bankrupt. At the very least this problem will not be resolved without a cut in current levels of benefits, and even lower levels of benefits being offered in the future. This is the approach being taken by Illinois, even though it means breaking the promises made to those drawing benefits. The union lawsuit is based on an Illinois law that makes it illegal to lower existing benefits. The first stage of this suit has upheld the union position and has ruled the legislation unconstitutional. The overall process is still underway, however, and appeals are being taken by the State of Illinois.

All in all these reductions in the value of real middle class assets coupled with the declining real value of middle class income clearly show the effect of the Great Recession in the United States. In the case of the wealthy, the following anecdote will explain what they are facing due to these rather technical problems. In an investment video discussion of the economic effect of the sovereign debt debacle, the following point was made. In 2003, an investment of $10 million in sovereign bonds would have produced a yearly income of $480,000 (approximately a 0.048% return) with almost zero risk. Today the same investment would produce a yearly income of $240,000 (approximately a 0.024% return) and carry the same risk as any investment made in the regular stock market. The real value of old money has also dropped significantly. The conclusion was that one could not retire in today's environment with a $10 million nest egg. While this may be true of the top 1% of income earners, there are, of course, many millions of people who are retired, or retiring, that do not have anything approaching that amount. Even more pertinent is the fact that many millions of people are working in a market that does not provide enough income for them to save or plan for retirement at all. These people will work all their lives or find a way to exist on Social Security benefits, as millions of others have already done. There can be no question, therefore, that the solution to these problems has very real consequences. The Japanese, and many European nations, are much closer to the realization of the stated consequences than the citizens of the US; but the problems and the consequences are the same everywhere in the industrialized world. These types of problems have tended to deepen the overall dependency of millions of Americans on the various federal and state welfare programs, which some claim is leading directly to a loss of individual freedom.

A technical problem that has come to the forefront on a social (civil rights) level is that of illegal immigration into the United States. This problem has many aspects, some of which are receiving little attention. The most technical portion of the problem is the long porous border shared by the United States and Mexico. Over the years it has proven next to impossible to stem the flow of illegal immigrants crossing this border. There are at least two major explanations for this, namely, it takes a very large sum of money and manpower to adequately guard the border, and further, it is to the benefit of both the United States and Mexico *not* to stop these migrants. It is estimated that the money returned to Mexico by these workers now amounts to nearly 30% of Mexico's national GDP. For the United States, the workers perform jobs that most American workers either cannot or will not do for the wages that are offered. One example would be the harvesting jobs found in American agriculture. Many growers, at least according to the growers themselves, could not provide an affordable product (if they could provide a product at all) without this source of low cost labor. The wages the workers receive are competitive with those offered by growers in low-wage countries and these workers receive little, if any, non-wage benefits. This latter is one of the most active complaints among the US citizen taxpayers who are footing the bill for the education of the migrants' children, as well as for their health care, school lunches, etc., etc. Another problem stems from the fact that nearly 11 million illegal immigrants, according to government figures, now reside in this country permanently. In many states, and especially in cities close to the border, immigrants represent a majority of the resident population. It is distressing that a significant number of these 11 million undocumented residents have found a way to participate in the various welfare benefits offered by the state and federal governments. And, although technically they are not supposed to vote, very few attempts are made to enforce this voting rule.

At any rate, the problem has now boiled down to two areas of concern. First, legislation is needed to determine the status of the 11 million people already residing in the US and who are in many ways participating in the society. The question remains how to allow them to become legal residents of the US, or how to deport them back to their country of origin. The latter seems to be out of the question for logistical reasons and the former has found serious resistance from, at least the employers who depend on this labor, at the federal level. The problem is most noticeable at the state government level through active lobbying activities. Second, the problem of what to do about stemming the flow of illegal immigrants coming across the border on a daily basis; especially the rapidly increasing numbers of unescorted juveniles; from Central America has become an emotionally charged issue. It has been suggested that a fence be built along the entire border with Mexico. This has been tried along sections of the border (California and Texas) but does not seem to have been particularly effective. Some states have been relatively rigorous in their enforcement of their deportation laws but also have had little overall success. These are apparently ineffective mainly due to the fact that those deported simply return at the first chance. In addition, the Obama administration through executive order has halted active deportation procedures, at least temporarily. A solution seems to be out of the question, even though one might exist, as long as illegal immigration remains in the interest of both nations. Should Central America find a way to control the existing violence; and should Mexico become economically robust enough to employ all of its unemployed workers, or even nearly all of them, the problem of immigration would dry up on its own. The US, in the belief of many, will no doubt legalize the 11 million people who currently reside permanently in the US and may also offer some effective resistance to further immigration; however, the latter seems to be unlikely. It would be more likely that the immigration laws will be reformed to allow a fast track to legal residency for those who come and little effort will continue to be made in reducing incoming illegal immigration. In addition it is already apparent that the US will do whatever it takes to house, educate and care for the estimated 90,000 unescorted juveniles expected to cross the border in 2014 alone. Once again it appears that this problem has deepened the need for a continued welfare system, if not a greatly expanded system.

Looking at these problems one at a time are there any obvious solutions that stand out? For example, we could take a look at the spending binge that the national government has been on for the last few decades. No one questions the fact that deficit financing is a major problem. From just the point of view of common sense everyone knows that one cannot sustain for long a situation in which more money is spent than is taken into the coffers. At some point the debt reaches a point where it cannot be repaid and the creditors call in their marks. The whole concept of a balanced budget is based on this simple fact of life. Most of the highly industrialized nations are spending amounts that exceed their revenue by many multiples. The US, for example, last year alone spent $1.5 trillion more than it had in revenue. The 1.5 trillion that was spent over revenue was obtained by borrowing it on the credit of the US through the sale of sovereign bonds. The $1.5 trillion was then added to the outstanding sovereign debt already accumulated by the federal government. This sovereign debt now stands at some $17 trillion. This currently represents, according to the experts in this field, about 90 to 100% of national GDP. In prospective it can be noted that only one nation has been able to survive a debt ratio of more than 100% of GDP and that was Great Britain nearly 100 years ago. The British debt at that time was estimated to be 150% of GDP. Today there are several nations that have exceeded even this amount. Greece is an example of a modern nation that was not able to survive this type debt ratio; and had to rely on a bail out by the EU and negotiating a deal with its bond holders to take a significant loss on their investment. Japan, on the other hand, has survived a debt ratio of nearly 350% of GDP for nearly 20 years. Only recently, however, Japan has asked for permission to devalue its currency and by this method eliminate much of its debt (by exporting it to other nations); in the end this again means a loss in value of the bonds and currency for those who invested in their bonds and who will suffer from the effects of the inflation produced. Most highly industrialized nations are in even worse shape than the US but are still hanging on with bailouts from the EU or internal reforms of some type. These include Italy, Portugal, Spain, Ireland and others. If Spain, Italy or France should go the route of Greece there would not be enough money available to bail them out and probably no investors capable of taking such a loss. It is for this reason that the holding of sovereign debt has gone from a zero risk game to a risk that is essentially equal to the risk of investment in the stock market. Although many expected the sovereign debt issue to explode in the short term it has not yet done so. However, all reasonable predictions would indicate that these debt ratios will become worse over the next three to five years no matter what is done. In the US, for example, it is predicted that the national debt will grow by another $5–7 trillion by 2020, that is, to the amount of $21 trillion or 150% of GDP.

The crisis has receded into the background for the time being, but the problem remains as strong as ever. Japan, the EU, or at least the EZ, could still collapse under the weight of its combined national debts. The US will also suffer a serious economic downturn although it may survive the short term talked about here. Should the stock market bubble that many believe is now in existence burst the situation will be much different. If the statement is correct that a very large amount of the money before being invested in sovereign bonds is now being invested in the stock market; and that this spike in investment has led to the over-evaluation of the stocks on the market, then one can expect a serious correction over the near term. There can be no question that such an event will have a very serious effect on the economy, including the possibility that it will hasten the growth of the sovereign debt ratio crisis. In short, there are still several scenarios that could produce the collapse of the national and global economies into something similar to the correction that took place in the 1930s.

One aspect of this problem that is not discussed in any detail is the total amount of debt that exists within the society. Some have predicted that if all debt in the private sector, the corporate sector and the state and local governmental institutions were added to the federal debt the total would be over $285 trillion, which represents something on the order of 16 times the GDP of the US. Most experts seem to agree that such large numbers are unsustainable for even the short term. Any series of defaults, even at the state and local levels, would force the bankruptcy of the investment and banking institutions in the US; and shortly thereafter the business institutions and the private sector. This is, in fact, what happened with the collapse of the global economy in the 1930s. Of course, most of the nations will survive but what the economic environment will look like after the correction is anyone's guess.

The most obvious choice is to accept the fact that a collapse is more likely to occur than not to occur. By accepting this fact the debate can shift from when and if to what will we need to do to survive. First, all the nations affected by this correction will need to adapt their policy to the fact that recovery will take a relatively long period of time. The shortest amount of time that is being predicted is five to seven years, the longest a generation. Recovery from the 1930 depression, if it is any guide, took over a decade to take place; and might not have happened even then without the economic stimulus of World War II production. It is reasonable, after taking a look at the current environment, to conclude that the conditions for a third World War do not exist. There will undoubtedly be large scale social upheaval, and much suffering, but the conditions do not exist for an all-out world war.

The correction itself will undoubtedly produce a society that will in many ways be unrecognizable by today's standard. A very significant lowering of the general standard of living will be pervasive. The increase in black market activity, crime, and violence will also be widespread even if it does not end in insurrection or civil war. The unemployment rate is likely to exceed even that of the 1930s and reach a general level of 35% or more; with pockets of unemployment, especially in the inner urban areas and very rural areas, reaching near 100%. In the end, large countries like China and India, among others, may find it possible to cope only by breaking up along already existing regional divisions. China and India have long had semi-autonomous regions within their federal structure and it would take little for these regions to return to a fully autonomous existence (as has happened in Iraq). The same is true of many other nations, such as the Russian Federation, some Eastern European nations, Indonesia, and the Middle East. The real basket cases would still be in Africa and Latin America, where poverty and starvation would be rampant. The result would likely be the largest movement of populations from south to north and from east to west ever experienced in the history of mankind. All of these issues would need to be faced realistically by the nations affected.

The issue is not that something along this line will happen, if the collapse does occur for whatever reason, but what will be the most likely reaction on the part of the state, local and federal governments; and even more importantly, on the part of the people, when it does happen.

Whatever reaction comes from the various governmental levels, it is likely that it will be the result of dealing with the reaction of the people under their jurisdiction. It is very difficult to imagine a situation in which people will be forced to live in some type of primitive lifestyle such as the one depicted in the movie "Mad Max"; but in certain areas this already appears to be close to the truth. The violence in some of the Central American countries has many factors similar to the movie; not to mention some of the inner urban areas of the United States. Life will remain basically social in nature; but it will be impossible to count on the various governments to maintain the level of services provided today. For example, we can anticipate that there will be no garbage services, a decaying sanitation system, a decaying of public water systems and a slowly decaying of infrastructure systems (bridges, roads). This will be the case even in those countries where such services are limited to the urban areas. The local and state governments will have no financing to respond to these breakdowns. Whatever will be done in these areas of concern will be done by the people themselves, just as they were years ago. In the areas of the US that will be affected, garbage will be burned or buried in the backyard, by those who make it; roads, bridges, streets will be repaired by the people who use them; water will be obtained from wells; and sewage will be treated by private septic systems constructed by the people who use them. Much of what is needed in terms of food, clothing, and shelter will be bartered for through a system of local trade-offs or produced locally through gardens, sewing clubs, and building parties. It would be reasonable to expect the rebirth of many of the social institutions that were abundant when life was more local. The church, the library, the schools, local chambers of commerce and many others would become more important in daily life than they are today. The state and federal governments will continue to exist but with much less responsibility, or duty, attached to them. The states will largely be responsible for the major highways, the collection of taxes, and the basic laws governing the society. The federal government will be back where it started, that is, responsible for the defense of the nation, or its parts, the regulation of the monetary system, the regulation of a standard system of weights and measures, a post office and the general welfare of the citizens of the country. There will be no "welfare" system as such; there will be no intervention into civil rights; no nation-wide regulatory system and no large professional bureaucracy. Manufacturing and business in general will again be focused on local, at most regional, systems of product creation and distribution. It will be all that can be made profitable for a considerable period of time, possibly a generation or so. This is one possible scenario; there are others, but they all would be similar to the one described but maybe not as drastic in nature in most cases. The problems will be so large that they will not be capable of being handled in any other way than in a piecemeal manner. The problems will have to be broken up into their local manifestations and be handled at the local level, whether that level is the lowest level or the state level.

It is also reasonable to conclude that the larger the country in terms of territory and population the more difficult it will be to get a handle on the reaction to the collapse. For example, the collapse of the Greek economy has created very little of significance in terms of an alteration of the standard of living in Greece. Unemployment has grown, emigration out of Greece, especially among young male adults has grown, the size of the population living in poverty has grown, but not as much as one would expect, and much is now being done through the black market and barter to relieve the pressure on the individual. Life in Greece has not become unrecognizable, however, even outside of Greece itself. What would have been the case had not the EU and the investors involved (EU central banks) stepped in to relieve the situation is unknown. It can justifiably be suggested that the situation could have been much worse. Some predict that social unrest would have been widespread and violent; even that the entire social structure of Greece might have eventually collapsed. Historically such a collapse has ended in the establishment of some form of totalitarian government capable of restoring some semblance of order. Indeed, such a collapse has often ended whatever freedom was enjoyed by the society prior to the collapse. This historical aspect of authoritarian response is the reason that some in today's environment are predicting the loss of American freedom.

When all is said and done it is very difficult to imagine the United States in the position that Greece found itself; or even the position in which Japan currently finds itself economically. Many people remained convinced that the US is still the preeminent power economically, politically and militarily, not only on the domestic level but also globally. These same people are convinced that the US although not yet fully recovered from the great recession will in fact be fully recovered and be entering into a period of robust economic growth within the next three years. The problems now being faced in the US, such as high unemployment, a sluggish economy, trillion dollar budget deficits, a $17 trillion sovereign debt, a slow erosion of the US position in regard to global trade and finance and the disappearance of the US manufacturing base are seen as mere bumps in the road. Although this position does not predict that budget deficits and sovereign debt will totally disappear they do predict that what remains will be indefinitely sustainable. They also do not predict that the economy will be able to avoid recessions or corrections on a permanent basis; but rather that such corrections are merely the manner in which a relatively free market system works. They see the erosion of the US position in global trade and finance as a figment of the imagination, or a manipulation of general facts in relation to the US position. They see the US position in both global trade and finance as changing in terms of the specificity of what is involved; but not in relation to the fact that the US still maintains preeminence in both areas. They also can accept the idea that the US for reasons beyond its control, such as the failure of the EU, or EZ, and the trauma caused by coping with such a crisis, may enter into another period of recession during the short term. However, even this would be a short term problem as it has always been in the past. That is to say, just another example of the cyclical nature of the free market system. They projected that by the end of 2014 the US rate of economic growth will meet or exceed 2.5% of national GDP (third quarter of 2014 came in at an annual rate of 3.5%). Even at this rather mild rate of growth they suggested that a significant beginning can be made towards a balanced budget and reduction of the sovereign debt level as occurred in the late 1990s. Shortly after the economy reaches this level of growth, unemployment will be reduced to more normal levels; and job creation will continue to grow, drawing many of those now on disability back into the labor market. They further project that over the five years following 2014, the US will maintain an economic growth rate between 3.5 and 3.8% of GDP. As a result the US will be in a position to increase its preeminent position in relation to global trade and finance. The US will also be in a position to maintain its position as the preeminent military power regardless of what type of military is required at that time. They agree that the US society of 2020, or thereabouts, may not be recognizable in terms of today's standards; but that a higher standard of living will have spread to all levels of the society. The rate of change found today in terms of new science and technology will increase altering life styles even more radically than they have been altered since 1960. Whether or not this is what will constitute the US environment when, and if, a robust economic growth occurs over an extended period remains to be seen.

In the past, if history can be seen as an accurate guide, good times merely brought higher levels of spending at both the private and public levels. It is, under this prediction, hard to imagine the replacement of the current welfare system, or even a significant reform being instituted; but rather only a continuation of the accumulating attempts to eliminate all "unfairness" to be found within society. Individual history would indicate that good times create a reaction which allows the individual to enjoy a new standard of living commensurate with the increased income. It is reasonable to expect that governmental reaction would be the same. In support of this prediction there are several signs that the US may in fact be entering a period of at least measurable economic growth. The unemployment rate, if the figures are reliable, is slowly dropping; the rate at which new jobs are created seems to be slowly increasing; corporate and business profits are on the rise; consumer spending is starting to rise among other things. There are still some signs of weakness, however, such as the stock valuation bubble, state and local financial problems, and overseas problems.

Some of these are within the control of the US and others are not. If this prediction of the future is accepted as the most likely, the reaction at the various governmental levels should consist of a do-nothing attitude to avoid interfering with the natural return of the economy to robust growth. One of the first steps has already occurred, as a determined effort was made to begin to ease the purchase of bonds by the central bank, aiming for a total withdrawal from this procedure in a relatively short time. The various governments should also begin to seriously look at the methods in which the infrastructure system can be repaired and expanded. The various governments should actively seek to create an environment that will make it possible for banks, investment institutions, and corporations to invest in long term production projects such as the refurbishing and creation of manufacturing facilities and equipment, and increased capacity for handling of inventory. This would mean creating a favorable environment to encourage savings. This may even include the institution of a modified "Marshall Plan" to aid the recovery of the other industrialized nations that make up the bulk of global trade and financial opportunities. This is the one scenario where no one sees a problem with the loss of American freedom, that is, it is the one scenario in which American freedom will continue to flourish.

Regardless of which scenario is chosen as most likely, a choice must be made rather quickly to keep the status quo from becoming a permanent feature of life in the US. Maintaining the status quo would mean accepting high levels of unemployment, large budget deficits, increasing sovereign debt, and a defeatist attitude as represented by the "new normal," as some pundits call it. This clearly is the least attractive alternative and the one that will most likely bring about the first scenario in its most virulent form.

Obviously the best choice would be the second scenario, if in fact it has any real connection to reality. There is already enough evidence, in eyes of some experts, to justify adopting this scenario. The state and local governments have begun the process of making the tough decisions to repair their fiscal problems where necessary; the business and investment communities are aware of their internal problems and seem to be also making the tough decisions to repair the situation; the public is also adapting to the new conditions and is beginning to save and plan as before; the housing and automobile industries are beginning to show signs of real recovery rather than nominal paper recovery. At the federal level, however, there are no signs that any action at all is being taken. The administration appears to have given up its domestic plans, especially since the flawed launch of the Affordable Care Act. It now seems to be concentrating on what are promising signs involving foreign affairs. Much effort is being put into the successful conclusion of the programs involving the destruction of the Syrian chemical weapons capability and the normalization of affairs with Iran, including the reduction of Iranian capability to produce nuclear weapons. Both of these initiatives are positive in regard to the current US administration and could produce some much needed credibility for US foreign policy. As a result, domestic policy has been left in the hands of congress. It is in relation to this state of affairs where the ideological stalemate finds its real importance. A detailed look at this will be taken a little later in this essay. For now it is important that the point be established that it is the federal level that still remains locked in the acceptance of the status quo. The status quo, especially if maintained over the longer term, represents the best chance that the current freedoms enjoyed by the American public may be lost due to growing levels of dependency and ennui.

Regardless of those who are looking ahead with rose colored glasses; and regardless of those who see only doom and gloom, one can still wonder whether events will truly be different this time as compared to earlier historical precedents. Some believe that the instability of the financial community, the fragility of sovereign nations as exemplified by uncontrollable spending, and the focus on short term profits versus long term investment, are truly harbingers of a new political and economic environment. It also does seem to be true that the time-tested methods associated with the ideas of Keynes have proven ineffective so far in this new economic environment. The increased governmental spending has had little or no effect on the growth rate of the economy, and indeed, may actually have depressed the economy even further. So far, significant spending reductions have not been instituted so one can only guess at what their effect on the economy might be, although if anything, the first round of automatic spending cuts seems to have again depressed the economy. This has shaken those in power enough to force them to present legislation that will reverse the next scheduled rounds of automatic cuts (sequester). This legislation may in the end pass but its effect on the economy is still some way down the road. The new approach of bailing out the corporations that have been labeled "too large to fail" seems to have worked, at least in the sense that those bailed out have not only recovered but have paid back the bailout funds with interest. The overall effect, however, has not been an increase in the number of jobs created by these companies, which are, in fact, still attempting to cut costs, especially labor and benefit costs. In the financial arena the results have been more negative than positive as compared with the corporate bailouts. In the financial areas the institutions targeted have been rescued from failure; but they are now either holding onto their investment funds or investing them overseas in short term profit investments. Indeed, there is evidence that the financial institutions, such as Bank of America, are returning to the use of shaky financial instruments equivalent to derivative swaps. This is the result of one of two possible reasons; that is, that there are no significant long term investments available in today's market; or that the concentration on short term profits cannot be avoided in providing for the bottom-line success required by the market. It appears that this type of behavior in the financial community may in fact have become the new normal. The loss of our manufacturing base is seen as the primary reason that long term investment is no longer a viable form of investment opportunity in the US market. What effect this will have on the overall economic picture is just now beginning to come into focus. All bets seem to be indicating that this behavior is having a negative effect on the rate of economic growth and job creation; as well as limiting the recovery of the housing market as interest rates slowly climb. Corporations also have been very reluctant to invest their available funds into domestic long term investment. The reason for this appears again to be two-fold; first, the cost burden of complying with a plethora of governmental regulations (this in fact, however, may be more of a rationale for the behavior rather than a cause); and second, the vast amount of spending that would be needed to refurbish existing manufacturing facilities and restock them with adequate equipment. Added to this is the vast cost of bringing the needed infrastructure back into a reasonable state of repair. Business leaders do not foresee the ability to return a profit on this size of investment for many years to come. They also are uncomfortable with the government being capable of providing the on-going funding for the replacement, repair, and creation of the needed infrastructure. For this reason alone a majority of the investment funds available to corporations are being invested overseas with much higher expectations of profit return over shorter periods of time.

This also appears to be the new normal in terms of corporate investment strategies. As a result the creation of high paying permanent jobs in the domestic market will likely remain flat or fall into negative territory over time. The jobs that are created will, of course, tend to remain in the service sector. This means a larger concentration of the total work force in temporary, part-time, unstable low paying, low- skill jobs. In turn this will mean a continuing trend towards a decrease in the real value of wages and over time the real value of assets. This also may be the new normal as concerns the overall economic picture in the US. The only real factor that could change this picture would be the invention of new industries that would return the cost of investment with profit over shorter periods of time. This is the hope of those who are relying on green technology to create new industrial opportunities. So far this has remained largely a dream and those which have successfully started up are short on job creation. The few jobs that are produced are very high-skilled, intellectually demanding jobs that are not within the reach of the majority of the US work force. Indeed, some claim that the current US educational system is totally inadequate for preparing its students for these new types of jobs, even though students stay in school much longer in today's world. Others turn to the return of manufacturing to the US from overseas. The prediction is that the trend that is seen in China, India and other emerging markets will accelerate to the point where the domestic labor market in the US will once again become competitive internationally. There is no doubt that the work forces in China, India, and emerging economies such as SE Asia and Brazil are demanding better wage structures, more benefit packages, and a larger concentration of consumer products than ever before. Both China and India are currently instituting programs to cope with these demands; but overall wages are increasing and benefit packages are becoming larger. As a result manufacturing costs have tended to level out in the international market. This has made it possible for some industries to return their manufacturing processes to the domestic market. This has been aided by the decrease in the power of organized labor in the US; coupled with the willingness of local governments to offer tax breaks for the return of manufacturing facilities. This movement, however, is so far miniscule in comparison with the amount of manufacturing facilities that went overseas earlier. This movement is also hampered by the tremendous cost of restarting operations in the domestic market. As a result the largest share of the new manufacturing jobs are being brought to the domestic market by foreign firms such as Toyota, BMW, BP and others. Many of these new facilities are highly automated and where 50 years ago they would have provided thousands of high paying permanent jobs they are today only providing a few hundred such jobs. All of these factors are relevant to the debate over whether or not a new normal for economic activity has come into being. If it has the old solutions may never be adequate to influence this new normal. It may even be impossible to alter this new normal until the environment adapts and changes to the new conditions in a natural manner. If this is correct then for some period of time, probably tending to be longer than shorter, the decline in the real value of income and assets will continue. The gap between those who have and those who have not, or who have much less, will continue to grow. These trends will be most evident in two segments of the US society, that is, the retired community, or the portion of the retirement community that is living on a fixed income, and those living at or below the poverty level. The former segment will continue to grow larger over the next few years as the "baby boomer generation" enters retirement age. The latter segment will also continue to grow at an accelerating rate as more people remain unemployable and incapable of obtaining the training to obtain the jobs available. The segment containing the "wealthy", especially those who hold the high paying, permanent stable jobs, will also continue to grow. Where 50 years ago this segment consisted of only 5 to 15% of income earners, it will in the near future contain around 20%. The very wealthy will still constitute about 1% of the population, as always. As a result there are currently some 58 million people drawing social security benefits; one third of the working population is using food stamps, rent subsidies or other forms of welfare programs. It can be expected that this number will continue to grow as the number of people entering the productive portion of the society continues to decease.

If the economic environment is accurately described as different this time and it is also correct that none of the old faithful remedies are working to resolve the issues a step must be taken to find a more creative or innovative response. The one issue that seems to be at the core of all the other issues, with the exception of political stalemate, is the persistently slow growth of the economy overall. The Great Recession officially began during the year 2007 and was officially ruled to be over late in 2009. Now, according to some economic experts, the recession actually began shortly after the destruction of the World Trade Center in Manhattan in 2001 and is still with us today. Others feel that we have made a weak recovery from the recession but that we are either entering into or will shortly enter a second recession. Either way the economic downturn, whether as a recession, or as a weak recovery, has lasted twelve years and may not end for another several years. Most economic experts are agreed that historically the recovery period from a severe recession is from five to seven years. If this is true, that is that the traditional time period for recovery is seven years, and the Great Recession ended in 2009 it should be coming to an end 2017. If the recession has not ended, or if the economy is entering a second recession, recovery may not be expected even under normal circumstances for at least seven more years. This would push the recovery time out to 2020 or beyond.

If this plays out, the last recession will easily double the historical average. When we compare what is happening in the US in the current economic environment to what has been occurring in Japan over the last 20 years, the parallel is striking. First, Japan has been experiencing a recessionary economic growth rate for nearly 20 years. This recessionary trend is marked by persistent low rates of economic growth, high levels of unemployment and declining real values in terms of income and assets. Japan, according to some economic experts, appears to be poised to enter into another serious recession in the near term. This will require that Japan significantly devalue the Yen; which will in turn trigger serious inflationary pressure that will retard economic growth even to a greater extent. Indeed, Japan made the necessary arrangement at the last economic summit of the industrialized nations to allow the devaluation of the Yen to proceed. In addition, the Japanese are carrying the largest sovereign debt in ratio to GDP of any highly industrialized nation One theory of how the Japanese were able to carry this debt is that they had the ability to print as much money as they needed without causing increasing inflationary pressure. The theory is that they were able to do this because they were doing so in a vacuum, so to speak, that is to say, they were the only nation that was at the time printing money on this scale. Today however the US, the UK, the EU and others are following the same process. A tacit agreement emerged at the G20 meeting approving the devaluation of the Yen, authorizing the Japanese to stop printing money and to devalue their economy in hopes that the deflation will result in greater economic growth. For the immediate future, however, most experts expect this move too will result only in a significant reduction in the value of Japanese saving accounts and other personal assets. In short, a good deal of pain for the average Japanese citizen; especially if, as some think, it leads to the collapse of the Japanese economy in the short term. If a collapse were to occur there is not enough currency even on a global scale to bail them out. There can be little, if any, doubt that the Japanese would then be forced to call in the sovereign debt they hold in the form of bonds. This would clearly deeply affect the US as the Japanese hold nearly a trillion dollars of our debt instruments. Other nations would also be adversely affected by such a crisis making this a truly global issue. In what condition the Japanese would emerge from this collapse is beyond current capability to calculate. In both the historical cases of comparable collapse, that is the German collapse in the early 1930s and an earlier Japanese collapse of the same period, the end result was the establishment of totalitarian governments. The same occurred in Russia in 1917 but the collapse in this case was more political and social rather than strictly economic. The same thinking applies to the peripheral members of the EU, that is, Greece, Spain, Portugal, Ireland and Italy, that is that they have avoided economic collapse only through the bail outs provided by the wealthier EU nations and EU central banks (the printing of money). This burden is seen as unsustainable over the long term and not even applicable should one of the larger economies, such as France enter into default. Once again in the case of the EU the most talked about solution to these growing problems is to either incorporate all the member economies into a true federal system of government; or to allow the failure of the euro allowing the reestablishment of local currencies after suffering a serious devaluation. Neither of these procedures has obtained much support from the political elite. The EU public would seem to favor the replacement of the euro, and the breakup of the EZ, and possibly even the EU. Either of these two events, that is, the collapse of either the Japanese or EU economies would without a doubt throw the US into a depression at least as serious as that of 2008 and maybe as serious as that of the 1930s. Such events may or may not have an impact on the issue of whether or not the US can maintain its current levels of personal freedom. It can be surmised, however, that these events, if any of them occur, will have a very profound negative effect on the US, and possibly require very stringent action on the part of the federal government to compensate.

Returning to a discussion of the United States specifically, two very interesting trends are to be followed. First, the state and local governments that have found themselves in fiscal trouble are calling on the two most ancient solutions. The governments in the worse shape, mostly limited to the smaller local governments, are filing for bankruptcy and defaulting on their debts, including the unfunded portion of their pension plans. In other cases, mostly the larger metro governments and the states, are instituting stringent austerity programs aimed at reducing spending and increasing revenue. The former includes rollback of earlier promised benefit levels involving pension plans, foregoing promised wage increases and other measures. The goal is to reach a point during the short term where debt is reduced to a sustainable level; and be completely eliminated in the long term. Most local and state governments are not allowed by law to operate on anything other than a balanced budget, but can, and do, fund short falls through the sale of bonds. These institutions are at the same time increasing revenue by increasing tax rates or by implementing new taxes, such as new sales taxes, etc. The most interesting aspect is that they seem to have the support of their citizens on both sides of the issue. The people are voting in the new taxes and increased tax rates; while at the same time accepting the austerity measures. The citizens of the governments that have actually defaulted also have accepted this as the price to be paid for uncontrolled or incompetent financial behavior on the part of the government involved. Most of the defaults occurred after 2008 and seem to have slowed down to a trickle at the current time. The austerity programs began after 2010 and have been increasing rapidly since. Even local and state governments that were not involved in a fiscal crisis are beginning to tighten their control of the fiscal ropes. Illinois, for example, has passed legislation specifically intended to reduce its unfunded pension fund liabilities from 110 billion to zero over the next three decades. This legislation quickly faced a lawsuit by the public employees' unions to have the legislation ruled unconstitutional. This will be a very important test case to determine where the political elite stand on this issue. If the legislation is passed, and enforced, it will be the first time that the public has taken a positive stand on this issue at this level of underfunding. If it is ruled unconstitutional then the State of Illinois will be back to square one in its attempts to resolve the issue. This would not bode well for Illinois as it has taken several years to obtain even this compromise legislation. As is clear the federal government at this point has not attempted to follow the local and state governments lead. This leads to the question of how the federal government would react to the onset of a fiscal crisis the depth of the ones found in Japan and the EU. There are some indicators that the same path will be followed in the US as was followed in both Japan and the EU, that is, the various bail outs that have already taken place, the QE programs, the reduction of interest rates to near zero among others. The result so far has been an astounding increase of the federal budget deficit and the national debt. These two factors have been coupled to the almost complete lack of savings on the part of the American public. There is no question that these programs have not stimulated the economy as was expected, but the claim is being made that the economy would be much worse off without them. This seems highly self-serving and is at the very least debatable. So far the federal government has shown no ability to obtain political compromise to institute solutions similar to the ones being taken by the states. Not only has the federal government been unable to come to agreement on reduced spending and increased tax revenue; they have shown an equal inability to attempt any real reform of the welfare system, the tax code, or the health care system. Although, in the latter case, the Affordable Care Act was passed, and now is being fought against tooth and nail by the far right wing of the Republican Party. At the inauguration of the act the roll out was so badly botched that it may die from its own self-inflicted wounds. A better example of how laws are passed in the US could not be found. The law was passed three years ago by both sides of the aisle; but had been read or studied by no one in congress. The administration was advised on what was included in the bill and how it would be implemented; but this advice was found to be unreliable when the act was ready for rollout. After it was actually put into force, for example, the President had obviously been advised that the act contained a clause that would allow people to keep their current insurance if they desired. This turned out not only to be untrue but some four million people had their old insurance cancelled due to the act. Even under the pressure of such dreadful events the congress once again was incapable of action to correct the problems.

What does seem to be happening is a rather open manipulation of the figures in relation to the number of people unemployed, the number of jobs being created and, of course, the real growth rate of the economy. A new congressional deal involves a more solid solution to the debt ceiling issue and the rollback of the sequester cuts that were to be implemented after Jan. 1, 2014. Included within this deal is also the rejection of the plea to continue the unemployment benefits for the long term unemployed. This will result in a drop in the unemployment rate due to all of those receiving the benefits not being counted in the unemployment numbers once they lose them, although they will remain unemployed or underemployed (about 1.3 million people). The end result is that the average American citizen does not have any real idea of what the real rate of unemployment might be; nor does he or she have real knowledge of how many, and what type, of jobs are being created. The public also has shown that it has no real confidence in the announcements made by the government as to the growth of the economy, or the health of the business and financial communities. The average American votes with his spending habits and it is plain to see that consumer spending has contracted significantly over the last year or so, although there has recently been a small rebound in consumer spending. There can be no question that the private sector overall is not yet comfortable with the pronouncement that the recession has ended and that recovery is under way. The government has used up the funds that were available under the TARP program (700 billion) and no new funding is being provided for economic stimulus, at least, in the area of promoting infrastructure projects, such as the repair and maintenance of bridges, roads, railroads, etc.. These infrastructure projects ostensibly brought the unemployment rate down from almost 9% to 7.3% and helped to promote a positive growth rate of 1.5% for the economy. Since the end of the stimulus programs the numbers have remained stable but show no signs of moving in a positive manner. There has, in addition, been no attempt to reform the American educational system in order to make it more competitive in comparison to international educational systems, especially those found in Japan, China and India. It is claimed that the American system is not competent in respect to preparing its students to obtain the types of jobs that will become available in the future. Indeed, it is distressing to read the numbers of those who have graduated from university and who either have not found employment, or are woefully underemployed. Lastly, it is being claimed that the educational system is also failing miserably in relation to remaining competitive with our international rivals in the scientific and technological fields. The stimulus package that was put together to stimulate the economy after the onset of the latest recession was essentially limited to infrastructure projects and appears to have been too small and too short lived to have a positive effect on the economy. Whatever effect the stimulus program had on the economy it was small and temporary in nature.

What has occurred is the solidification of the ideological positions of the two parties in the federal government. The conservatives refuse to allow any new spending programs to be instituted; coupled with the refusal to consider any new taxes as they believe them to be a drag on stimulation of the economy and the creation of jobs. The Democrats, on the other hand, have sought extensions of expiring welfare benefits; supported the increase of tax rates on the wealthy and corporations; while at the same time opposing any legislation that restricts spending, in the belief that such policies will enhance consumer spending and stimulate the economy. Currently the only federal program still in affect is the Federal Reserve QE program by which it buys $85 billion in sovereign debt per month suppressing interest rates to near zero. The central bank ended this program in Oct. 2014). As a result there are no federal programs aimed at resolving the perceived problems. Some would claim that this is just what is needed, that is, no federal intervention in the natural operation of the free market system, or at least a market that is as free as circumstances will allow. Others feel that the loss of federal governmental lead will result in even worse conditions. On the economic and political front it appears clear that there is a growing dependency on the part of a very significant segment of the American population in relation to welfare benefits. It is also clear that the government intervention into the daily lives of the people, especially at the state and federal level of government, has become increasingly pervasive and complete. It can be claimed, and sometimes is, that such a dependency, coupled with the complacency of allowing further government intrusions, equates directly to the amount of freedom the individual is willing to give up for the sake of maintaining government benefits. This will be looked at in more detail later.

CHAPTER 4. HEALTH CARE: AN ECONOMIC AND A POLITICAL PROBLEM

The major economic and political problems on the domestic level have now been briefly set forth and discussed. They can be put in a summary form as follows:

A. Economic problems (private level)

    a. The persistent sluggishness of the overall economy.

    b. The persistent high rate of unemployment.

    c. Increasing dependence on the welfare system for a sustainable standard of living.

    d. Lack of a comfort zone for the long term investment of funds in productive projects by both the business and investment communities, coupled with an almost complete lack of private savings on the part of the public.

    e. The exponential growth of health care costs.

    f. The gradual decrease in the real value of middle class income and the real value of middle class assets.

    g. The hesitation of the American public to spend as freely as it did before 2008.

B. Economic Problems (Public level)

    a. The growing levels of budget deficits.

    b. The growing levels of sovereign debt; coupled to the issue of their sustainability.

    c. The slowly decreasing revenue base as the US finishes its conversion from a manufacturing base to a service orientated base.

    d. The almost complete loss of fiscal responsibility at the federal level.

e. The slow deterioration of both the infrastructure system and the education system.

C. Political problems (state and local governmental levels)

f. A rapidly shrinking revenue base, particularly in the areas of property tax revenue and sales tax revenue.

g. The growing age of the population, as represented by the shrinking number of those working to pay for the retirement benefits of those who have entered the non-productive segment of the population.

h. The slow drying up of the employment opportunities available in the local and state markets.

i. The growing inability of state and local governments to fund existing educational institutions.

j. The increase in spending obligations related to the repair and maintenance of roads, highways, pension funds, sanitation systems, etc.

D. Political problems (federal level)

k. The growing number of illegal immigrants into the US.

l. The growing effects of the longstanding gridlock bordering on dysfunction, especially in congress.

m. The loss of revenue created by the dysfunction of the existing tax code.

n. The growing level of health care costs, and decrease in the quality of health care, even after the passing of the Affordable Care Act.

o. A growing discontent among the American public as represented by the approval rates given to congress and the administration.

All of these problems are recognized as currently existing and in need of serious attention, but to date they have been addressed only by the various local and state governments who don't have a choice to "kick the can a little further down the road." The latest round of government shutdown and reluctance to raise the debt ceiling clearly indicates that the federal government has not yet taken these problems seriously. At every opportunity to provide leadership and viable solutions to the problems it faces, the federal government opts to kick the can a little further down the road. As the analogy goes, sooner or later one more kick will send the can flying off the road and in many cases it cannot be retrieved. The state and local governments have clearly recognized that little, if any, help can be expected from the federal level and have instituted the steps listed below to resolve the issues facing them. They have taken steps to reduce their spending on wages, benefits, and pension plans; and have increased their revenue by increasing sales and property taxes to fund new spending on infrastructure, educational facilities and programs, hospitals, and the attraction of new business to their area or state. Even so, the consensus is that it will take at least a generation for these problems to be rectified.

The federal government as stated above has failed to set forth even a single plan for the solution of the problems facing it let alone to resolve the issues. A new super-committee was formed as a result of the latest crisis of a 16-day government shutdown; and another last minute temporary extension of the debt ceiling issue. One major difference between this new committee and the first super committee is that no power has been given to the new committee to institute automatic spending cuts or tax increases. The committee has, in fact, announced that a compromise on the two issues assigned to it have been reached. As we have seen the first portion was a requirement of finding a long term solution to the debt ceiling issue to avoid the possibility of further government shut downs. The legislation presented expanded the debt to avoid the next round of debate scheduled for Jan. 2014. It did however only allow spending under the new ceiling for six months to allow time for a more permanent solution.

The second issue is to deal with the upcoming automatic spending legislated by the first super committee; as well as deciding the fate of the extended unemployment benefits for those who have lost their two year benefits. Most of the automatic cuts have been reversed by this new legislation maintaining the current levels of spending in the various affected departments. The unemployment benefits, however, were allowed to expire at the end of 2013; a concession to the right wing of the Republican Party. As noted earlier the legislation has not yet passed through congress, or the administration, however, the administration has issued its agreement to sign the legislation if passed by congress. Both houses of congress have also indicated that the legislation will pass (in fact the House passed it on December 11, 2013). The bill has now passed and has been signed into law by the administration relieving the immediate pressure. Only time will tell whether this initial compromise is a harbinger of future ability to get the job done; if so, then the credit for this change should be given to the low ratings given by the public to congress, the administration and to the political parties.

The much expected collapse of the EZ and/or the EU has apparently passed without much drama. Indeed, the financial and economic problems facing both the EZ and the EU have receded into the background, at least in terms of the mainstream media coverage and the minds of the American public. Whether or not the potential for severe crisis still exists does not seem to have been resolved, although there are definite signs that the crisis is under control. The problems starting in Ireland and then spreading to Greece do not seem to have spread to Italy, Spain and Portugal as expected, although again there are signs that they all are far from being in sound financial condition. The political problems which had arisen due to the economic stress, especially in relation to Greece, also seem to have faded into the background. In addition, the expected slowdown of the Chinese and Indian economies has not yet taken place, at least, to the extent where it is causing them problems, however, recent reports indicate that the initial slowdown has not stopped but rather accelerated. Both nations have acted in a timely fashion to the issues and it seems to have worked in their favor. The emerging world, that is, such nations as Russia, Brazil and the SE Asian nations are still booming, however, indications are clear that their economies are fragile due to single resource reliance, for example, the Russian reliance on energy exports. The situation as regards the expected events on the international scene and their failure to materialize seems to be based on one of two things. First, either a serious misinterpretation of what was actually happening in the nations studied; or second, the attempt to manipulate information by the various industrialized nations, especially the US and the EU, to present events as if a crisis existed when in fact none did. This manipulation, of course, would have to provide cover for the obtaining of an objective not actually involved with the pretended crisis; for example, in the case of the EU the goal could be the fostering of further integration of the member nations into a true supranational government. In fact within the US the term "manufactured crisis" has been used quite freely. This was particularly true of the discussion surrounding the 16 day government shut down and the deadlock over the debt ceiling issue. In fact, it is claimed by some that the shutdown was manufactured to provide leverage for the defunding, or delay, of the inauguration of the Affordable Care Act (Obamacare). Up until its actual roll out date the battle was between those who favored limited government and those who favor pro-active government. Nothing was resolved by the shutdown and the last minute deal on the debt ceiling; and if it was a manufactured crisis the only thing that it manufactured was a large degree of cynicism on the part of the public and historically low credibility ratings for both political parties and the current administration. All in all, however, it appears that the American public places the most responsibility for the shutdown and last minute heroics on the Republican Party. It will only be a short period of time before it will be known if this translates into definitive losses at the polls for the Republicans.

If in fact these various crises that have been so severely and loudly declaimed are the result of one party, or the other, creating them to accomplish unrelated goals the cost to the global community has been immense and unnecessary. The use of such terms, especially without fear of reprisal, only suggests that the political elite feel confident that they will retain their power no matter what they do. It also suggests that if the unrelated goals sought by the political elite are driven by private sector interests that the interest group system in the US has become more powerful than most believe.

These interest groups, especially grassroots movements, such as the Heritage Foundation, have obtained a large degree of cooperation from both the state and federal governmental structure. Conspiracy theories, on the other hand, are always the weakest form of argument that can be made; even if they do at times contain a grain of truth, and rarely even the truth. In this case there are only two candidates for the manufacturing of a crisis, the political parties and the interest groups. The Republicans, of course, are blaming the shutdown, etc. on the administration in particular and on the Democratic Party generally. The Democrats are blaming the Republicans, especially the far right wing of the party known as the Tea Party. No one is attempting to place the blame on interest groups although the far right interest groups, such as the Heritage Foundation, have definitely had a say in the way individual members of congress voted. There is apparently enough blame to go around; but the important point for the American public, and the world at large, is that a crisis of this nature and magnitude could be manufactured in the first place.

Such a tactic would seem to be an abuse of public trust in the most blatant fashion. This would be even more the case if the only goal or objective that was to be obtained was a stronger stance in terms of results of the various state and federal elections. If that is indeed truly the goal of both parties then it can be expected that manufactured crises will continue to appear on a regular basis.

The proof will be in what happens if one party, or the other, obtains a landslide victory in one of these elections. In fact, the Republicans won control of congress in a landslide in 2014 and now have the power to force the passage of many pieces of legislation that have been stuck in congress. As we saw, however, many are expecting only continued deadlock. Whether or not this would translate into a resolution of the problems facing the US is an entirely different question. One must note that the political blame game has always focused on obtaining power through influencing the votes given by the public. The manufacturing of crises would merely be a more severe form of the blame game. Even if the crisis was not manufactured the objective for saying it was remains the same. In the end it is wise to set aside the conspiracy theories and to concentrate on who is doing what in relation to the demands of the American public. At the current moment it is accurate to answer that inquiry with a resounding "no one." It is interesting to note that the political elite appear to feel "safe" enough in relation to the upcoming elections to ignore the demands and needs being expressed by their constituency.

A good example of how the public's demands and needs are ignored is the continuing debate revolving around the Affordable Care Act. The inauguration of this legislation began on Oct. 1, 2013, after lying at rest for three years to allow time to bring on line all the software required to make it operate. The roll out on Oct. 1 was an almost total failure from a technical point of view. The computer was off line due to problems with the software for over 90% of the time and after two months there still had been only some 342,000 people making application to the program. In addition, the program is not working in the way that those responsible for it claimed that it would. Millions of existing insurance policies have been cancelled since the insurance companies found that it was easier and less costly to cancel the old policy and issue a new one, and they were not prohibited by the act from doing so. Those people who had their old policies cancelled found, if they were successful in getting online at all, that the new policies included forms coverage that they didn't need or didn't want, and certainly didn't want to pay for; and they were faced with a significant increase in premium cost. Prior to the roll out, the House of Representatives passed legislation that would have delayed it for one year, allowing the system more time to fix any glitches and allowing the citizens a longer time to enroll before fines could be applied.

As it turned out, this would have been a very good idea. Even earlier the House of Representatives attempted to sponsor legislation that effectively would have defunded the act. It is clear that these attempts were driven by the far right wing of the Republican Party and were not even brought to a vote in the Democrat-controlled Senate. After the roll out, those who were attempting to repeal, or delay, the implementation of the act are now leading the complaints that it has been nearly paralyzed by technical problems. The Republicans are using this paralysis as support for claiming that the law is broken and should be either repealed or delayed. In fact, however, it would appear that neither will happen as the law has been confirmed as constitutional by the Supreme Court; and has in fact been implemented regardless of how poorly.

As with any big national legislation it will take a significant period of time to reach any level of operating efficiency. This is, of course, the position being taken by the administration and the Democratic Party generally. In other words, they are downplaying the significance of the roll out problems and stressing the good things that will result from implementation of the law. These latter include the ability to obtain insurance by the 40 million uninsured citizens of the country; the elimination of the use of pre-existing medical conditions clauses by the insurance industry; the ability to maintain insurance on students through the parents' policy until the age of 26; among other points. Whatever turns out to be the true nature of the act over time one point is clearly evident; that is, one political party is doing everything in its power to get the act repealed while the other political party is doing everything in its power to complete the implementation and enforcement processes. The two sides are implacable in their positions and will not back down an inch. A better example of ideological gridlock could not be found.

It is equally evident that it is too early to accurately judge how the American people will weigh in on the Act as time goes on. The initial reaction has largely been negative due to the technical problems and the smear campaign related to them. Many of the formerly uninsured, especially in the states with local enrollment procedures, are investigating the coverage available and the cost of such coverage. It is to be expected that if they can find what they want, at a price they can pay, or be qualified for subsidized premiums, they will sign up for it and vice versa. This procedure is now being considered by the Supreme Court as to the constitutionality of the subsidies under state exchanges. If ruled unconstitutional the efforts of the uninsured in the state exchanges will be nullified. Most people favor the elimination of pre-existing conditions clauses, etc.; however, few are aware of how the extension of Medicaid provisions are going to be used to subsidize the newly insured. A few states, such as Florida, are refusing to abide by the act, preventing their uninsured citizens from complying with the law. The cost of this, as with everything else, is being borne by the taxpayer.

One aspect that is just now beginning to come into focus is the creation of a national risk pool. As with all risk pools the affordability of the insurance is based upon a balanced participation by those who use the insurance. In this case, this translates into a balance between high end users (the sickly, the elderly, etc.) and the low end users (young healthy people). In short, the quickest means for destroying the affordability of the insurance is to skew the above balance. The young, under the conditions that currently exist, may find both that they can't find the coverage they want at a price that they are willing to pay; and that paying the fine is less expensive than the insurance. Without them the cost of the program will skyrocket beyond anything yet calculated by the government. This is in essence what has happened over the years to Social Security, that is, the workers who pay for the program are rapidly becoming so small in number compared to those drawing the benefits that the program is no longer sustainable over the long run. There are other reasons for this lack of sustainability, but this is claimed to be the major problem faced by the Social Security system. Over the next few decades the taxes collected (FICA taxes) will continue to shrink and the number of those seeking, or getting, benefits will continue to grow. The deficit will, as it is now, have to be met by borrowing more money. The taxes on the working population can be compared to the premiums paid by those who never, or seldom, use the benefits. Should these premiums dip below a certain level then the insurance premiums of those least able to afford it; especially those whose premiums are subsidized, will automatically have to be increased to make the risk pool work. The only other option would be to truly nationalize the program and operate in the same manner as they do in Canada and the UK. Should the unbalance spoken of occur without the program being nationalized it will quickly become apparent that those who were intended to benefit most from the program will not be able to afford it; and/or the federal subsidy program will become unsustainable. It is for this reason that the legislation requires the assessment of a penalty for anyone who is qualified for, and required to take, the insurance but decides not to in fact become insured. It was considered likely that the largest share of those who would voluntarily decline to take the insurance would be the young and the healthy. This category is absolutely required for the risk pool concept to work, and they are also the group least likely to be able to sustain the ongoing penalties. Over the long term the risk pool concept will determine whether or not enough is being paid in premiums to cover the use of the insurance. If it turns out that the premiums taken in will not support the costs then the premiums must go up or the plan must be altered to fit the new circumstances. This is exactly what happened in the case of the drug prescription program added to the Medicare coverages. Even with the penalties the subsidized premiums and cost rose faster than expected. In the end the American public will make the final decision, hopefully through the action of their elected representatives.

As one issue, or another, as the health care debacle has shown, takes the attention of the public the other issues will be temporarily pushed onto the back burner. A crisis could easily reappear in any one of the economic issues; as well as in any one of the political issues. Crisis level debate is not so likely on the social issues, such as immigration, tax reform, welfare reform or educational reform. The public appears to see these as issues in need of reform, or some level of attention, but not as front burner problems. This, however, may be changing with "crisis" level coverage being given to the unescorted juveniles entering the US illegally. Is this another example of crisis manufacturing, that is, to create a crisis to force action on another issue, in this case generalized immigration reform? This will only change should circumstances change, for example, if in the near future it becomes necessary to reform the benefits being currently received, or which will be drawn within the next couple of years, under Social Security. Such a necessity would automatically move welfare reform to the front burner and force whatever issue was on the front burner to a back burner position. The same is true of the chronically unemployed in the US and other highly industrialized nations. It would be expected that those unemployed for long periods would also be the most vocal in their calls for federal action on this front. This is not true for the simple reason that most of the chronically unemployed are being taken into the welfare system as permanently disabled workers. Should it become expedient to remove these newly qualified people off the disability benefits this would automatically become a front burner issue. Some 1.8 million chronically unemployed workers have been moved onto the disability rolls; and 48 million families are participating at some level in the federal food stamp program. Under the health care act millions of chronically-ill citizens will be moved into the extended Medicaid program.

All of these recent moves have led to some sarcastically denoting the federal government as a kind of "nanny state." The real concern, however, in all of this is whether or not the costs of all these programs are within the ability of the US to sustain. As stated earlier, the current deadlock in the federal government boils down to a battle over whether or not the current welfare system, coupled with the new additions such as the Affordable Care Act, are sustainable. The Republican Party following the lead of the economic experts who claim that welfare benefits are either not now sustainable, or will become unsustainable in the short term, are seeking to substantially reduce spending in these areas. The Democratic Party appears to accept the fact that under current conditions the costs will become unsustainable in the long term; they are following the lead of economic experts that claim the US has more than enough time to gently reform the system into a sustainable position. The Republicans, as we have seen, view the situation as critical at the current moment and are seeking massive spending cuts; large decreases in tax rates for small and medium sized businesses; and substantial relaxation of the regulatory burden currently imposed by the federal government. The Democrats, on the other hand, see the situation as stable with resolution being possible through elevated tax rates for the wealthiest taxpayers and the largest corporations, coupled with increased spending on infrastructure, research and development, and education. Under this view spending would be restricted mainly through the closing of fraudulent purchases, the streamlining of government departments, and other cost saving methods.

As a sort of middle position a group of economists, financiers, investment professionals and others holds that instituting either of these positions completely would send the US economy back into recession. They are calling for a different approach altogether. This bloc has not yet offered any specific programs but has set forth in general terms what the solution would need to be. They call for significant spending cuts coupled with significant tax increases across the board. They are also calling for the institution of a regulatory reform program aimed at producing a level of comfort in the private sector that will stimulate long term investment in productive projects and private savings programs. At this point they have not offered a plan indicating where the cuts could most painlessly be applied or exactly where and how the tax increases would come about. Two suggestions offered in the latter case are to change the tax code to a flat rate system rather than a progressive taxing system. This would, of course, eliminate most of the tax credits and other loopholes that severely reduce the income obtained by the government under the current system. The other suggestion would be to close the loopholes, etc., while at the same time adding some new taxes, such as a tax earmarked for infrastructure repair. None of the approaches, however, expects a resolution of these problems in a time period shorter than ten to fifteen years. In the meantime the number of unemployed and/or underemployed workers continues to grow, as do the budget deficits and national debt. It is crystal clear, however, that the American public has noticed, and is complaining about, the fact that they do not feel any relief when they are told things are getting better.

The Affordable Care Act (ACA) exemplifies several aspects important to the determination of the question regarding whether or not the US is still operating as a representative democracy under a free market economy. First, the original bill was some 2300 pages long. Very few people inside (or outside) the government had read or understood the act in total when it was passed. It became apparent that the legislators and the President were carrying clear misunderstandings as to what the act required and as to what its effect on the American public would be. The very least that can be expected under a representative democracy is that those responsible for passing the laws would have read and understood what the laws contained, but the ACA is an important example of how modern legislation is introduced, debated and passed into law.

Second, the rollout of the ACA, after a three-year waiting period, as shown earlier, was an unmitigated disaster. The software programs did not work 90% of the time, and many of the states opted to offer their own state-sponsored sign up sites with the remainder going through the official federal site. After several months it was obvious that many people were either unable or unwilling to take the time to go through the process and only some 340,000 people had actually begun the application process.

People had been told that if they wished to keep their policies, they could, but soon 4 million policies had been cancelled. Those who were able to use state sponsored sites were able to at least research the program. Many found that they would be forced to take coverages they didn't want, or need, at a price much higher than the former policy that was cancelled.

Third, the ACA is now under court scrutiny to determine who qualifies for premium subsidies and whether the law as written is constitutional in regard to this section. Whether the attempt to create an effective national risk pool will prove to be a success is seriously questioned. In the end, the people affected are required to take the insurance whether they want it or not, or be subject to yearly fines that increase and will eventually make the insurance unaffordable.

In short, the ACA is an excellent case in point to show how large scale social planning is effecting the traditional principles which are the purpose of this inquiry. The bill was introduced, debated and passed without the people's representatives understanding what they had passed and the people had no choice but to accept this haphazard work. Both parties now contain a segment that wishes to see the ACA repealed or put in a position where it can die on the vine. Without any question the act restricts the operation of the free market system in terms of health care, and is openly a denial of the democratic principles that normally would be in place in the health care industry.

CHAPTER 5. AMERICAN PROBLEMS AND THE EFFECT ON AMERICAN PRINCIPLES

A beginning can be made by analyzing each factor set forth above and attempting to determine what effect, if any, it has on the status of the US as a representative democracy. The first factor listed was the economic situation in which the US finds itself.

The American system of representative democracy in terms of economic philosophy is based on two main ingredients: the protection of rights based in private property and the use of the free market system. The actual practice in the US is to support the operation of the economic system as closely as possible with both the sanctity of private property and the free operation of market forces. Private property, as one might suspect, is the underlying source of capitalism as represented by the profit system. The free market is represented by the relative interaction of all market forces; such as labor costs, price determination, levels of employment and types of investment among others. The mainstay of a free market, at least in relation to democratic political systems, is a demand that governments don't interfere with this free interplay of market forces. Historically, however, there have always been manmade factors that have limited the amount of free interplay of market forces. Monopolies, for example, were formed with the intent of providing corporate (business) control of all levels of the manufacturing system; that is, the obtaining of the materials needed in manufacturing, the actual cost of producing a product, control of the method by which the product was distributed and the final price that would be charged for the product. Control of all the phases of manufacturing resulted in the ability of large corporations to control the cost of materials, the cost of production (labor and equipment costs), the cost of distribution and the ability to charge a price without having to account for the free interplay of market forces (competition). The result was a series of abuses represented by labor abuse (artificially low wages, child labor, very long hours, lack of safety provisions, etc.), product abuses (shoddy goods, inadequate facilities, etc.), and price fixing. The public eventually reacted to these abuses and forced the state and federal governments to pass legislation to prevent these abuses from taking place. The result was state laws instituting the eight-hour day and regulatory health legislation, among other things. At the federal level legislation was passed to limit the level of monopoly that could be established, that is, the Sherman Anti-Trust legislation, and later the Clayton Anti-Trust Act. Although the legislation did manage to reduce the abusive effects of private corporate interference with the interplay of market forces it opened the door to the other major form of restriction on the free interplay of market forces; that is, government regulation of economic activity. Market forces are still restricted in their free interplay on the private level through corporate policies and union activities but by far the most important restrictions are now found in government regulation.

It is, of course, at this point that any direct effect on the political system of representative democracy will be found. As stated earlier one of the basic foundations of representative democracy is a dependence on the free interplay of market forces known generally as the free market. Any government regulation which artificially increases, or decreases, the cost of materials needed for a product, the cost of producing the product, the cost of distributing the product, or the price of the product being sold is a direct attack upon this principle. This being the case the economic model that is most appropriate in the case of the US is the maintaining of the free interplay among market forces; or at least as free a play as possible under conditions found in the existing economic environment. What is being suggested here is that we determine whether or not the economic environment now existing in the US meets the above definition. Is, or has, the state and federal governments reacted in a manner to the issues involved that results in an overly restrictive interplay of market forces? It would appear, for example, that the federal loosing of the qualifications for benefits under the Social Security disability provisions has artificially kept the price of labor higher than it normally would be in a free market. By incorporating the chronically unemployed into the disability category they have been removed permanently from the labor market reducing the number of people available to take work. As a result the cost of finding and using a more limited supply of labor tends to raise the cost of that labor. In a like manner it can be claimed that all forms of government stimulus, whether it be creating jobs not naturally in the market; putting money in the pockets of those who have not earned it or otherwise reducing the work force; is an attempt to artificially support an economic growth rate not to be found in the free market place. As stated before there has never been an environment where the interplay of market forces has been truly free; however, in the US it can be claimed that the interplay of market forces is as free as possible under normal conditions. This is the assumption that is being challenged here.

It might be useful to follow these thoughts through to their conclusion in one specific instance. For example, we could follow what effects unemployment has on the operation of the free market system. It is claimed that high levels of unemployment; coupled in the US with both long term unemployment and permanent unemployment, restricts the free interplay of labor costs with the other forces of the marketplace. What are the effects of unemployment in this sense, at least, as it applies to the US situation? First, high levels of unemployment directly reduce the amount of discretionary funds that are available for people to spend as consumers. Most economists agree, at least in relation to the US economy (Keynesian theory), that consumer spending represents one of the major factors driving the economic growth rate of the economy. In order to bolster consumer spending levels the federal and state governments have taken the approach of providing funds to those who are unemployed in the form of unemployment insurance benefits. These funds are, according to the experts, spent largely on the necessities of life, that is, food, clothing and shelter and do not make their way into consumption that will improve economic performance. The funds spent on unemployment benefits are also a one for one trade off on government spending in other areas, such as infrastructure maintenance, pension fund contributions, etc.

The official unemployment rate only includes those who are still actively seeking employment in the regular labor market. This group, assuming they find work during the period allowed for them, in this case 2 years of benefits, will not directly affect the cost of labor. When they become long term unemployed, or permanently unemployed, they are no longer actively seeking employment and have used up their unemployment benefits. They instead have been forced onto the welfare rolls adding to the overall cost of maintaining them as non-productive members of society. The long term effect of this system is to one, keep the amount of labor available to take employment artificially low and costly; and two, to withdraw large sums of funds for investment in productive areas of the economy artificially increasing the cost of investment to accomplish the same goals. It also encourages large scale immigration to take the low paying jobs not taken domestically. Unemployment in this way, among other more technical ways, directly affects the free interplay of market forces. One can ask whether or not this interference with the market represents a force strong enough to actually prevent the market from operating freely under the conditions created by high unemployment rates.

It does not appear that there is a definitive answer to this question but it is claimed that if carried on over extended periods of time that it does produce direct interference with the free play of market forces. The strongest claim being made currently along these lines is that the welfare system in all its parts is the greatest source of interference with the free interplay of market forces and represents an example of controlled economic activity not unlike socialism. The welfare system artificially protects the non-productive forces in the economy at the expense of the productive forces. As such it depresses the ability of the economy to grow at robust rates due to the lack of funds available to maintain long term investment in productive activities vital to the operation of a free market. All welfare programs, at least in the US, were intended to be temporary stop-gaps to help people cope with the vicissitudes of life. They were not intended to replace income earned in the productive segments of the society, at least for any length of time. Social Security, for example, began as a program intended to provide a basic safety net for those too old or infirm to stay in the work force. It was not intended to provide them with an income that would maintain the standard of living they had while they were in the work force. Today, however, Social Security, Medicare and Medicaid replace nearly all of the income lost when a lower or middle class worker retires or becomes too infirm to stay in the work force. Currently in the US there are claimed to be somewhere between 11 and 18 million able-bodied people unemployed and receiving welfare benefits. Not normally taken into account are the unknown number of people who are in the workplace but who are working part-time, or who are working at poverty levels (at federal minimum wage). It is estimated that 19 million people are working at the minimum wage level. In addition there are estimated to be 58 million people receiving some level of support from Social Security. Lastly, there are another 48 million people who are taking benefits under the state and federal food stamp programs. If one assumes that the total work force of the US currently stands at between 130 and 160 million people then almost two-thirds of the available work force is drawing some type of welfare benefit while remaining essentially non-productive, or working at or below the poverty level. No one doubts that these numbers have a negative effect on the health of the economy.

Our search is to determine whether or not this effect is strong enough to destroy the free market upon which democracy depends. Few would, I think, claim that democracy, in terms of the free market, has already been destroyed in the US; but there are many who are claiming that this is the definite trend should these issues remain unresolved. As the work force becomes more and more reliant upon receiving income for non-productive activities, that is, for not working, they lose their economic freedom of choice. Were those who are among the unemployed, (but still seeking employment and not receiving benefits) still in the workplace the labor market would clearly be suffering from an oversupply of labor. Such conditions have historically resulted in an abundance of so-called cheap labor, that is, workers who will take employment at low wages and benefits in order to provide the necessities of life, in short, a free competition for jobs takes place. It is this natural effect of unemployment that is being interfered with by the intervention of the state and local governments. The argument can be advanced, and often is, that the ability to obtain unemployment benefits definitely restricts the free interplay of market forces in terms of labor costs. During the period that the currently officially unemployed are getting benefits they are effectively removed from the labor market; even though technically they are supposed to be still actively seeking employment. Left in the labor market without benefits they would be directly competing for any job available at whatever price they could obtain for their labor skills. Historically a glut on the labor market results in labor being sold at a lower price than under normal conditions, that is, periods where the labor force available is limited. People are both willing and eager to take less pay and fewer benefits to maintain a living income under such conditions. This is clearly borne out by the fact that those who have lost their benefits are mostly willing to accept lower paying jobs; or even one or more temporary or part-time jobs. In lieu of not taking underemployment, which many have chosen to do in today's economy, the only option left is to apply for disability benefits or other welfare benefits. One of the complaints that is often made in regard to the immigration problem is that the immigrants are willing to take the jobs that Americans will not, or cannot, take at a lower cost than Americans who will do the job are willing to take. This directly interferes with the free play of market forces in two ways; first, the public welfare system permanently lowers the amount of labor in the market artificially; and second, the arrival of illegal immigrants artificially deflates the cost of labor that is available for hire.

The conclusion, therefore, can be fairly drawn that unemployment in all its forms, in the economic conditions that prevail in the US, has a definite negative effect on the free interplay of market forces. In addition the funds made available for paying temporary unemployment benefits (two years in the US); and for supporting the disability programs for the permanently unemployed directly removes these funds from being used for investment in productive segments of the market. If the figures available are accurate the welfare system in the US involves nearly 48% of the total GDP of the US. The military takes another 25% of the total GDP and the interest on the national debt takes another 10% leaving only 17% for all other productive expenses from incoming revenue. This is still a relatively large amount of funds but nothing nearly close to what is needed for even the maintenance and creation of needed infrastructure. The failure to maintain the existing infrastructure in turn automatically increases the costs of both production and distribution of products making up the total market. These increased costs in turn require higher prices for the products eventually bringing them into a position where they are no longer competitive with the same products coming into the US from the international market place. In short, a free interplay of market forces, both domestically and internationally, are necessary for the establishment of the competitive levels of business operations expected in a democratic political system. The claim is made that for a democracy to survive it must have as one of its major pillars of support a free market system. Therefore, the economic problems that currently face the US in regard to the economy do directly affect the free operation of market forces in a negative way and as a result also negatively impact the democratic political structure of the US.

It has now been determined that unemployment, in the current environment, restricts the free interplay of market forces. This restrictive factor has been set forth in two different ways; first the restriction it places on the free play of the labor cost portion of the market and second the restriction it places on the funds available for investment in productive segments of the economy. It now remains to be seen how, if in any way, these restricting factors can be removed or overcome. However, this portion of the debate will be postponed until a look has been taken at all the factors set forth in an earlier chapter.

The second issue listed in regard to economic problems facing the US is the erosion of the middle class, both in terms of the value of real income and the real value of middle class assets. This factor also has been looked at from two different points of view. As discussed above, the largest single asset held by the middle class is their home. When the housing bubble burst in 2008, the value of residential real estate dropped by 30 to 70% in most cases. This asset has never recovered. The second largest asset held by the middle class is their retirement programs, that is, 401Ks, company retirement benefits, and/or public retirement pensions. As we have seen, the near meltdown of the financial community reduced by 30% or more the value of the 401Ks after 2008. Some 401Ks have nearly recovered by now, with the exception of those funds that are being actively used by retirees who have to withdraw money to live upon. These 401Ks will never regain the loss they suffered. Corporate retirement programs are all essentially fully funded and have retained their value; however, most companies have moved away from providing pension type retirement benefits, replacing them with the 401K and similar individual investment vehicles. In the case of public pensions, we have seen that many of them are currently underfunded and in jeopardy of total failure. What has been promised in this case is likely never to be received; or the real value of a public pension has been drastically reduced.

Secondly, the middle class has been placed in a position where they are not receiving increases in wages that match or go beyond the rate of inflation or increase in living costs; or they have lost a manufacturing job and found a replacement job at lower pay and with fewer benefits. Overall during the last decade or so, some seven million jobs were lost in the US, a majority of these being middle class manufacturing jobs. These jobs were moved overseas where the products could be produced more cheaply. These seven million jobs have never been fully replaced, as whatever new jobs have been created are, in large part, temporary, part-time, unstable jobs which pay less and do not include benefit packages; hence the term underemployed. This is what is meant when people say that the middle class is seeing a reduction in the real value of their income.

This trend has also affected the children of the middle class in regard to employment after graduating from college. A very large number of those graduating from college are unable to obtain jobs in the field for which they trained. As a result they are taking jobs equivalent to those held by their parents and also are classified as underemployed. In regard to the young people, underemployment has created two further consequences, that is, one, that the children are remaining in the parent's home for extended periods; and two, they are delaying getting married and having a family for periods way beyond that which was normal 25 years ago. If it is correct to state that the lost manufacturing jobs will never return to the US in numbers necessary to restock the middle class; and that education will remain uncompetitive for the good paying jobs that remain, these trends will deepen over the next couple of decades.

Some claim that within 20 years or so, there will essentially only be two classes in the US, that is, an upper class and a lower class. The consequences of the reduction of the real value of middle class income and assets are numerous, indeed, too numerous to follow in detail in an essay such as this one. The immediate effect of the loss of income is that a larger percentage of the total income must be spent upon the necessities of life; that is, food, clothing, shelter and what is needed to maintain employment, leaving very little for discretionary spending, such as college education for the children, health care, not to mention a new car every two years, among other things.

This is coupled to the overall effects of lower income, that is, the direct reduction in consumer spending in the economy generally, and the fact that less taxes will be paid to the various governments.

In the case of the loss of real value of assets what is meant is that the normal investments in long term vehicles related to the middle class, such as residence, pension and retirement vehicles, savings accounts, etc. are all losing real value over time. Until quite recently these types of assets almost invariably have seen steady increases in value. Home values, for example, until 2008 were increasing at astonishing rates. With the bursting of the housing bubble, however, they may never fully recover the value levels that they held pre-2008 and the Great Recession. The artificially low interest rates being paid in the current environment have created a situation where saving in the traditional manner is a money losing proposition.

For that reason such funds, if any are available, are being invested in other ways, such as the stock market. Many investment experts claim that the stock market is currently undergoing the process of bubble creation. If that's the case, all the additional money moving into the stock market has allowed corporate stock values to far exceed the normal valuations given to corporate operations and income; that is, the stocks are seriously overvalued due to size of the demand in the market. In the view of many financial experts a serious correction is coming, essentially a bursting of the bubble, such that the loss of real value in the stock market will dwarf even that seen in the housing debacle. In both the case of the housing bubble and current overvaluation of stock values, the correction has and will bring the prices back in line with what they would have been had the free interplay of market forces established the value; or at least, that is the expectation or assumption being made. This being the case, the values may or may not return to the artificial levels, but either way the real values will be determined by the market system.

The question is whether or not the housing market and the stock market are any longer subject to the free interplay of market forces. Many experts feel that the housing market is outside the free market system now that the federal government has taken over the ownership of the vast majority of home mortgages. The Central Bank, that is the Federal Reserve System (FED), has the power to dictate the terms under which mortgages will be created, how they are sold and how much return in the form of interest will be paid. With these powers it still remains true that mortgages are being obtained by people who cannot afford them and who will default on them in the short term. In the case of the stock market the lack of regulation by the federal government has allowed the stock market to be driven by short term profit seeking, speculation, fraudulent bookkeeping practices and other operating factors that have resulted in the current overvaluation. However, in this case it does not appear that the values have been set outside the free interplay of market forces. The drive for short term profits, the decision to speculate, and shaky bookkeeping are all part of the forces which are at play in this segment of the economy. Even when a look is taken at the shrinking, and possible disappearance, of the middle class the conclusion can be drawn that this result is not because of interference with the free interplay of market forces. The movement of the economy from a manufacturing base to a service base is the result of the free interplay of market forces. The decline in the real value of middle class income is also the result of the free interplay of market forces, that is, the loss of job availability, the lack of adequate educational or other job preparation, and the competition for these jobs. The final conclusion then in this case is that the solutions to these problems are to be looked for somewhere other than in the free market system.

Lastly, a short look will be taken at the current middle class in the US in an attempt to determine whether or not it is actually decreasing in size. The existence of a healthy middle class, as was the case with a free market economy, is seen as one of the major pillars supporting the American democracy. The middle class has ever since the industrial revolution been by far the largest class in terms of numbers in the US society. During most of the 20th century it was estimated that 60 to 70% of all Americans belonged to the middle class. This percentage was established on the basis of where total income and asset holding fell in relation to the highest and lowest levels of income and asset wealth. Roughly 20% of the American population had income and asset wealth below that of the average productive citizen while about 10% had income and asset wealth that exceeded the average productive American. Those living below the official poverty level or at a subsistence level, make up only 5% of the lower class and only 1% of the upper class were deemed to be truly wealthy. All classes have, at least in the US, been broken up into tiers, usually three. They are, for example, the lower middle, middle and upper middle class. A look at the current environment will clearly show that those who were formerly solidly in the middle class due to their holding good paying, stable, permanent jobs; and who now are holding temporary, part-time lower paying jobs have fallen into the lower levels of the middle class and in many cases into the upper levels of the lower classes. On the other end of the spectrum those who have obtained the so-called core jobs that constitute technological employment, government jobs, etc. have moved from the upper middle class into the lower upper class. It is now estimated (at the end of the first decade of the 21st century) that the lower class holds nearly 40% of the population and that the upper class holds roughly 20% of the population. If accurate then the middle class has been reduced by nearly 30% since the last quarter of the 20th century. During the last quarter of the 20th century the lower classes did not pay any taxes at all on average, while the upper classes paid at a lower effective rate of taxation than the middle class (largely due to loopholes and other income deductions). In a nut shell, during this period, and probably up to the great recession, the middle class provided the lion's share of all tax revenue to all levels of government. A 30% reduction in the size of the middle class represents a tremendous loss of governmental revenue. There is little wonder why revenue falls short of need in both state and federal government. This loss appears to be permanent although it may in fact get worse depending on which events occur and when. At any rate, in the near term the middle class does not seem to be positioned to recover its former status in terms of percentage of the population and proportion of revenue.

One result of this trend is the increasing size of the gap between the lower and upper classes in terms of wealth. The top 20% of income earners (upper class) now controls, according to most economic reports, about 70% of the total wealth of the US. This means, of course, that 80% of the population is in control of only 30% of the total wealth. The measured gap between the wealth of the lower two classes as compared to the upper class is the largest in the world, at least, for highly industrialized nations. A continued trend involving further losses to the middle class will only increase the size of this gap. Some claim the eventual result will be the total collapse of the middle class.

One of the major supports of all democratic systems is found in the maintenance of a healthy middle class. It remains to be seen whether democracy can be maintained if in fact the middle class disappears, or becomes a non-factor economically. In every case where the middle class has disappeared democracy has been replaced by some form of totalitarian government (1930s Germany and Japan, for example). It is concluded, therefore, that even though the changes involved in this second category are economic in nature they do not directly affect the interplay of the forces of the free market system. They may; however, be one of the reasons that many are claiming that the US is no longer a true democracy. This aspect of the problem will be looked at in detail later in the essay.

The third issue of the general category of economic problems revolves around the fact that the American Public is not saving money. First, it should be noted that the middle class as a rule saved approximately 10% of their yearly income throughout most of the 20th century. Today the savings rate is near 4%, although recently it appears that the public has again been attempting to actively save. This reluctance to save can be expected when banks are paying only .001% on the funds deposited with them. Saving accounts are almost a sure way to lose money in today's investment market. From a different point of view it can very simply be stated that you cannot save money you don't have in the first place. If everything that constitutes revenue to a household that is, earnings, welfare benefits, etc. is consumed on the purchases necessary to survive nothing is left for discretionary spending. This is an informal way of expressing the fact that savings are discretionary spending, and indeed, in some cases would be classified as luxury consumption. It is claimed by some economic analysts that research has clearly shown that a growing number of households cannot provide for the necessities of life (without borrowing on credit cards, food stamps, etc.) let alone afford the luxury of saving money. This outcome seems to be the result both of the shrinking value of real income in the middle class and the fast rising costs of necessary consumption, that is, such items as gas for the auto, heating fuel, electricity, food and health care. Even in the case of those surviving on the fixed income represented by welfare benefits the rising benefit structure (pegged normally to cost of living) over the last few years has not kept pace with the rising cost of necessities, although they have kept pace with the overall pace of inflation for the economy as a whole. This is only one example of how the official numbers can be misleading in relation to specific issues.

What is of most interest is that this trend has been covered the closest in relation to the middle class; but is now also becoming apparent to the lower and upper classes. The lower classes are slowly slipping into a position where their benefits, or income, or both, are not even keeping pace with the slow increase of the official poverty level. For those working at the mandated federal minimum wage of $7.75 per hour, a full time job produces something less than $15,500 per year. This amount even for a single member family is below the national poverty level. The same is true of a three member family where two members work full time at minimum wage. It is important to note that many of the minimum wage jobs, especially those in the fast food industry, are not full time jobs making the poverty level even further out of reach for those working in that field. The lower and middle upper classes are also finding it harder to make ends meet on the income they have; even though that income may be in the range of $250,000 per year. These households are experiencing the same squeeze as the middle class. At this level, however, it is not the necessary items that are causing the squeeze; but rather, the escalating costs of education for the children, the escalating costs of exchanging automobiles on a regular basis, and other such luxury spending. In order to maintain the standard of living currently held by a household at this level of income it also seems to be a necessity to carry some level of debt. Most experts now accept the fact that only those in the top 5 or 10% of income have escaped any real effect in terms of real income or real asset value losses. The end result of this trend, at least in the US, is that for the first time in its history the majority of the national wealth is being held by the top 5% of income earners. In turn, since money carries with it political power this power is also being concentrated in smaller and smaller numbers of individuals and entities, e.g., corporations, investment firms, international conglomerates, banks, etc. With this concentration of wealth and power in decreasing numbers of individuals comes the automatic conversion of the political system from a democracy to an aristocracy or oligarchy. History also shows that most aristocracies and oligarchies are relatively unstable until they are converted to some form of authoritarian, or totalitarian, governmental system. This conversion allows the aristocracy, or oligarchy, to hide behind the formal government and conduct affairs without any transparency as concerns the public in general.

One can use the EU as a current example of how democracies are slowly being converted into a powerful aristocracy of the political elite. This, of course, directly affects the question as to whether this trend is contributing to the decline of democracy in America, if it occurs at all; it equally shows that this trend is beyond the economic system. That is to say, this trend is not one that has any appreciable effect on the free interplay of market forces. Indeed, it may in fact have been the result of the free play of market forces. However, the lack of savings in the private sector is directly related to the fact that there is a real lack of investment in the productive sectors of the economy. This in turn directly results in the production of fewer good paying permanent jobs and the income they represent. This in turn reduces the revenue available to government and increases the need to borrow. Lastly, this creates directly an economy that is very sluggish in terms of rates of growth. Therefore once again this issue will directly affect both the free market system and democracy in America in a negative manner. It appears that the cumulative effects of the economic issues facing the US are to be feared as much for their involvement with the loss of the free market system as with the loss of democracy claimed to be taking place in America; but again this will be sorted out later in the essay.

The third and fourth issues of the general category of economic problems can be looked at together. We have in essence incorporated the third feature into a portion of the second feature. The lack of saving on the part of individual citizens is in part a result of the loss of real income mentioned above. One aspect of this feature, however, remains to be discussed, that is to say, the credit binge that has swept over the American public over the last several decades. The level of personal debt, as represented by credit card balances and other short term debt vehicles, has exploded. A good share of this debt in all levels of the class structure was obtained in an effort to maintain a standard of living that had grown unsustainable at the level of income available. In order to pay down this debt, especially in the case of the middle class, it has been necessary to lower the standard of living that can be maintained. This has been done by spending less on non-essentials and more on debt reduction. This pay down has left considerably less money available for funding retirement programs, savings, education and other investment planning. In the lower and middle levels of the upper class this issue is reflected in a reduction of investment in luxury items, such as yachts, foreign vehicles, luxury dining and other expensive but discretionary spending. The reduced spending is again a function of reducing overall debt levels.

When the realm of the individual is set aside and a look is taken at the business communities the same issue arises but has different resolutions. Long term debt in the case of businesses is in one of two forms. First, money that is directly borrowed from the financial community to provide for physical goods such as plants, equipment etc.; second, funding that is obtained through the sale of stocks and bonds and used for refurbishing plants, equipment or for expansion of the business. In either case the borrowed funds have cost in the form of interest, dividends, or capital value increases. The near melt down of the financial community, including the banking community, combined with several other factors over the last couple of decades has changed the way businesses operate in terms of debt. After the onset of the great recession businesses became much more conservative in relation to debt. In order to control the level of debt they adopted other methods aimed at increasing the bottom line profit earned. These methods included severe cost cutting, usually represented by reducing the number of employees, increasing the efficiency of the business, and outsourcing many aspects of the business. It also included a withdrawal of available profit from investment in long term debt for plants, equipment, expansion and other productive uses. These were some of the functions that were outsourced to overseas operations, some affiliated with the business and others not affiliated. This did allow for businesses, especially large inefficient businesses, to reduce their debt structure, to pay back the bailout funds given to them, and to once again be competitive in the international market. On the domestic level, however, these were also part of the reason that permanent unemployment rates rose and part of why the economy was seeing such low rates of growth. At the same time the funds that historically would have been spent on productive projects domestically were being invested overseas where a higher return over shorter time periods could be obtained. In addition the financial institutions, after nearly imploding, also took the stance that they would withdraw from the long term investment market. In short, they withdrew

$3 trillion from the traditional long term investment market and invested it in vehicles that would bring them short term profits at a higher level. The money was withdrawn from business investment, home mortgages, small and medium sized business startup costs, and put into stocks, bonds, auto loans, sovereign debt (bonds) a majority of which were overseas. The net effect was to depress the ability of small and medium size businesses to start up in the first place; or to expand if a successful startup was already accomplished. The financial institutions, however, according to some investment experts, are still essentially risk tolerate. This in effect means that they tend to overlook the risk involved in their investments to gain the higher returns offered. This is most pronounced today in two specific areas. One, sovereign bonds have become much more risky than they were even five years ago, but the financial institutions continue to hold vast amounts of sovereign debt. Two, the funding of shipping containers (those huge ships that carry oil, ore, commodities, etc.). Many financial institutions ignored the risks involved to become involved in the massive profits that seemed available. Without going into much detail the shipping industry, or at least this portion of the shipping industry, is now in a serious decline. The ships that were built during the goods times for 40 million each are now being sold as scrape. Ironically, it is the Greeks who have benefited most from this movement that is, they sold the various financial institutions on the idea of funding the building of the ships when the market was really at its peak and are now buying them back at bargain basement prices. This, however, is not the important point. The real point is that the various financial institutions who either directly provided the funds, or those who provided the funds for them to invest, are facing a complete loss of their investments. The Central bank of Germany, being one of the largest institutions holding these worthless assets, may survive, but all of their second cousins who were in the market are failing. Experts see this bubble as being almost as large as the derivative swap debacle of the housing bubble of 2007 and 2008.

The effects of this type of investment philosophy (both on the part of the corporate community and the financial community) are expected to show up over the short term with the end result being another serious global recession. This trend towards a second recession is already evident in Germany. The main effect of this policy on the domestic market is the artificial restriction of funds available for long term investment, especially at the level of small and medium sized businesses. It is claimed that it is small and medium sized businesses in the US that drive both the creation of good jobs and the growth rate of the economy. The argument along these lines include the claim that without a healthy economic environment which supports growth and startup of small and medium sized businesses a free market system cannot be sustained. The lack of discretionary cash for investment opportunities, especially in relation to the middle class, has stifled the normal free interplay of market forces in this regard. In addition, the uncertainty of the current economic environment has repressed the normal cycle of long term investment by both wealthy individuals and big business. It is estimated that big business has withdrawn $1.8 trillion that would normally have been invested in productive projects and put the funds to work overseas for the production of short term profits. The same process has already been seen in the case of the investment community and its $3 trillion withheld from productive investment. Much of the money that has been withdrawn from long term investment has been flowing into the domestic market for stocks and bonds. Experts are beginning to claim that such huge amounts of money flowing into the New York Stock Exchange has had two major effects. First, it has fueled the growth of the overall evaluation of the stock market, which under this influence has recouped all the value lost during the great recession. Second, the money has tended to artificially inflate the value of individual stocks beyond that which would naturally be produced by the fundamentals of stock evaluation; that is, earnings, sales, product research and development, etc. They expect that this has caused an investment bubble very similar to that created in the housing market. The result, they expect, will be a massive correction of these over-evaluations. This they expect to appear during the year of 2015 or 2016. Once again such a result will put the US, and possibly the global economy, back into a serious recession. Speculation has artificially inflated economic value beyond the levels that would have obtained had the free interplay of market conditions been allowed to operate.

The crash of the stock market, today just as in 1930, will not be the cause of the following recession but merely a symptom of the problems that led to it. The 1930 depression was caused by the vast overproduction of American corporations and the glut on the supply side of the market with products that couldn't be sold. This resulted in the closing down of production to levels that could be sustained by the consumption segment of the domestic economy. Many millions were thrown out of work, and could not find any form of work to replace their lost job. Businesses, banks, governments all went bankrupt leaving the population essentially without assets to sell. The crash of the stock market in today's environment will still, indeed, be a symptom of the problems, but the problems themselves will be different. It is not overproduction of the manufacturing sector that will be to blame, it is rather, the over development of debt and the inability to repay it that is the cause. This cause is mainly to be found in the spending binge of industrialized governments and the shaky investment policies of the financial institutions.

The end result will, however, be the same, that is, many people will lose all means of working for an income; businesses, especially small and medium sized businesses will fail; and financial institutions will be forced to close without the ability to liquidate assets. The economic malaise may be as severe as that in the 1930s, but most expect it to be somewhat less severe, if it happens at all.

There are, of course, as many experts that see the situation differently as see it in the manner set forth above. This group would clearly reject the claim that the business and financial climate is currently unfavorable. Business, at least for this group, appears to be healthier than it has been for two decades. The financial community, although problems remain, is also healthier than it has been in decades, at least in the US. The economy is expected to show real signs of improvement both in terms of good jobs and growth rate over the next couple of years. It can be wondered by those who do not have access to the wealth of knowledge available to both sides in this matter how they can be so diametrically opposed in their conclusions. What is important is that the accumulative effect of the economic problems facing the US is negative in regard to both the operation of a free interplay of market forces, and the democratic tradition of the US political system. In the former case negative in the sense that government intervention and private policies are restricting the free play of the market system intentionally. In the case of the latter economic trends are resulting in a loss of choice on the part of the individual. In some cases this is found in welfare dependency and in others in a lack of motivation to make choices involving individual freedom and responsibility.

It may be of interest to take a little side trip into US history between 1920 and 1990. This seven decade period did, in fact, contain the whole of the Great Depression, World War II, The Korean War, The space and weapon race (cold war), and the Vietnam War among others. By 1920, or a little later, the US economy was undergoing the effects of full production. Unemployment was so low as to be unnoticeable; good paying jobs were plentiful even to those lowest on the income scale; production was supplying an abundance of products at prices that people could afford; and science had begun to discover labor saving devices for the home and business, such as refrigerators, electric ovens, and many others. Times were so good; in fact, that this era was labeled the "roaring twenties." The Great Depression, as we know, officially lasted from late 1930 until the engagement of US manufacturing capacity in the task of supplying our World War II allies with materials in 1939. The October 1929 crash of the stock market was merely an early sign of what was to come. In a manner of speaking, it is possible to look at the Great Depression as the first bursting of a value bubble, and by far, the most serious of any yet known. The official unemployment rate reached 25%, but in some rural areas, and some inner urban areas, the unemployment rates were nearly 100%. The loss of real value of income and real value of assets reached into all levels of society, but of course, most strongly affected the lower and middle classes. The savings of the private sector were completely lost and no new savings were generated. The business and investment communities were brought virtually to a standstill although some survived and may actually have benefited from the economic turndown. The massive spending programs initiated by the state and federal governments (what today would be classified as economic stimulus, Quantitative Easing, and welfare expansion) under the "New Deal" was the first attempt to follow Keynesian economics. Under this system it was projected that the main, if not the sole, engine that produced economic growth was consumer spending. If the private sector of consumer spending could not provide the purchasing flow it should be filled by temporary government spending. However, by the end of the 1930s decade the Keynesian economics had proven to be relatively ineffective; although everyone seemed to accept the argument that things would have been so much worse without it. Indeed, the New Deal program may in fact have reduced the amount of suffering and discontent that could have been generated by the prevailing economic conditions; but by 1938 the economic situation was actually getting worse. It is today accepted relatively generally that the Great Depression came to an end with the onset of World War II. The US manufacturing sector was again operating at full capacity, unemployment was non-existent, a welfare safety net had been established through the New Deal, and the economy was growing at a 5% of GDP per year over the next decade (the decade of the 1940s). By 1950 the US had obtained to a preeminent position economically, politically, and militarily in the global market. As a result the domestic economy was still growing at a very robust rate. Even the Korean police action did not put a dent into the economic growth rate. The Cold War which replaced the shooting of World War II also acted as a stimulus with the various races that it produced, that is, the arms race, the nuclear weapons race, the space race among others.

Between 1950 and 1970, however, the second major evaluation bubble came into existence. This was the bubble created by the tying up of non-productive funds in the military budget and the growing cost of the various welfare programs both of which were representative of growing levels of debt. The first evidence that this bubble had burst was to be found in the failure of the Great Society Program instituted under the administration of Lyndon Johnson. This program was intended for all intents and purposes to be another New Deal for the American people. Instead the funds intended for the program were spent on the Vietnam War, the space race, and various smaller entitlement programs. The second shock came with the oil embargo of the early 1970s. The era of cheap oil had come to an end and with it the low cost of production that American manufacturing depended upon. The manufacturing bubble had burst and the reaction of the business community was to move manufacturing to less costly environments. It was a market driven decision, that is, it was apparent that the cost of refurbishing worn out, or out dated, manufacturing plants and equipment was much higher than moving the facilities and equipment to nations where labor, materials, taxation and regulation were all at lower levels than comparable services in the US. The conversion period saw runaway inflation combined with sluggish economic growth which came to be known as stagflation. The result was a very substantial loss of good paying jobs, high levels of unemployment, high interest rates and increased levels of welfare benefits and high rates of inflation.

What followed was a series of relatively shallow recessions after the 1970s. These were all associated with evaluation bubbles, that is, segments of the economy that for one reason or the other were forced into over evaluation of assets and a sudden devaluation (or correction) of them when the bubble burst. The first was a mild over evaluation of certain types of investment vehicles through manipulation, that is, junk bonds and the S&L's. The loss of value of savings held by the Savings and Loan Associations was the largest public haircut taken by the American people up to that time. The junk bonds, and leveraged buy outs (LBO's), represented an over evaluation of investment vehicles through fraudulent and/or immoral business procedures. The next to follow was the over evaluation of the high tech companies involved in the rapidly expanding information field. By the end of the 1980s and early 1990s these companies were forced to devalue their projections for income with the investors again losing much of the asset value that had been artificially created through pure speculation on short term stock profits. The last was the housing bubble that has already been discussed in this essay. The point being that both the causes of modern recessions (those occurring after 1970) and the solutions to them (Keynesian economics and temporary welfare programs) have been around for a long time and have for an equally long time been ignored in terms of the problems involved and their real solutions. No substantive solutions have been offered to resolve the issue of how the causes came into effect; or as to how they could be resolved once they came into effect. We are at exactly the same point today after the passage of forty years or so.

The point of this history side track is to show that the environment which existed during the whole span of time running from 1920 to at least 1990, or a little later, no longer exists. The first three decades of this time span where dominated by the manufacturing vacuum created by the destruction of World War I and the depression, as well as the fighting of World War II. Germany, the UK, Russia, Japan, China, and the rest of Europe generally had been reduced to virtually non-existent manufacturing capacity. That vacuum was filled by the undamaged manufacturing capacity of the US during this period. There can be no doubt of the vastly superior position of the US both in the manufacture of products for the domestic and international markets; and in the control of distribution of these products (domestic and global trade) from 1920 through 1950s. The dominance was so great in fact that both big business and big government ignored the effect that union demands for high wages and large benefit packages was going to create in the near future (not to mention constant increases in benefits and qualifications for welfare). By the 1960s this preeminent position had begun to deteriorate. Both the Japanese and the Germans had, through adapting American investment, manufacturing and technological procedures, developed a large manufacturing base which was producing products of higher quality at lower prices than their American counterparts. By the time that the US began to notice that it was losing its manufacturing preeminence a significant share had already been lost. It was also becoming very clear that American manufacturing concerns were no longer competitive on either the domestic or international market. The end of the period of unlimited growth in manufacturing, investment opportunity and rapidly increasing standards of living at all levels of society had come to an end. All of this should have been evident to both big businesses and big government as early as the 1950s; but did not become part of the business and governmental consciousness until near the end of the 1960s; by which time the opportunity to resolve the problems at a reasonable cost in terms of money and effort had passed. The early signs were clearly recognizable by the late 1950s and were evidenced by the rapid growth of the EU in direct competition with the US, Japan, and SE Asia.

By 1970 the US had lost its preeminent position, at least to a substantial degree, in the manufacturing segment of the global economy. It still held the premier position in global finance, trade and information technology. However, even these were beginning to come under challenge, particularly the information technology sector. The US today, according to some experts, is now faced not only with the loss of preeminence in manufacturing but also in the area of global financing (the conversion of the US from the largest creditor nation to the largest debtor nation) and global trade (the impact of China, Japan and Greece on the global container industry). The US today remains preeminent, without any reason for doubt, as a military power. This, however, may in fact be a deficit rather than an asset. The US is now claimed to be facing an economic and political environment where the most she can hope for is to remain a preeminent regional power in the view of those who see the US as in decline. This latter prediction may be a little unrealistic, at least for the foreseeable future, but without a resolution on a permanent basis of the current economic, political and social problems facing the US it could, of course, become more accurate over the long term. The conclusion can be drawn that the current set of economic problems is having a negative effect on both the free market system and American democracy.

CHAPTER 6. THE OVERALL EFFECT OF THE WELFARE SYSTEM

A second category of problems revolves around the slow erosion, in the eyes of the American public, of the credibility and competence of those who make up their representatives at all levels of government. There are, of course, many different aspects to this slow erosion problem and only a few can be set forth in this essay. A few have been arbitrarily selected, not necessarily for their overall importance; but rather as a means for expressing the point that is trying to be made. First, the American public senses the detrimental effect of the various governmental penchants for budget deficits and long term debt. Most can easily compare such activities to their own lives, that is to say, most can recognize the importance of a balanced budget and competence in running a household. They understand that if you spend more than you bring in, and do not have a plan in place for paying down this debt, that at some point the debt will become so large it can't be paid off. When this occurs they also clearly understand that the only option is to default and possibly to go bankrupt. Although they may not see the reasons for government behavior along these lines, they instinctively know where it will lead over the long term. Coupled with this basic understanding of economics is the further misunderstanding which arises when they see the federal government intentionally approaching a point where it will have to go into default on current obligations. In their own lives, people have a deep understanding that society requires we make every possible effort to prevent ourselves from going into default on our debt. Adding to this confusion is the perception that the various governments cannot come up with any method or plan for reducing the current level of budget deficits or for funding a program paying down the national debt. Once again, in their own household, when debt becomes overblown, as it has in recent decades, most people find a way to reduce spending and plan a debt reduction program. This may even include sacrificing of some aspects of their current standard of living. In some circumstances, as with the housing crisis, many people were unable to accomplish this feat and were forced to go into default resulting in the loss of the asset covering that debt. This was both a moral and a social crisis for those who underwent foreclosure.

The American public understands that debt, of whatever kind, puts a restriction on actions to be taken in the future if there is any intention of repaying the debt. The actions of the federal government in particular seems to tell the public that the government does not expect any results affecting the future; or that it does not intend to ever pay back the debt. These in combination bring the public to question both the credibility and competence of its elected representatives. Today the performance rating of those serving in the federal government, at least those elected by the public, has reached historical lows. This reflects not so much a blame game as a plea for rational action focused on problem solving. The wisdom of the masses, who know that you cannot indefinitely spend more than you earn, is seen as not being applicable to the government elite. The sale of bonds, the preferred method of borrowing on the part of governments, was detached from reality in the sense that they were seen as long term investments that held near zero risk of default. No one ever called them in, fearing that the government involved would default. In fact, however, this has happened many times in the past, that is, governments have defaulted on their debts and suffered a serious devaluation of their currency as a result and paid off the debt with depreciated funds, while investors incurred large losses on their investment. This is the same as making only a partial restitution on the whole debt owed.

With the failure of Greece a combination of things occurred. The EU, mainly the German banking system, provided funds to pay a percentage of the Greek debt while the investors holding the bonds agreed to a seriously reduced return on the money invested to carry the remaining debt. As a result sovereign debt was no longer unrealistically evaluated as a zero sum risk; but rather it was assigned the same risk as any investment in the stock market. Over time this will make borrowing much more expensive in terms of interest paid. This in turn makes it even more likely that governments will at some point find debt unsustainable and be required to default. Unlike a small debtor, such as Greece, a much larger economy, such as France, could not be bailed out and the default would have a proportionally larger effect on the global economy. It appears from the fact that Japan has sought relief from its debt by seeking permission to significantly devalue its currency (the yen) that this nation has come to the brink of sustainability in terms of its sovereign debt issues. Many expect that Japan will default in the near future, but nothing is certain in this case. The EU over the last couple of years has seen several of its member economies reach a point where their debt could not be sustained, or their banking systems had become unable to carry their debt, especially in the Euro zone. To date none of the governments, or banking systems, has been allowed to fail, but according to many experts neither are they out of the woods yet.

The situation in the US appears to be much more stable, with the caveat that we do seem to be heading along the same road. In the US the short term would be more likely to see the default of local and state governments rather than the federal government. Several small towns and counties have already gone into default and claimed the protection of bankruptcy. No state has yet entered into default but several have come to the brink including New York, California and Illinois. California, for example, if it was a nation, would be in the top 15 largest economies in the world. Should an economy this size collapse, it could not help but put the whole nation, at the very least, back into a serious recession.

The people have a right to fear an artificial default on the part of the federal government as it would mean real suffering and privations for the whole population. We have seen two intentional near defaults in the very recent past and others will arise on a periodic basis if the current political deadlock is not abated. There is no question that such financial brinkmanship is cause for wondering about the credibility and competence of those who opt for such actions; let alone questions concerning their sanity. As stated earlier the collapse of national economies in the past has led to the establishment of some type of authoritarian or totalitarian political system, especially during the Great Depression, as is seen in the rise of Nazism in Germany and Fascism in Japan. There is no reason to doubt that the same result would follow the collapse of the American economy if it were to occur. This, of course, means that the democratic system of government found in the US at all levels is being challenged by any action that leads to default.

The continuance of the welfare state at its current level also appears to be a direct challenge to the democratic way of life. For a growing number of people, support received from these programs represents nearly all of the income they have to survive upon. Any attempt to deprive them of even a portion of this funding will cause them to protest long and loud. It is for this reason that all plans so far offered for controlling the growth of the welfare state are based on the same format, leaving the benefit structure in place for those who are already drawing benefits from the programs and leaving the expected benefits in place for those who are within 10 years of becoming eligible to draw them. Any reform to the system would be pushed out beyond this time span and would not affect the sustainability of the existing program for at least another decade.

It is a good question to ask whether or not anyone has actually taken the time to determine whether or not the people currently receiving benefits, or those who will become eligible in the next 10 years, would be willing to take a little less in order to make the system sustainable. In order to do this the government would first have to make a realistic determination as to which benefits could be most effectively cut and how much would need to be cut from them to make the reform effective. The government would then have to make the information readily available to all current recipients and to those who will become eligible within 10 years. This information would need to be presented in such a way that those involved could make a truly informed decision on this issue. Lastly, the government would need to find a means of recording what the conclusions were of those involved, and if positive, how to institute them with the least amount of disruption to those affected. The roll out of the Affordable Care Act at least makes it questionable as to whether or not the current government is capable of such a feat. The issue, however, is of major importance because the answer may be the source of whether or not the US economy (free market system) and political system (democracy) will survive in the long term. Many believe that the American public is much better off than most give them credit for and that those currently accepting welfare benefits, of all kinds, are much more capable of taking less than one would expect (the public reaction to state and local austerity programs is a good indicator). It is also reasonable to believe that they will not give up any of these existing benefits, or expectations, unless they can be convinced that it is in their long term best interest to do so. There are, of course, a minority of people on welfare programs who are truly riding the system and can be expected to resist any reductions regardless of their long term interest (this may include such interest groups as AARP). They will, like all others, do what has to be done if they are made to do so, hence the justification for authoritarian government to be established, or instituted if all else fails. It is something very difficult to understand why those who represent the public in congress have not been asking people those questions. Polls clearly show that the majority of the American public not only realizes that both significant spending cuts and increased revenues are needed to resolve these issues. It has also been shown that the American public shows a willingness to participate in both spending reductions and revenue increases as long as they are distributed among the population in a fair and honest manner. The rub comes when the public hears the political rhetoric that clearly is ideological in nature. The Republicans claim loud and clear that the Democrats want to take wealth from the wealthy and the business community and "redistribute it to the poor." The Democrats, on the other hand, claim loud and clear that they do not want spending cuts focused on the reduction of welfare programs, such as food stamps, rent subsidies, school lunch programs, student loans, etc. and that the revenue increases should come from tax rate increases for the wealthy and the business community. Neither side is being completely honest about what the other side is asking, or presenting, nor are they being honest about where and how spending reductions and revenue increases could be obtained fairly. Indeed, none of the solutions offered by either side so far can even be fairly graded as a solution. The conclusion can be drawn, however, that even though these problems are largely technical in nature they have a very practical and important impact on both the free market system and American democracy.

These technical issues are by and large outside the operational interest of most of the public; at least in the sense of the public making a contribution to the actual programs that would put the solutions in action. They expect that the elected representatives will hear their call to find a solution that is fair and honest in terms of the burden borne by the various segments of society; and that the elected representatives will do their job and put together the programs that will accomplish these demands. The public demands begin with the requirement that a budget be built; and that this budget become balanced as quickly as possible. The public has clearly told its representatives that it will no longer accept the operation of the government without a balanced budget. The second demand being made by the public is that whether or not the existing national debt is sustainable they want a program put in place that ends the yearly increases and also begins a process whereby the debt will be significantly reduced. As stated earlier the American people realize that both spending cuts and increased revenue will be needed to accomplish these goals. They are demanding that the government put together a program, or programs, that will accomplish this goal with as little sacrifice as possible to all segments of the society. The American public appears to feel confident that if these demands were met that the economy would in a relatively short period of time recover from the last recession and again enter into healthy rates of growth. They seem to accept the concept that an economic and political environment that makes the business and financial communities comfortable with investing in the future of America will make it happen. As a result the public is clearly demanding an end to the ideological stalemate it has been witnessing for the last three years.

The general societal issues all revolve around issues that have a direct effect on the quality of the individual citizen's life. First, and most important, as the conversion of the US economy from one based on manufacturing to one based on the service industry proceeded the loss of high paying stable permanent employment has become painfully evident. The former base in manufacturing was essentially made up of large scale employment located in relatively small areas, that is, large manufacturing plants that hired into the thousands of workers and were usually located in or near large cities. These workers by 1950 were largely organized into effective bargaining units by the large unions that supported them. The workers that made up the manufacturing base by 1960 represented approximately 60% of the total work force of the US. This same group of people represented a majority of the segment of the society that was labeled as the middle class. This work force, in comparison to those of other industrialized nations, held the highest standard of living in the world. When after 1970 the manufacturing competitiveness began to be reduced due to these factors, and later lost to other industrialized nation's companies, the reaction of the large manufacturers, with the smaller company's later following suit, was to move their facilities, equipment and labor overseas. Many of the largest of the manufacturing facilities, that is, those involved in the production of automobiles and consumer appliances closed their American facilities completely. Some were torn down, others were left to deteriorate, and others were converted to other uses. The point being that the facilities no longer existed, the equipment had been removed and the labor force had been released. The labor was, and still is, essentially unable to replace the high paying, stable and permanent employment represented by the earlier manufacturing base. Instead they have been forced into taking less well paying, less stable and temporary or part-time employment in a great many cases. Those who were particularly unfortunate were forced into long term or chronic unemployment. The cities that were the centers for the manufacturing base, such as Flint, Pontiac and Detroit, Michigan lost their revenue base and slowly descended into poverty with large losses of population and infrastructure erosion. This happened not just in Michigan but throughout the nation. The end result has been the persistently high level of permanent unemployment, the rapid increase of long term unemployment and the movement of former workers into the disability programs adapted to absorb them. The issue now facing the US is the discontent surrounding the forced reduction of the standard of living of the middle class, coupled with the shrinking size of the class itself. Sometimes this is expressed as the decline of the real value of middle class income and middle class assets. Bottom line, however, is that the lower and middle classes in the US have seen a definite decline in the standard of living they are able to command. So far the reduction of the standard of living has not proceeded to the point at which society will need to cope with violent social protest, with the possible exception of the inner urban environment. It is estimated that the number of workers whose standard of living has been negatively affected by this process has now reached approximately 79% of the total working population. It has, however, reached a level at which public demands for action to reduce unemployment, to create "good jobs", and to bring manufacturing back to the US are being made more often and more to the point. Up to this point no one is listening, or if listening, capable of doing anything about these demands. It is important to remember the statistics that are now being used to explain the current environment of the US work force are truly estimates. It is estimated that 70%, and maybe a little more, of the work force is made up of lower and middle class workers (approximately 30% in the lower class and 40% in the middle class. That only about 20% of these workers (mostly in the upper middle class) are employed in what has come to be known as "core" employment, that is, jobs, such as truck drivers, construction workers, etc. Another 25% of the work force are employed by the various governments, large corporations, or are business entrepreneurs of some type. This group consists of jobs that require high levels of training (college education or long apprenticeships), and are high paying, stable and permanent jobs. People in these professions, businesses or jobs represent about 10% of the workers lost to the middle class, and which, have been brought forward to the lower and middle levels of the upper class. The truly wealthy that represent the upper levels of the upper class represent about 1 to 5% of the work force. These are people who do not hold productive jobs but rather are locked into the investment, banking and high level government positions. The wealthiest of Americans, such as Bill Gates, the Walton's and Warren Buffett do not even get counted in the work force and represent no more than 1% of the upper level of the upper class.

The result of all this was a massive conversion of the long term, relatively unskilled, high paying jobs that supported the upper lower class, all of the middle class, and a good share of the lower upper class. These jobs were replaced by low skill, temporary/part-time, low-paying jobs that made up the service industry or medium wage jobs also in the various service categories of employment. In addition those unwilling to convert to the new jobs were temporarily supported by unemployment benefits, and later settled for the option of removing themselves from the labor force by going on permanent disability status. Those taking the new jobs after exhausting their unemployment benefits found they were increasingly unable to support their former life style and quietly slipped back to a lower standard of living. All of this has been aggravated by the dysfunctional status of the American health care system. 40 million people are estimated to either be unwilling, or incapable, of obtaining health insurance and therefore adequate health care. Added to this is the dysfunction of the existing tax code where the bottom 48% of tax payers pay no tax at all, and the top 5% pays much less than would be expected under a graduated tax system. The influx of 11 million illegal immigrants who are working at low paying, unskilled jobs and in many cases benefiting from the various state social welfare programs have also added to the problem.

The least advertised segment of issues which affect the operation of the democratic system in the US is the importance of the interest group system that has grown up. Large well organized, well-funded, interest groups currently have found that they have the power to influence congressional actions in their favor almost without restraint. These include such groups as the Chamber of Commerce, big business, environmental groups, women's rights groups, gay rights groups, etc. These are active on the domestic level, but all in all, the most powerful groups may be the two political parties, international conglomerates, and the non-elected bureaucracy. All of these groups have gained the ear of the federal and state governments on issues that affected them; and have been able to get legislation passed to support their positions regardless of the desire of the American public (a form of entitlement benefit). As a result the American public does not feel that it has a credible voice in any government level. This over time has resulted in a loss of faith on the part of the American public and is reflected in the very low voting ratios seen particularly at the local and state levels, but also at the national level. Several recent Presidential elections have seen voter turnout in the range of 47 to 53% (while other industrialized nations see rates approaching 70 to 80%). On the state and local level the voter turnout has been sometimes less than 10% of those registered to vote. Whether this reflects a feeling among a large segment of the population that they already do not live under a democratic system can only be guessed at without further study. It is fair to conclude, however, that a large degree of cynicism, marked by political apathy, has grown up among the general population. Should this trend deepen it will be most likely expressed as a failure of the American democratic system.

Chapter 7. A New Day Ahead

What would the end result be if all the predictions being made of gloom and doom ahead for America were wrong? What predictions would be made to replace the ones of gloom and doom? Could there be a new day ahead for America? Everything seems to revolve around the catch phrase the "new normal." Within this catch phrase one finds the predictions of constant states of high unemployment; a consistently and long term sluggish, if not negative growth, economy; an imminent financial meltdown associated with the stock market bubble; unsustainable budget deficits and national debt; the loss of democracy and federalism; and the decline of American superiority in the global manufacturing, financial and trading sectors. In short, the demise of the American system as we know it. Added to this is the prediction that political incompetence and gridlock will continue to plaque the American scene. The scenario is a bleak one and is well expressed by Mark Steyn in his book "After America." It is this attitude that should be questioned by those who believe that the US has better days ahead. All in all, therefore, the new normal includes anything and everything that anyone cares to claim is wrong with the US. It can be fairly predicted that if the new normal is an inaccurate, or false, assessment that the opposite might in fact be more accurate. In that case it can be claimed that high levels of unemployment will be replaced, in the short term, with essentially full employment; budget deficits will in the short term return to sustainable levels, as will the national debt; the economy over the next couple of years will return to a robust rate of growth; the middle class will be reconstituted through the cultivation of permanent, good paying, low to medium skill jobs appearing due to advances in technology and science; the free market system will again be the most important adjunct to the economic system overall; and the US will see success in its foreign policies that are beyond sight at the moment. These events will overall support the strength of democracy in the US and reduce the existing burden of the welfare state. Political deadlock will end with the election of 2016 regardless of which party wins. It is likely that the candidates for President and Vice-President will be seen as much stronger than has been the case in recent years. The state and local governments will continue the current trend of instituting spending cuts and revenue increases until they have returned to a state of financial health. As such they will be in a much better position to reassert their constitutional powers and duties. Lastly, the American public, white, brown and black, will return to a conscious commitment to self-reliance, personal responsibility, honesty and acceptance of a solid work ethic.

Accepting that the latter predictions are accurate, one must consider what supports these predictions at the present time; and what must be done to assure that the predictions are given the support that they need to obtain the objectives desired. The following can be offered as support for the predictions being made:

- The rate of unemployment has been reduced from near 10% to 5.8% over the last few years. There is some debate as to the accuracy of these figures and how they are obtained, but it appears that the unemployment picture is slowly becoming better over time.

- There are strong indications that both the business and financial communities have adjusted to the new conditions facing them and are poised to begin large scale investment in domestic projects of a productive type.

- Consumer confidence in the economy is slowly returning to normal as is the rate of consumer spending.

- The economy is showing signs that it is recovering from the great recession and will enter into more robust growth rates over the next two years, hence, the 3.5% annual rate of growth for the 3rd quarter of 2014.

- The work force is slowly coming to adapt itself to the new type of jobs that are available and are getting the training needed to take these jobs reducing the rate of chronic unemployment and underemployment.

- Over the last two years the size of the budget deficit has been reduced by half (to $750 billion); and the rate of growth of the national debt has also slowed to the same extent.

- The US has slowly come to a solid foreign policy stance and this stance will continue to harden over the next few years. This policy accepts our limitations in today's environment while at the same time emphasizing our strong points.

- Lastly, the American public has shown itself weary of political gridlock and will over the next two years bring it to an end. The result will be most evident in economic growth rates that run near 3.5% of GDP;

a return to normal rates of unemployment; a slowly stabilizing financial community, including the stock market; a solid reduction in the activities of the organizations now labeled as terrorist organizations by the US.; and a growing confidence in the American public that all is well.

There is a lot of room for improvement that will become possible should the above events occur as predicted. The value of homes, the largest single asset of the middle class, will gain back most of, if not all, of the value lost during the great recession. The value of 401K's and other investment vehicles, the second biggest asset of the middle class, have already gained back all of the value lost in the great recession; but this gain is seen as somewhat fragile and subject to a massive correction. There undoubtedly will be a correction of some type if stocks are truly over-valued but it will not be catastrophic as predicted by the gloom and doom crowd. Values will stabilize over the next two years and these investments will again begin to grow at traditional rates. Employment will continue to be converted from a manufacturing base to one based on the service industry; and the middle class will be invigorated by the conversion of temporary and part-time jobs into full time employment. It may be several years before this last change is fully realized in regard to the middle class but it will become recognizable over the next two years. Lastly, without political deadlock it will become possible to truly reform the existing tax code; the existing regulatory system; to reduce the footprint of the national government; and to return the economy to a point at which the free market system is again operating efficiently.

The heartbeat of the American public has been seen in the results of the 2014 mid-term election and may prove to be even more so in the 2016 Presidential election. After 2016 it is very likely that a serious effort will be made to reform the welfare system in order to bring it into a sustainable condition. The same will be true in regard to the fate of the Affordable Care Act and the reform of the health system generally. The American public has shown a strong desire, for example, that the national government take the measures needed to bring the Social Security, Medicare, and Medicaid systems into a sustainable condition prior to 2030. There is also a strong desire on the part of the public to reduce the size of other welfare programs, such as the food stamp program, the various subsidy programs, both for individuals and businesses and the school lunch program (school free or subsidized food programs). The latter currently affects 95,000 schools and some 26 million children on a daily basis. All of these trends support the prediction that there is in fact a better day ahead for the US and that the US is not in eminent danger of collapse.

Whether or not the above trends represent an adequate base of support for the predictions being made is, of course, still debatable. It is, in fact, the essence of the on-going debate one faces every day in the various media outlets and academia. It seems everyone has an opinion on what will happen, how what will happen will be triggered, and what will be the result of what happens. Since at least as late as 2007, if not before, the general consensus has been in favor of the new normal and its consequences. Many explanations have been offered to show how the new normal came about and what the results of it being established will be over the long term. Some prefer to talk about the failure of the new normal theory and how everything is going to get better in the near term, or at the very least, that we are at the bottom of a deep bust cycle. This group, which includes many government advisors, believes that the economy periodically goes through a cycle consisting of a boom (high rates of economic growth) and bust (periods of sluggish or negative growth in the economy) as part of the operation of the free market system. This group has been in the minority for some time but that is exactly the theory that is being suggested here. It has been suggested here that this is, in fact, the course that America finds itself on today.

The next question is what must be done to bring this prediction into existence. It will be contended that at a minimum the following actions must be taken to assure that the predictions given stay on course. On the most general level it must be consciously acknowledged that the operation of the free market system is crucial to the success of the above predictions. This includes, but is not limited, to making sure that the national and state governments do not interfere with the free operation of the market forces. Also on the most general level democracy must be consciously promoted in regard to the valuing of innovation and creativity. Boom cycles, according to this theory, have always been introduced by putting in place the results of innovative and creative approaches to economic problems. On a more specific level, a real attempt must be made to reform the current regulatory system to provide a degree of comfort in both the business and financial communities in regard to the actual costs of doing business. A reform of the existing tax code must also be undertaken, first, to provide businesses the luxury of being able to calculate the amount of profit they will be allowed to keep, and second, to increase the effective revenue received by both the national and state governments. The educational system must be reformed, preferably through the combined effort of both business and government, to insure that the students are adequately trained and ready to take the jobs that will be available in the future job market. This reform should include an attempt to make this education affordable without government subsidy; most likely with the establishment of some type of apprenticeship program where work and training are combined. Lastly, a conscious effort must be made to reform the welfare system with the goal in mind being the sustainability of the system at least while the current beneficiaries are using it. All of these ideas, or reforms, are essentially aimed at the national and state governments, but it must be remembered that nearly as many restrictions arise from the private sector. Private restrictions on the market forces include such things as union wage and benefits policies, corporate outsourcing policies, shipping jobs overseas, investment policies and others. In the eyes of many the combined restrictions currently in place within the economy, both public and private, have already advanced to the point that the free market system cannot be saved. The current trend towards a controlled economy, through regulations, bureaucratic actions, and taxation policies, has already been put in place and awaits only the failure of the free market system completely for its full implementation. There is some level of truth in the claims being made by this side of the debate. Here it is only being claimed that the conclusion drawn from the truths found in the argument are wrong, that is, that the free market system no longer exists, or will disappear in the short term, within the US. The contention being made here is that the free market system is still active and of great importance to the health of the US economic system, but that it is in need of some tender loving care. This attention needs to be focused on the reforms set forth above and the real interest of the American public in assuring that the goals are accomplished. The only way in which a reform of the regulatory, tax and welfare systems is going to happen is for the public to demand that it be done in a manner that cannot be denied.

There are other economic measures that need attention, such as the reform of the health care industry. No one denies that the system is broken in regard to the 40 million people who were uninsured; in regard to the use of pre-existing coverage clauses in medical insurance programs; in regard to the high cost of doing business as a health care giver due in part to frivolous and exorbitant legal cases; and in regard to the blatant practices of the drug industry. Although the Affordable Care Act has been passed and is in the process of implementation it does not appear that it is resolving many, if any, of these issues. In this case it can be claimed that government interference in regard to the act has restricted the ability of the problem to be solved by the operation of the free market system. If so the law should be repealed to allow a free playing field for market forces. What legislation is passed should be limited to relieving the system of private restrictions on the free market, such as drug and medical facility monopolies.

Attention must also be turned to the decaying US infrastructure system. Over the years this responsibility has shifted from the states to the national government. The reason for this shift has always been stated to be the scope of infrastructure maintenance and repair, and the gigantic cost involved. Again there is truth in this argument. The problem arises from the fact that the shift that was made not only shifted the duty to help pay for and plan infrastructure maintenance and repair to the national government; but also included shifting the responsibility for overseeing and conducting the actual maintenance and repair to the national government.

Last but not least, a reform of the US immigration policy must be undertaken. The use of illegal immigrants as a cost cutting measure in many ways does not differ from the former policy of using child labor to accomplish the same goal. It is in fact a restriction that is being place on the operation of the free market system. It also needs to be accomplished as part of a humanitarian response to the 11 to 14 million illegal immigrants who are already in the country and to some degree participating in the society.

It can only be guessed as to the stimulus such reforms would bring to the economy of the US and the free market system. It is being suggested here that it would result in the revitalization of the US as a nation both domestically and internationally. Indeed, if properly instituted the US would again be operating as it did during most of the 20th century.

In the case of democracy a less specific approach will be needed. In the modern debate the question of the loss of democratic traditions is usually tied to the increasing size of the welfare state and the loss of traditional social standards. The new normal in relation to the welfare state is based upon the following set of assumptions: one, that the welfare system on the national level alone takes approximately 48% of the national wealth. Two, that the cost of the system in relative terms is what drives the ongoing budget deficits and the expanding national debt. Three that the level of benefits delivered to the American public has made them dependent upon the national and state governments for their standard of living. Four, the dependency of the public has fostered the willingness of the public to give up its traditional social principles for a check. The national government has used the payment of benefits to extend its ability to intervene in nearly every aspect of American life. Over one half of the working population of the US receives some form of benefit from the welfare system. This would include such benefits as food stamps, rent or home ownership subsidies, unemployment benefits, free or subsidized meals at school, student loans, among many others. When one adds in retirement benefits under Social Security; medical benefits under Medicare and Medicaid, nearly one half of the total population in the US receives some level of benefit. This would seem to be pervasive enough on its own but when one adds in the fact that about 60% of all jobs on the market are government jobs the problem truly comes into perspective. Lastly, the problems created by the size of the welfare system are further aggravated by the demographic problem facing the US and other industrialized nations, that is, the working population is tending to grow smaller due to falling birth rates; and the number of people receiving benefits is growing due to a falling death rate. If it can be assumed that the number of good paying, permanent, low skilled jobs is also shrinking then there can be no wonder at why the US and other industrialized nations find themselves in the position they are in today. This is a description of the new normal as it exists in the political and economic realms. It can be claimed that all of these trends when put together result in the loss of democratic traditions. Actually it would be more accurate to say that the democratic traditions have not been lost, as they still exist, but rather that they are being traded for the convenience of not having to make any real life decisions. Once again it is fair to say that there is a modicum of truth in the position being presented here; but the conclusion is again wrong, that is, democracy still exists in the US, but is, as we found with the free market system, under attack and in need of some tender loving care.

The other side of the argument is presented in the following manner: one, that the business and financial communities have adapted to the conditions brought on by the great recession. They have not only adapted but are beginning to take advantage of the new conditions. Investment in the productive aspects of the economy are beginning to rise; Americans are again beginning to save, at least for retirement, which over time will tend to accelerate the investment process; and the local and state governments are beginning to get their debt issues under control, as is the private sector. Most important of all, however, is that the business and financial sectors are again beginning to reward those who are willing to take innovative and creative steps in the creation of wealth. From a historical perspective one finds that all recessions since the 1970s have ended with an explosion of creativity and innovation in business. This has not always been a positive factor over the long run but has in the short run always stimulated the economy into more robust growth rates. The training necessary to bring new employees up to par in new industries is, of course, always a little behind the need for them. It does appear that this lack in the educational system has been recognized and is in the process of being dealt with in the private sector. Hence, the increasing number of large corporations willing to cooperate with the educational institutions in instituting the programs needed to prepare the students for employment. This latter represents a new type of apprentice program called work/study. These are all positive signs that there is indeed a better day ahead for the US, but there are still problems that need to be attended too.

First of all it must be clearly recognized that predictions based on gloom and doom have always sold better than predictions based upon rose colored glasses. Regardless, it must be understood that for those unemployed, chronically unemployed, and under employed there is no fast fix. Although helpful in getting these people over the hump, if the stretch of unemployment is short, unemployment benefits will not replace the benefits of a permanent job. It is also true that one, two or three temporary or part-time jobs will also not replace the wage and benefit packages that were lost when the manufacturing job ended. Government benefits under the welfare system will at best only support a long term life style if one is agreeable to taking a serious reduction in their standard of living. It appears that a growing number of people are willing to take this reduction in standard of living for the convenience of not having to work for a living. Such a decision does not just affect the individual, or individuals that make this decision, but also seems to lock succeeding generations into the same life style. This generational dependency seems to be at least partially responsible for the growing rate of crime, drug usage and gang membership. This type of behavior has historically been considered anti-social but seems to have become acceptable to some sections of the current population. The real fear should be whether or not the current government policies in regard to welfare are in fact creating a permanent underclass of citizens. This was in fact what happened within the Roman Empire as it converted from a Republic to an Empire. If so then this is reason enough to end, or at least seriously reform, the manner in which the welfare system delivers its benefits. As always the public has accepted the damage done by the great recession and appears to have gotten past the stage where blame is the game. They are now prepared to move on to a better day ahead.

The national government, as was pointed out by Ronald Reagan, is the problem. The entire public system seems to be out of touch with the real needs and issues that drive the private sector. The legislative branch for whatever reasons has brought itself to the point that nothing can be accomplished. The executive branch has for various reasons determined that it cannot work with the legislative branch and is attempting to operate on the basis of executive order and the bypassing of the legislature. The bureaucracy has grown so large over the decades, and so independent of supervision that it essentially acts on its own in accord with what it thinks is the desire of the executive branch. The bureaucracy has for all intent and purposes become a fourth branch of government mainly responsible for the implementation and enforcement of the laws passed and the executive orders issued. The judicial branch remains independent of the other two branches but is locked into an agenda that no longer represents the concerns of the people. They are still locked in the debate over civil rights that have long become out of date with the public, that is, abortion rights, gay rights, women's rights and prayer in schools (leaving these decisions to the people).

The federal government should forget about same sex marriages, abortion rights, prayer in schools, etc. and begin to focus on the issues that matter today. The latter would include the constitutional limits on the use of the executive power, the limit on the ability of the bureaucracy to act on its own initiative, and the limit on congressional power to bring the government to financial default and shut the government down. These are constitutional questions that loom large in the public eye and are essentially ignored today. The civil rights issues remain an important undercurrent of American society but it seems reasonable to allow the people to make the choices rather being dictated to by the national government, in other words, return the control of these issues to the people and the state governments. This may lead to a non-uniform treatment of these issues, but it will in fact come closer to satisfying the citizens of the various states.

There is much work that needs the attention of the legislature of the US. Attention is seriously needed to resolve the immigration issue, whether done by the national government, or maybe better by the state governments. There is a real need for legislation that will reform, if not scrap, the current tax code. Legislation is needed to resolve the ongoing issues in regard to the Affordable Care Act. If these problems cannot be resolved then the act should be repealed and the reform of the health care system returned to the private sector. Legislation is needed quickly to reform the major welfare programs to make them sustainable beyond 2030. These alone would keep the legislative branch busy and earning their money for several years. It would also pose an answer to the question of who the members of the national government represent, that is, special interests or the public as a whole. The administration also must stop whining about congress and quit attempting to operate the entire government with a pen. There is real work that needs attention on this side of government also. A concise and long term foreign policy strategy must be developed to handle the type of international events that are occurring in today's world. Whether or not one plan would fit the issue in the Ukraine, the issue in Iraq and Syria and the issue with the South and East China seas is debatable. Regardless, the administration must focus on these problems from both a short term and long term view point. There are many who claim that the US has lost most of its influence in the international arena due to the failure to develop a consistent foreign policy since 1989. Russia and China both see the weakness of the current lack of focus and are pushing the envelope to see how far they can go before resistance is offered by the US. The Islamic State is acting with impunity in both Iraq and Syria as far as the reaction of the US is concerned. Iran and N. Korea continue to flaunt their nuclear programs and anti-western dialog without fear of reprisal on the part of the US and its allies. Putting economic sanctions on a nation is not a foreign policy but rather an economic policy. The administration should focus on the sustainability of our current commitments to continue to carry the defensive burden for Europe, Japan and Israel. Japan apparently sees the lack of response on the part of the US in regard to the South China Sea issue and has started to rearm itself. Israel has long known that when push comes to shove that they are largely on their own in the region. Europe, on the other hand, still has not done anything of note to promote its own self-defense and is up in arms over the lack of response on the part of the US to the Russian moves in the Crimea and the Ukraine. The load facing the administration on the domestic front may be even heavier than that facing them on the international front. The administration must focus on producing a written budget that is submitted to and passed by congress; with the intent to reach a balanced budget as soon as possible. This would satisfy one consistent demand being made by the American public. A focus must be taken on the revitalization of the military to meet the demands of the modern world. Real decisions about the size and maintenance of the nuclear stockpile must be made; real decisions about the size and components of the conventional military must be made; and a real focus on the sustainability of a military budget that controls 25% of national GDP must be made; and the US must decide whether or not it wants to maintain its current control of the world's oceans. Beyond all this the executive branch must submit for legislation that will reform the tax code, the welfare system and the regulatory atmosphere. If this were not enough the executive branch must face the growing problem of infrastructure decay, the decline of education to prepare students for real jobs, and inept monetary policy of the Federal Reserve System. Problems can be studied and talked about for only so long and then action is required. It would appear that the latter point has been reached on most of the issues outlined above, and some action must be taken.

For example, in regard to the immigration issue the following can be done: one, amnesty for all 11 million illegal resident aliens could be given through legislation adjusted to the conditions and demands of the public. Two, the border with Mexico could be made less porous by passing legislation that makes it easy for those wanting to work in the US to get a work visa, a green card, or whatever else would make it unnecessary to cross into the US illegally. As an alternative, should the people decide that they do want to make it easier for workers to become legal, legislation could be passed that allows the actual protection of the border to be a state duty with the national government providing much of the financing. Three, over the long term legislation should be passed making it possible for the national government to cooperate with Mexico and other Central American nations to control the drug traffic, the social violence brought by the gang mentality, and the growth of economic opportunity within the subject nations. Fourth, the US has no choice in the matter of unescorted minors who are crossing the border. We are obviously going to take care of these children and a process should be established by law that makes this task as easy and straight forward as possible. The real issue, however, can be found in the claim that is being made that neither country finds it in their interest to deal with the immigration problems. This claim suggests that 30% of the total GDP of Mexico, for example, is produced by the monies sent back to Mexico by the illegal Mexicans working in the US. This is a large amount of benefit for Mexico and makes it difficult to find the will to stop the illegals from coming to the US. On the other hand, the US business community is stoutly resisting any attempts to stop illegal immigration as they need low-wage workers to produce a profit. This may be particularly true of the agricultural industry where a large percentage of illegals work. The industry claims that it could not produce a competitive product, if it could produce a product at all, without the influx of this cheap labor. They have also shown that very few American workers are willing to work that hard for that level of wage. In short, for this reason, among others, American business does not find it in its interest to stop illegal workers coming into the US.

At any rate, the point being made is that the business world and the American public have accepted the outcome of the great recession and are beginning to adapt to the new conditions. The same is true of the local and state governments which are attempting to seriously reduce spending and increase revenue. This has historically been the point at which the economy shifted into a healthier level of growth rate, that is, at this point the recessions in the past have come to an end. If there is a difference from those past experiences today the difference is undoubtedly in the fact that the national government is standing in the way of the recovery. It is a given that when money can be obtained cheaply it is usually invested with a lack of risk aversion (invested in bad debts). This appears to be the current case with the banking industry and its ability to obtain cheap money through the Federal Reserve policies. Add to this the fact that some 1500 new regulations were proposed at the federal level for the month of Jan. 2014 alone. Little question remains that with such a heavy burden of regulatory compliance and financial uncertainty that the environment is not a comfortable one for business opportunities. The national government is the problem.

Having established the reasons that a claim is being made that the economy is poised to return to a healthy rate of growth, if not exactly a robust rate of growth; and that the one remaining stumbling block is the policies of the federal government a look must be taken at what can be done to remove the stumbling block. The programs that are most widely held to be involved in the national governments reaction to the problems are the following: First that the Federal Reserve QE programs are in fact removing money from long term investment in the economy and putting it in the pockets of the consumer. This is claimed to have placed a negative drag on the growth rate of the economy. Indeed, this is a very simplistic explanation but it is beyond the scope of this book to detail the economic effect of the QE programs. The point being that the sooner the government stopped this program the better it would be for the overall economic recovery (the program ended in Oct. 2014). One of the claimed results of this program is that artificial inflation of assets has taken place which will in the end have to be corrected (this is usually done through a recession). Overall this has depressed the availability of funds, or raised the cost of these funds beyond the ability of small and medium sized business to accommodate. Even successful businesses are finding it difficult to find funds for expansion. Second, the artificial inflation of asset value has again brought the housing market back into focus. The banks, through the ability to obtain cheap credit, have again begun to loan money to people who cannot afford their mortgage and who will default as soon as the economy slows down again. This bad debt is largely found in the banking industry and will undoubtedly lead to another round of failures if a second recession appears. Third, the current policy of attempting to control the growth rate of the economy through consumer funding has removed these same funds from use as investment in the productive sectors of the economy. The unsolved problem in this area is to determine whether there are enough productive projects available to absorb the funds if they were made available. This is a different look at the result of the US economy converting from a base of manufacturing to one based upon the delivery of services. The service based economy appears not to have the same level of need for long term investment as did the manufacturing economy. As a result more money is funneled into other types of investments or used overseas for long term investment in manufacturing. This is also the underlying reason for the continued high rates of unemployment and particularly long term or chronic unemployment. What long term investment that is being made in the domestic manufacturing market is being made by foreign companies, such as Volkswagen, Toyota, BP and others. The returns on these investments go overseas to those who make the loans. The same problem can be traced to the activities of the domestic companies, such as Burger King buying the Canadian company Tom's Donuts. The main reason for the purchase was to take advantage of a tax loop hole to avoid taxes at US rates (tax reversion). Lastly, the regulatory system within the US is claimed to have grown to the point that it has become impossible for a business to calculate the cost of doing business with any consistency. This inconsistency or inability makes it difficult for them to invest their free cash into the economy.

The issue is not whether these statements are accurate; but whether they are putting any real restrictions on the operation of democracy within the US system of government. There is no doubt that a large number of the candidates that run for office are professional politicians, that is, they see politics and office holding as their means of earning a living. As with all professionals they are extremely reluctant to give up any aspect of their efforts that will lead to success. In short, they learn the rules of the game and play the game by the rules; with the rules being set by the political parties and the special interest groups. In this case it boils down to the political pro staying in the good graces of the party and doing what is necessary to control the vast amounts of money needed to get elected. In the end this means that a certain amount of deference to the needs of organized business, the financial community, wealthy individuals, unions, and specialized interest groups must be paid. Each of these groups expects that its influence will be increased as the amount of money spent on the candidate increases. Each group also has a relatively narrow range of interests and needs that it wants met. It goes without saying that these interests and needs do not necessarily match up with the interests and needs of the society as a whole. While the majority of the people of the US may in fact be involved, either actively or passively, in one or another of the special interests; no one is being represented as an individual by any of the professional politicians. If for no other reason it can be claimed that the US is no longer a representative democracy. The sovereign power that was to have been retained by the people (local governments) over time has been shifted to the national government. The sovereign power found in the national government to a large extent is being exercised at the direction of the two political parties and the special interests. Meanwhile the real business of the nation is implemented by and carried out under the direction of the federal and state bureaucracies. In combination these bureaucracies represent a shadow government that exercises the real power but without the restriction of supervision on the part of the people or their representatives. Over the last few decades it appears that the national bureaucracy has come to the point that it represents the font from which all powers flow to the state and local governments. This is in reality the basis for saying that most of the duties and responsibilities intended for the state and local governments have found their way into the hands of the national government. It is also the basis of the claim that the US is no longer operating on the basis of federalism.

Today very little can be done at the local or state level without the consent, financing and mandate of the federal government. The various departments and agencies of the federal bureaucracy are increasing in control of the delegation of this consent and financing to the state and local governments. A prime example of this phenomena is the Affordable Care Act. This law was passed by both houses of congress after some changes with no one in either house having read or understood the entire bill (a 2300 page document, which is now a 20,000 page document). It was signed into law by the President who clearly did not know what the law contained; and the law was then given to the bureaucracy to implement and enforce. What is of most interest is that the bureaucracy has succeeded in implementing the law (regardless of the problems with the actual implementation procedure) and continues to prosecute the enforcement of the law without regard to consequences. The media for the most part has shifted to other issues and the process continues essentially unchecked. The point being that once the law becomes the property of the bureaucracy it moves beyond the ability of the public to securitize. In this sense the deadlock between the two houses of the legislature and between the administration and congress is something of a non-issue. The administration has the constitutional right to issue executive orders, mandates and edicts to insure the enforcement of the laws of the US and the current President is using the power to its fullest extent; indeed, his use of the power has caused some to claim that he has exceeded the constitutional power granted to his office. With the federal government exercising the majority of sovereign power and the bureaucracy delegating most of the powers held by the state and local governments it is possible to say both that the US is no longer a federal system or a representative democracy. It is claimed by some that the US has evolved into an oligarchy supported by a technocracy. In short, it is claimed the US is now ruled by a shadow government made up of a hidden political elite (wealthy individuals, wealthy corporations and wealthy interest groups) supported by a professional bureaucracy. It is hard to argue with this point of view considering the fact that for almost a decade, or more, the elected representatives of the people have done nothing more than talk. All actions that have been taken are the result of the bureaucratic processes prompted by signals received by whoever they see as their employer. This employer is obviously not the people. This fact has brought about the call for reducing the size of the various bureaucracies in both number of employees and scope of responsibilities. This appears to be a self-defeating proposition in today's world with the various governments providing employment to nearly 60% of the total work force. This percentage is likely to grow even larger when one takes into consideration only those jobs that provide stable, high paying, and permanent employment. In the short and middle term it does not seem feasible to expect a large scale spending reduction in government employment at any level of government.

It has often been suggested that the reduction of the federal work force could be obtained by returning duties to the state and local governments. It does not appear that the state and local governments will be in a position to accept these new responsibilities for some years to come. This leaves only the option of raising revenue for the reduction of budget deficits and reduction of the national debt. The fastest and easiest manner in which revenue can be increased is for the economy to enter a phase of robust growth. A 10 year period, for example, with an average economic growth rate of 3.5% per year would eliminate the budget deficits and pay down the national debt substantially assuming that the additional revenue was not spent in some other way. For this to happen the federal government would have to be subject to a legal mandate to create a balanced budget for each of these 10 years. In addition the government would have to be required to earmark at least a percentage of any surplus generated for payment on the national debt, or a budgetary item, would need to be included for debt reduction. There have been periods of time in US history where balanced budgets were made, kept, and the surpluses used to reduce debt; the latest being a four year stretch in the 1990s. Barring a robust economy there are a few other likely alternatives. These would include scrapping the current tax code to eliminate all exemptions, deductions, and loopholes to escape paying taxes due. Tax rates could, and likely will over time, be raised on all segments of the working population. There will also be many new taxes installed to cover specific items in the budget as has happened in the past. As in the past these new temporary taxes will become permanent in time. It is estimated that currently the lowest 48% of income earners do not pay any taxes at all. It is further being suggested that the wealthy corporations and wealthy income earners pay far less than their fair share of taxes due to exemptions, deductions and loopholes. One cure for this massive loss of revenue would be to install a flat rate tax code. There would be no exemptions, deductions or loopholes. Each individual, corporation, or entity would pay a flat percentage on all income earned whether in this country or abroad. This tax rate could be graduated, that is, the percentage required could be raised as the level of income increases. For example, anyone making less than the then established poverty level would pay nothing. Those making between the poverty level and say $125,000 a year would pay 10%. Anyone earning between $125,000 and $250,000 would pay 15%. It might also be possible to structure a flat rate corporate tax code where all corporations pay a flat rate of 18% on all income earned either domestically or internationally. This is approximately the rate claimed to be paid domestically by most companies in the industrialized world. The exact numbers, of course, would have to be established after a careful study of the revenue needed and the revenue expected under the different percentages. The current acceptance on the part of the American public for the austerity programs being instituted at the state and local levels; as well as the acceptance by the public of increased tax rates, and new taxes, bodes well for this type of reform on the federal level. This reflects the fact that the US public is the least taxed of any citizenry in the industrialized world. This may not be true of the business community, but with the exemptions, deductions, and loopholes it is likely true of the business community also.

Currently there is no comprehensive plan being offered at the federal level to control spending or to increase revenue. The professional politicians seem to be putting all their eggs in the basket of expected robust growth in the economy in the short term. No action will, according to most experts, be taken and in the long run will cost the US its opportunity to fix the problems voluntarily. There is no other means by which the federal government, or any other entity, can obtain to a balanced budget than by spending no more than it takes in revenue. Currently, this would mean that both significant spending reductions and increases in revenue would have to be found in regard to the federal government. This is even more the case should the US decide that it would be wise to significantly reduce its national debt. In addition, because of the size of the needed spending cuts and revenue increases it is likely that the goal cannot be accomplished without a relatively long period of economic growth rates at 3.5% or above per year. Such a combination of events would in a very reasonable time period (three to five years) bring about a much rosier outlook on life for the American Public. This does not mean that the current generation will not feel the pain of the adjustment to the new conditions. This generation will on average, because of what is necessary for the future, end up with a standard of living that is somewhat lower than the generation that preceded them. Regardless of this fact it is still true that life, liberty and the pursuit of happiness have to be earned through the expenditure of blood, sweat and tears. American's have traditionally been up this task and there is no reason to believe that they will not be up to the task this time around, therefore, one can predict that better days are ahead for the American Public.

A look must be taken at what type of austerity measures might be needed; and where they might be found. The same will also have to be done in regard to the production of additional revenue. First, it must be noted that the American Public did not resist the automatic cuts authorized by the Simpson-Bowles Commission. The politicians failed to allow the cuts to be fully instituted due to warnings issued by various experts; but the public did not ask that the cuts not be made. This was done by the various interest groups in relation to selected proposed reductions. It was obvious that the public was prepared to accept not only the cuts but the suffering, if any, which would accompany them.

Second, the same attitude has been seen in the public in regard to the various austerity programs and increased revenue plans instituted by the state and local governments to repair their economic condition. This includes even the public willingness to accept the consequences of bankruptcy as with the City of Detroit.

Third, not only the public but also the business and investment communities appear to have accepted the consequences of their former actions and have prepared themselves to move ahead under the new conditions prevailing. The problem, therefore, is not the expected resistance on the part of the public to accept both the needed austerity programs and increased revenue programs; but rather, the resistance that is coming from the political parties, the major interest groups and the professional bureaucracy, that is to say, the existing vested interests. Having said this, however, it is probable that this would change under certain conditions. Should the burdens of the austerity programs, or the programs for increasing revenue, be unfairly imposed upon selected segments of the population a negative reaction would occur immediately. For example, if the burdens of the austerity programs should fall mainly on the backs of those already paying the largest price, that is, the middle and lower classes, protest would be significant. This would include removing any extensions to benefits for the unemployed, restricting the eligibility requirements, or benefits, under the food stamp program, the free meals programs at the schools, etc. It would result in large scale reductions in spending but would also directly affect the standard of living of nearly 50 million people, nearly all of whom are in the middle or lower classes. The protest might essentially be silent as the people who benefit from these programs traditionally do not have much of a voice when it comes to being heard by the political elite. This being the major reason that these types of cuts are usually targeted by the same elite.

Therefore, short term reductions in spending that effect mainly the middle and lower classes, the young, or the maintenance and repair of the infrastructure are not to be recommended. However, it seems likely that significant cuts could be made in the welfare benefits currently being paid without causing irreparable harm. The reduction of benefits under the food stamp program, if coupled with reductions of the subsidies paid to farmers; cuts in the benefits given for fuel and rent subsidies, if coupled with reductions in subsidies to energy companies; cuts in the school meals programs, if coupled with cuts in the price supports for agricultural products, would be acceptable to the public as being at least an attempt to spread the burden fairly across the whole of the society. The same is true of the programs to increase revenue, that is to say, as long as it is the public's belief that the burden is being spread across the society in a fair manner it would be acceptable. It is only when the revenue increases are loaded on the back of only the middle class, or any class for that matter, will they be resisted. What is very unfortunate is that this is exactly how the federal government appears to be approaching the matter, that is, by fostering reductions of spending, or increases, in revenue that fall disproportionately on one segment of the society. It is one aspect of the frozen ideological positions being taken by the political parties, that is, as the public views the situation the Republicans would like the burdens to fall on the middle and lower classes; and the Democrats would like for the burdens to be borne by the wealthy and the corporations. Neither is seen as justified by the public as a whole. It is not really possible to predict where the best sources of spending reductions will be found; nor how many people will be affected by them, but it is imperative that the sources used be spread fairly evenly throughout the society. The same will be true of the programs, or sources, for increasing the needed revenue. It is most likely that the short term reductions in spending, especially at the federal level, will come from a reform of the existing mandatory programs, such as the military, the various departments and agencies of the bureaucracy, and governmental salaries. In the case of revenue it is most likely these also will result from the reform of the tax system, a withdrawal from the federal programs, such as the QE programs; and the creation of new taxes, such as luxury taxes, sin taxes, and other user based taxes. This might even include the expansion of the use of toll roads with the funds earmarked for maintenance and repair of the infrastructure involved. Both the austerity and revenue programs would be greatly affected by the economy entering into a period of robust growth. This is a possibility that is argued both ways by the various experts, that is, some argue from the data available that the economy will not go into robust growth rates before the arrival of a second recession and recovery (probably a period of five to seven years or before 2020). A second group claims that both the business and investment communities are poised to take off as the economy warms up. They see the economy reaching grow rates of 3.5% per year by as early as 2015 (actually hit in third quarter of 2014). It is beginning to look like the latter group is making the best prediction, but only time will tell.

Regardless of the growth rate of the economy over the next five years the federal government must make an effort to reduce its spending, increase its revenue and attempt to operate within whatever revenue it has to work with. Some promising signs can be seen in the process being instituted by many state and local governments. Unions are showing themselves, and their membership, willing to negotiate reductions in wages, retirement and health benefits, and other cost saving agreements. Government contractors are showing themselves open to bidding reforms, reductions in requested cost overrides, and other cost saving measures. The state and local governments are willing to reduce the level of services they offer and to reduce their non-essential staffing requirements. They are also raising tax rates, and instituting new taxes to insure the full funding of public employee pension funds, essential infrastructure projects, and other needed social programs. The federal government per se has not yet taken notice of these new trends in the private sector and the local and state governments. Here the arguments are still over reducing spending only in the area of welfare benefits and increasing revenue only in the case of increased tax rates on the wealthy and corporations. Both sides seem to be depending on the hoped for robust growth rates in the economy. It is obvious that both sides of the debate are not serious about installing programs that will result in serious reductions in spending or serious increases in revenue. They can count on every suggestion they make being buried dead in the dust by their opponents. The American public in the meantime is left to go begging for solutions.

CHAPTER 8. DO DEMOCRACY AND FEDERALISM STILL EXIST IN THE US ?

The federal government will remain in the way of real solutions until the broken system that exists is repaired or replaced. As pointed out earlier many believe that the American system is not only broken but in danger of imminent collapse. It may also be claimed that the majority of power in Washington is being exercised by a political elite that is supported by well financed interest groups and a professional bureaucracy and is well beyond the ability of the American public to control. This has led to the claim that the US is no longer a representative democracy even though many of the officials are elected to their office. There is no question that the two political parties are beyond the control of the people as they blandly ignore the demands made by the public. Interest groups were never expected to be responsive to the people as a whole as they represent only a small portion of the citizens of the US. They have over the years been able through the explosion of costs in regard to campaigning for office garnered more power than would have been expected. They, of course, do not spend this money on political parties, and their campaigns, without expecting something in return. The something in return is not just influence with the political elite but real benefits, such as legislation favorable to their cause. The bureaucracy technically is under the control of the people through the elected representatives they send to Washington or the state capitals. As we have seen, however, the various bureaucracies have grown so large and complex that the elected elite are no longer capable of adequately supervising bureaucratic activity. It is easy to see that the parties select the list of candidates for nearly all elected offices; that they set the agenda for those candidates; and have the power to punish them if they do not follow the party platform. The interest groups through their donation of campaign funds do to a large degree determine the platform that the political parties will enforce on the office holders. It does not take a very close look to see that the officeholders do not represent the needs and wants of the citizenry that elects them; in fact, it is obvious that they can often ignore the public entirely. As a result the Republican Party platform has many planks that are favorable to the business community and to the wealthy individuals within the citizenry. The Democratic Party platform has many planks that are favorable to the interest of unions, civil rights groups and the academic community. For each party the groups mentioned represent a majority of the funding needed by the parties to conduct the numerous costly campaigns that come up every two years. Therefore, even though the members of the House of Representatives and the Senate are elected by the people; as well as the President and Vice-President in the executive branch, they do not represent the people, but at most only some of the people. For many decades it has been known that there exists a large silent majority. In short, a majority of the people in the US have no voice nor anyone to talk for them. Groups of people, who do vote, have their representatives who talk for them through lobbyists, financing of campaigns, and other methods, that is, people represented by labor unions, by business concerns, by AARP and many others. If this representation by group qualifies for inclusion in the traditional meaning of representative democracy then the US is definitely a representative democracy. The contention is, however, that group representation does not fit the definition as it was understood in 1789. At this time the definition of representative democracy was clearly regarded as a government by the people and for the people as individuals. What the group wants or needs may or may not fit with what is seen as good for the society as a whole. The people per se have very little input in who will run for office; what they will stand for once they are in office; and have no way of punishing an office holder who does not heed what the people need or want. In this sense none of the "candidates" represent the wishes or desires of the people other than as a part of campaign rhetoric.

The state and federal bureaucracies are a different type of problem. They are not elected to office by the people and never have been. In most cases the highest offices within the bureaucracy are appointed by the head of the various executive branches. It is only natural that these appointments would tend to be political in nature, that is, rewards for service to the party and the political elite. Many of them are not particularly qualified for the type of department or agency they head. By far, however, the majority of the people who actually carry out the day to day operations of the various departments and agencies of the bureaucracy are hired for their positions as professionals in the field. They tend to be stable regardless of which party comes to office and thereby provide expertise needed to operate the government effectively. They are only secondarily responsible to the people through the appointment process and the legislative requirement of confirmation. This first of all only applies to the highest level positions, most of which are not truly involved with the day to day activities of the department or agency in question. The bureaucracy as it stands today can be seen as a sort of fourth branch of government responsible for the implementation and enforcement of the laws passed by congress, the executive orders issued by the President, and the various edicts and mandates given to them from many sources. They are authorized to exercise this power by the constitution and their exercising of this power is not subject to the control of the people. In most cases it is not likely that most Americans would recognize the names of the people who head up the various departments and agencies or know anything of importance about them or their duties. A quick survey on the street will reveal that most people cannot even name the most important of the appointees, for example, the current Secretary of State. The distance between the people and those who man the bureaucracies is greater than one would like to admit considering the amount of power they exercise.

Accepting for the moment that the US is no longer truly operating as a federal system of representative democracy it is fair to ask under what kind of political system is the US operating? In the case of federalism it has been submitted that the US is now operating under the political system known as the national state. Under this system the sovereign power is held by the national government and the duties and responsibilities of the lower governments, and the people, are delegated to them from the national government. Although it can still be argued that many features of the federal system still remain in place it can also be claimed that the US is much more under the influence of the national system. This is, of course, the exact opposite of what was the rule during the first century or so of American history. In the case of representative democracy it has been submitted that the US is now operating as a confused combination of Oligarchy, Technocracy and Aristocracy. It is clear that the US can be at least seen as some form of democracy other than a representative democracy; but it is difficult to determine just what type of democracy that might be. If all that is needed is for the people to have the technical right to vote for office holders to be classified as a representative democracy then the US is still a representative democracy. If the political parties, office holders, and professional politicians only represent the interests of the wealthy (whether individuals, corporations or interest groups) then the US could be described as an oligarchy operating as a democracy. If the majority of governmental decisions are being made by the various professional bureaucracies then the US could be labeled a technocracy operating as a democracy. From what has been said before it is possible to see some aspects of all of these in the US today. This is not only a problem in relation to the US, but is a problem in the definition applied to a large majority of democracies that exist globally. The wealthy, the business community, and the interest groups all clearly have more clout with the political elite than the amorphous group known as the public, or the voting public. The same is true of the ability to make actual operating decisions of day to day importance that is found in the bureaucracies. The bottom line being that the people no longer hold or exercise any real power, duties or responsibilities, at least in comparison to those envisioned by the founding fathers. It is fair to conclude that the new conditions that have come into effect since 1945 have left the US technically a democracy, but one that cannot be classified as a representative democracy as defined by the constitution.

Today it would appear that the political parties through a sort of elitism do in fact control who will be a candidate for office; what and how the candidate will vote on various issues important to the party platform; but they do not seem capable of controlling the outcome of the elections themselves. Both parties must acknowledge to some degree the wants and needs of the voting public. This deference may be given most often to the various groups represented by formal organizations, such as the league of women voters, or to campaign donors, but they do take some part of the public into consideration. The public, therefore, does have some degree of say in what the candidates will campaign on and how they will vote once in office. There does not, however, seem to be any reason to believe that public opinion is as powerful as it was in the past. This being true it is fair to say that the US does not operate on the basis of aristocracy even though the wealthy may in fact be a sort of new economic aristocracy in the US. The wealthy (individuals, corporations, and interest groups) do have a lot of power and say in how things are done but they also do not control the outcome of elections. The end result is that the people do have the power to scrutinize the actions of office holders and to punish them. Therefore the term oligarchy also does not apply to the current US political system even though it does show some likenesses to that form of government. The bureaucracy also is very powerful but they do not at present truly control any part of the political process. They are powerful enough that at times they can and do act independently of supervision but they are incapable of dispensing with the other branches of government. The US for this reason cannot be labeled as a technocracy although there are some similarities between the EU (which is seen as a technocracy) and the US. Lastly, all of these interests, including the legislative and executive branches, are still subject to the decisions of the Supreme Court concerning the constitutionality of their actions.

The conclusion seems inescapable that the US remains a representative democracy but that this democracy is not as directly responsible to the people as was intended by the founding fathers, or even as late as 1900.

There does not seem to be any fear of overstatement when one claims that the majority of sovereign power now rests with the federal government. The state and local governments still have independent duties and responsibilities that they maintain; but even at this level the federal government is pervasive through its control of project financing, mandates and orders. The state and local governments are also under some degree of compliance in regard to the federal taxation policies and regulatory powers. For example, one of the most important duties and responsibilities that remain at the local level are the creation and maintenance of the public K-12 school systems. The state and local governments are responsible for building the facilities, hiring the employees that will run the schools, budgeting the money necessary to run the schools, and for collecting and distributing the property tax revenues taken in for the schools. The states also provide most of the funding over and above what is taken in property taxes if need be. This appears to be straight forward enough. The federal government, however, is involved at every stage. The states receive billions of dollars each year from the federal government for expenditure on the construction, operation and maintenance of the K–12 schools. The federal government funds the school meals programs that affect 95,000 schools and 26 million students on a daily basis. The federal government has recently also taken the lead in legislation that establishes the standards that the schools must meet for teacher competence and student achievement, such as the "no child left behind program." Although it is certainly true that the federal government is much more deeply involved in local and state affairs than it was even 50 years ago, it is not true that the local and state governments exercise no sovereign power of any type. The conclusion is that the US is still a federal system and operates as one even though many of the former duties and responsibilities of the local and state governments now rest with the federal government. As pointed out earlier, the trend appears to be that more and more of the sovereign powers still held at the local and state level are being transferred to the federal government, that is, the federal principle remains under attack.

It can clearly be established that the US is a representative democracy operating within a system of federalism. At the same time it can be clearly established that representative democracy and federalism do not operate in the manner that was intended under the original constitutional convention. The overall trend in American history has been one in which the sovereign power of the national government has increased at the expense of the sovereign power of the local and state governments. If this overall trend continues, and at this point there is no reason to believe that it will not, it is possible that some time in the future the US will no longer be a representative democracy operating within federalism. More than likely the US will still be a democracy but will be operating under the dictates of a truly national form of government. The additional trend that is found in American history shows the slow drift of power being exercised for the benefit of the society as a whole; to one in which power is exercised for the benefit of the wealthy (individuals, corporations, interest groups, etc.). Should this trend in the manner in which representation is exercised continue then it is possible that the US at some point will no longer operate as a democracy of any type. History has shown that when a democracy is converted to either an aristocracy or an oligarchy that it tends to be unstable. As a result both of these forms of government have tended to relatively quickly morph into some type of authoritarian government. It is fair to claim that democracy, the free market, federalism, and liberty have not yet been lost in the US; but that all of them are currently being challenged by negative trends within the society. The gloom and doom people are clearly warning of what the result of such trends will be if continued and that this should be attended to by the public.

The political and economic issues are not alone in determining whether or not the US is still operating under its traditional principles in regard to democracy and the rule of law. They are also affected by what has been happening in the social arena since the end of World War II. The cold war was overwhelmingly fought with the weapons of propaganda and money. The arms race, the race into space, and the race to obtain clients (foreign aid of all types) all were conducted with massive expenditure of money and lavish use of propaganda. The whole purpose for both sides was twofold, first, to convince their public that the other side wished to exterminate them; and second, to obtain control of world opinion in favor of their propaganda position. There were several actual combat arenas, however, that developed during the cold war. The first was the invasion of S. Korea by N. Korea. The newly created United Nations organization (UN) mandated the use of force to remove N. Korea; and the US, as the only war-capable nation at that time, took charge of exercising the mandate. After several years the status quo was reestablished due largely to the willingness of China to commit a million troops in aid of the N. Koreans. This conflict tended to enhance the status of the US within the international community and with the people at home.

The next conflict arose in relation to the ending of the French colonial hold on Vietnam. The French were pushed out of the area by the N. Vietnamese in 1954. The Americans stepped in to support the S. Vietnamese regime against its own people and N. Vietnam. After a decade of fighting, the

American public wearied of the monetary drain on the nation as well as the large loss of life. Through protests the federal government was made to see that they could not continue in Vietnam and they withdrew. Immediately S. Vietnam was incorporated into Communist N. Vietnam. This was clearly a loss of prestige, and a military defeat, for the US, but one the people seemed to accept.

The last major event was not a military event but rather the implosion of the Soviet Union in 1989. This event seemed to take place very quickly and took most experts by surprise, but hindsight clearly reveals that the Soviet Union had been economically strapped for many decades, and the people there were ready for change.

The Vietnam police action had a very significant effect on the US domestic scene. The people, especially the young people, grew weary of the materialism that bound their lives. They had seen the failure of Johnson's Great Society program due to funds being shifted to the war effort; and the US had already expended some 58,000 lives in a conflict that seemed to have no purpose. They began protesting against the federal government's involvement in Vietnam; which effort was resisted by the authorities. The anti-war protests, however, were merely the tip of the iceberg. During the 1960s and early 1970s young people had become cynical in regard to authority of all types, that is, family, church, school, government, and business. They fomented social revolutions in the conduct of sex, family life, religious belief, business relations, and many others with the goal of becoming truly capable of ordering their own lives. This revolt encouraged the use of drugs, disobedience (largely social rather than legal) and a faith in the simplification of life in general. As with other periods of narcissism, the event turned out badly and the young people as they grew older became a solid part of the society. This episode was highlighted by the conversion of the protest generation from social rebellion to proactive political involvement through good jobs and the formation of powerful interest groups.

In 1990 the US was the only remaining superpower. The US had not yet had time to even contemplate what this meant in terms of new policy decisions, etc., before it faced its first challenge as sole superpower. Iraq under cover of a historical land claim, invaded the nation of Kuwait. The administration of George H. W. Bush not having had time to develop a new foreign policy returned to the cold war policy. The US sought and obtained a mandate from the UN to forcefully remove Iraq from Kuwait. The US, having this mandate, then succeeded in putting together a very effective coalition to remove Iraq. Many of the coalition members committed ground troops and others provided the financing needed. The result was a very quick and successful removal of Iraq from Kuwait. As part of the cold war strategy, the

Bush administration is believed to also have had plans to foment revolution within Iraq with the goal of entering Iraq and deposing the ruler, Saddam Hussein. Had the administration approached this as they did the initial removal of Iraq, that is, openly and above board, there is little doubt that they would have been successful. As it turned out the coalition, world opinion and the home front all resisted invasion of Iraq and the idea, if it existed, was quietly dropped. This was, however, a major boost to the prestige and influence of the US in international affairs.

The international scene remained relatively quiet for a period of nine or ten years. The only real opportunity for a development of foreign policy came with the breakup of the Yugoslav Soviet. The civil war that followed included an attempt by Serbia to ethnically cleanse its nation of non-Serbs. Once again a mandate was obtained from the UN to put together a peace keeping mission. The mission was undertaken by NATO under US command. The Clinton administration put together a plan that combined diplomacy with US air support for the NATO peacekeepers. The diplomatic charge was led by the US Secretary of State Madeleine Albright. Both the diplomatic and military offensives were effective. The civil war ended by treaty signed in Dayton, Ohio. It was the first real use by the US of a rapid deployment force and a diplomatic solution at the same time. It was very successful under the conditions that existed at that time. This was also seen as a positive western response to a military crisis. All of this was to change very rapidly after 2001. Claiming retribution for the US polluting Islamic holy ground in the first Gulf War the organization known as Al Qaeda launched an attack on America. The attack combined the hijacking of four jet airliners by members of Al Qaeda and their suicide by flying the planes into the World Trade Towers in Manhattan, the Pentagon in Washington D.C.; and the crash of the fourth plane in a field in Pennsylvania. The attack was immediately labeled an act of terrorism akin to that being used against Israel. The administration of George W. Bush again reverted to the tactics of the cold war. Al Qaeda was based in Afghanistan where it jointly ruled with the Taliban regime. The US sought and obtained a UN mandate to forcefully eject Al Qaeda from Afghanistan. In order to accomplish this the US again turned to putting together a coalition. Having done this the US invaded Afghanistan with its allies and quickly deposed both the Taliban and Al Qaeda. Both, however, remained in Afghanistan and began fomenting civil war among the various tribal leaders of Afghanistan just as they had done earlier when the Soviet Union had invaded Afghanistan. The result was that the US was forced to attempt to build a stable nation from nothing. A puppet government was installed and the US continued to provide protection from the assaults launched by the various fighting factions in Afghanistan, including both the Taliban and Al Qaeda. This would continue for the next decade or more.

As part of the new war on terrorism, as it was designated by the US, was the desire to return to Iraq and finished the job not accomplished in the first Gulf War. An attempt was made to obtain a UN mandate to forcefully remove suspected weapons of mass destruction from Iraq but this attempt failed. The US next attempted to put together a coalition to invade Iraq without UN mandate. This effort essentially failed also. As a result the US, and few of its allies, unilaterally invaded Iraq and once again quickly deposed Saddam Hussein. Once again civil war was the result of US involvement and nation building efforts were also a failure in Iraq. Meanwhile the American public had again grown weary of war and demanded the withdrawal from both Iraq and Afghanistan. This was the platform that got Barrack Obama elected in 2008. Under this administration the withdrawal from Iraq was completed in 2011, and the majority of America's presence in Afghanistan was removed in 2014. Afghan leaders requested and received a stay on the removal of all American troops to avoid the result that arose in Iraq (early in 2015).

The Afghan situation is still volatile but much less so than Iraq. In Iraq, the withdrawal was followed by the development of an organization known as the Islamic State (believed to be an outgrowth of Al Qaeda) to move from its base in Syria into Iraq. This organization is labeled as a terrorist organization by the US and is known by the acronyms of ISIS, ISIL or IS. The Iraq security forces that were trained and armed by the US prior to withdrawal proved to be no match for the troops of the Islamic State (or they were unwilling to fight them). The forces of the Islamic State now hold a stretch of land running across central Iraq from the Syrian border to near Baghdad. The US has opted to fight this development with air support of the fighters on the ground (largely Shia and Kurdish forces). This has been extended into Syria where the civil war between the ruling Assad family and the moderate Syrian rebels continues. This has been complicated by the fact that the forces of the Islamic State are fighting both sides in this civil war. Once again the troops of the moderate Syrian rebels appear to be unable to hold their own. Here also the Kurdish population is providing the bulk of the defense against ISIS. The US is providing air support for their efforts. It is too early in the game to predict what might happen in either Iraq or Syria. So far the US and its allies have refused to commit ground troops to the effort even though the Islamic State forces have committed several large scale massacres and beheaded several western journalists.

The American media has convinced the public that this organization poses a serious threat to the homeland, although the truth of this is doubtful. There are some 100 Americans fighting with ISIS and capable of carrying out an attack in the US. Several attacks in Canada recently were attributed to this organization and its recruiting efforts, and at least one copycat beheading took place in the US. The general consensus, however, is that ISIS offers no substantial threat to the US public, outside of random attacks, which are impossible to completely prevent.

The military and many government officials believe that the current plan cannot successfully destroy ISIS and that ground troops will eventually be used. The congress and the public so far have not taken any action to force the administration to change its policy.

The 21st century has not been kind to the United States. The early success in the Middle East was followed by the collapse of the high tech bubble and early signs of real financial instability in the economic system. The high tech recession was followed by the disasters of Sept. 11, 2001. These attacks on the American homeland, in addition to being a real shock for the US public, had two further long term effects. They brought about an economic dislocation mentioned early after the attack but which was not really closely followed by the media. The real economic impact of the 9/11 attack was its role in the turn down of economic activity that resulted in a very sluggish economic growth rate and the eventual collapse of the housing market bubble. The US has been suffering the economic doldrums from at least 2008 and is still feeling the pain.

The war on terrorism, when coupled with the corporate and financial sector bailouts and the various attempts to stimulate the economy, brought on trillion dollar budget deficits and ran the national debt to $17.5 trillion. The debate concerning the sustainability of the status quo continues with no clear end in sight. There are a few bright spots when one considers that this year's budget deficit is only $750 billion; the upswing in business community activity; the slowly increasing economic growth rate and slowly growing consumer confidence. This recovery, if it can truly be labeled a recovery, is very fragile. There are many factors outside the control of the US that could easily bring the global economy back into recession. Germany is seen as just now entering into a second recession and there still could be sovereign failures among the members of the Eurozone. Either of these events could stop the US recovery in its tracks. It is plain that so far the first two decades of the 21st century have involved two decade long military conflicts, which for all intents and purposes continue to this day; the near melt down of the US financial sector; the collapse of the housing and retirement fund assets of the American public, and the decade long recession. It is no wonder that the domestic market is filled with books predicting the end of the American way of life. As we have seen this prediction could well be just whistling in the wind, but only time will tell. Even if the industrialized world goes through another 1930s type of correction, or worse, the likelihood of the failure of the US system is not large. It is likely that a very large adjustment will be needed to adapt to the new conditions, and that such an adaption could take a generation, but the better day ahead will soon be on the horizon.

The most obvious speculations that can be drawn from what has already been said are not particularly appealing. First, it does appear that there will be another global recession, probably bringing the US back into recessionary conditions. This recession will probably occur sooner rather than later. This recession is seen to be on the scale of the 1930s depression, but there is no real way to predict the depth of the upcoming recession. Second, it seems equally likely that there will be a worldwide war generated by this recession. The war will have two major aspects, one, it will be a war of the have nations against those who have not. The war will be a test of the ability of the west to survive a massive attempt to redistribute the world's wealth. Third, it will be a religious war, that is, the Islamic peoples versus everyone else. These three factors will tend to keep the fighting at a conventional level and very barbaric in nature. Most of the conflicts will be regional in nature but fought around the globe. The recession will merely escalate the regional conflicts now taking place in the Middle East, Eastern Europe and Eastern Asia. The Muslims will be attempting to establish a global Caliphate while everyone else will be attempting to maintain their own way of life. The war will be a short one. The west will either collapse joining the rest of the world in chaos; or it will create a temporary coalition and use all weapons necessary to end the Islamic threat. The end of the shooting war will not mean the end to the conflict. It may take decades, even generations, to work out the means by which global stability can be reestablished. One thing is certain the world that arises from these events will not be recognizable by today's standards. For example, it is likely that the current nations of China and India will emerge as ten or more independent nations. It is at least possible that Europe will continue its seventy year march towards consolidation and emerge as one large federation rather than 40 or so independent nations. The places least likely to change to any great degree are Central America and South America. They may, in fact, find themselves in a position of being capable of leading the return to civilization. Africa, of course, will be the basket case that it has been for centuries. The Middle East and possibly SE Asia may emerge virtually devastated from losing the war. It is possible that the US and Canada will at least temporary unite to provide security and maintain the democratic way of life found in them today. If nuclear weapons are not used the New Caliphate may extend across N. Africa, through the Middle East into Central Asia and SE Asia. This really appears unlikely, and if established at all, the new Caliphate will only incorporate the nations now controlled by fundamentalist Islamic sects. Israel is likely to disappear from the face of the earth. Africa below the Sahara will probably return to tribalism or colonial status of some type. It is difficult to imagine but certainly not beyond the realm of possibility.

Although a total economic collapse of the existing global economy as predicted by the gloom and doom people may not happen it is still likely that a serious correction of proportions will take place. Currently the EU, and in particular the EZ portion of the EU, is already entering into a serious recession. The EU is the third largest economy on the planet and its failure, or lack of economic vigor, cannot help but affect the rest of the globe. The smaller economies of this union, that is, Greece, Italy, Portugal, Ireland, and Spain are being kept afloat by bailout programs offered by the healthier economies of the union. This may soon change, however, as the largest economy in the union (Germany) appears to be entering into a new recession. There is much talk within the Union about disbanding at least the Eurozone if not the whole European Union. So far this has not gone very far, but with worsening economic conditions it could proceed. The failure of the euro, the failure of the Eurozone, or the failure of even one major economy within the EU would be a catastrophe for the global economy. Some see the US slipping into a depression the equal of the 1930s but it is equally likely that the US will be able to take advantage of the opportunities created by a global economic recession and to come out the other end in better shape than it is in today. In short, it may provide the opportunity for the US to reestablish the dominance it had after World War II in the manufacturing, financial, and military fields. In short, this may be the equivalent of the Second World War in regard to the 1930s depression.

CHAPTER 9. SOLUTIONS AND THEIR FEASIBILITY

The next step will be to attempt to outline the possible solutions that are being offered and to determine their success, or probable success, if they have not yet been instituted. Let us begin with arguably the most powerful of interest groups, that is, the political parties. In a simplistic manner the Democratic Party can be seen as the liberal faction of the federal government. Under their scheme the solution is for the federal government to continue to spend money in stimulating the economy and fostering both job growth and increasingly healthy economic growth rates. The way in which the Democrats would have this money spent generally is as follows: first, and foremost, the Democrats want to continue, and wherever possible to expand, the existing welfare programs with the intention of putting cash in the hands of consumers. At the moment this includes extending both the disability benefits available under Social Security, and the medical payments made under the Medicaid system. These programs are intended to absorb the nearly 18 million people who are suffering from chronic unemployment and the 40 million people who are currently medically uninsured. The disability roles of the Social Security system have been recently expanded by several millions mainly through executive order aimed at reducing the qualifications needed to become rated as permanently disabled (essentially to include as a qualification stress related to unemployment). The Medicaid program is to be expanded mostly through the institution of the Affordable Care Act and through expansion of the State portions of this program. In both cases the inclusions, or expansions, in spending are justified in terms of increasing consumer spending; which in turn will stimulate the economy. Within the Democratic scheme consumer spending is the main driving engine in the creation of new jobs and robust growth in the economy. These types of programs are, on the other hand, seen as the major driving engine of both budget deficits and long term national debt by those of the opposite ilk. In addition, the Democrats are calling for increased (new) spending programs for infrastructure maintenance and repair, education and research and development. The spending on infrastructure is without a doubt intended to relate to direct increases in consumer spending. The spending on education and research and development will, as the democrats claim, increase the possibility of creating good jobs and innovative business opportunities, such as green technology on a sustained basis. There is, of course, no denying that the Democratic approach will include additional growth in government deficit spending.

Of equal concern, however, is the rationale of the Democratic Party in relation to how this additional spending is to be paid for by increased revenue. We can start with the constant Democratic mantra that budget deficits and the national debt are to be constrained within the limits of sustainability, as they believe they currently are. They do concede, however, that increased revenue will be needed to obtain this goal of sustainability. The bottom line, from the democratic point of view, is that this increased revenue will be obtained in two main ways. First, the stimulated economy will produce an abundance of revenue through tax receipts even without the need for increased tax rates. This will be the result of the natural creation of stable, high paying permanent jobs by the robust growth of the economy (a rejuvenation of the middle class). Second, the reform of the tax code, through the elimination of tax credits and loopholes, will insure that the wealthiest Americans and large corporations pay their fair share of the tax burden.

Without further ado, the weakness of this scheme is as follows: first, from a historical point of view increased government spending, in particular on new expanded entitlement programs, have never positively affected either the growth rate of the economy or job creation. Indeed, it has been clearly shown that increased government spending in the area of welfare programs has had the opposite effect on both the economy and job creation, that is, both have been impacted in a negative manner by such spending. The reason, of course, is explained in the following manner; the taking of productive dollars and putting them into the non-productive segment of the economy (welfare benefits) reduces dollar for dollar the amount of money available for investment in the productive segments of the economy, which in turn, is how all good paying jobs and increases in overall income are generated. The latter in turn account dollar for dollar in any sustained increases in consumer spending. On the other hand, government investment in infrastructure, education, research and development may in fact produce positive results in both the economy and job creation as they increase the efficiency of the productive segment of the economy. In order for the US to be competitive in the international market (arguably the most important) the US infrastructure system, the education system, and its research and development system must compare favorably with that of its international competitors. It has been pointed out by many experts in these fields, as well as in this essay, that currently the US infrastructure system is deteriorating and has become outdated; that our educational system has dropped below even the average available to the children of our competitors; and that we have lost our technological edge as compared to our competitors due to a lack of viable research and development programs. This became evident several decades ago with the lack of competitiveness of the US manufacturing sector when compared to that of Germany, Japan and other emerging industrial powers. Currently it is being claimed that the US is once again providing an environment that is conducive to manufacturing industries. This competitiveness is claimed to be the result of both a general demand on the part of workers in low paying countries for higher wages and benefits; and the continued emphasis in the US on the informational sciences. The manufacturing that is returning to the US, however, is not the older system of massive hiring of employees. The new industrial facility is composed of several hundred high skilled, very technically trained core employees who control the computer operation of the robotics systems, and a few unskilled laborers that maintain the shipping docks and other unskilled functions. The thousands of employees once needed for the direct manufacturing, assembly and distribution operations are no longer needed. Therefore, it is claimed that even if manufacturing returned to the US at the level that existed in the 1960s it would not appreciably affect the unemployed labor market. The weakness of the Democratic Party platform, therefore, appears to be essentially two fold. The spending on welfare programs is actually a drag on the growth rate seen in the economy and the spending to increase the competitiveness of the US in the international market has no appreciable effect on the growth of good jobs in the domestic market. As a result the expected increases in revenue from the natural growth of the economy is not going to materialize and reforming the tax code will not produce the level of revenue needed; nor will it provide a sustained increase in the amount of money invested in productive projects. Added to these considerations is the fact that the Republican Party has consistently blocked any attempts to institute this program.

In the case of the Republican Party, without getting into the benefit or detriment of the argument between the various wings of the party, it appears that two main elements make up the stance taken: first, the reduction of government spending, especially in the area of non-productive spending associated with the various welfare programs. Second, the increase of revenue that will be produced through the stimulation of economic growth; in this case the stimulation is to be produced by the reduction of tax rates on businesses, in particular, the small and medium size businesses coupled with a reform of the tax code. Under this view the major engine that drives both job growth and robust economic growth rates is to be found in the health of the small and medium sized businesses in the US. This appears to take into consideration the conversion of the US economy from one based on manufacturing to one based on service industries. Small and medium sized businesses will, in the future under this view, be the only natural source of good, high paying, permanent jobs. They will also be the only source of increased revenue due to increased business income. The reform of the tax code, coupled with a reduction of governmental regulation, will stimulate the economy by producing a business environment conducive to long term investment in small and medium sized business startups.

Once again we need to step directly to the weaknesses of this Republican approach. First, small and medium sized businesses are not starting up, nor are they expanding, under the current business environment at anywhere near the rate that is needed to accomplish the Republican goal of job creation. Actually there is some question about this last statement. Those who claim that small and medium sized businesses are not making an impact are focusing on the kind of jobs that are being created. Instead of the so-called "good" jobs touted by the President the jobs are largely in the low end service industry and are low paying part-time jobs, that is, in the food service and health service industries. As such they are not creating the type of economic impact expected, and touted, by the Republican viewpoint. Second, the regulatory environment has at least two aspects to it. On one hand, the lack of regulations, or the non-enforcement of the regulations on the books, is believed to have been a major reason for the activities that led to the great recession. This is to say, that the less than above board transactions that took place in the banking and investment banking industries were capable of taking place due to lack of regulation, or enforcement of regulations on the books. On the other hand, the fact that so many regulations, such as the environmental regulations that exist are very expensive to comply with; and are updated so rapidly that businesses, both large and small, feel uncomfortable committing their assets to long term investments. The Republicans are claiming that a reduction, or in some fields elimination, of regulation will bring about an economic environment that will promote the use of funds for long term investment. However, this is totally dependent upon the type of long term investments that are available in the current market. From the fact that both big business and big investment are investing their funds overseas to enhance return would indicate that similar opportunities are not available in the domestic market. If such investments were available it is likely that the same funds invested domestically would carry a slightly lower risk than the investment made in the international market. Indeed, the fact is that long term investment, for whatever reason, is not being made in the domestic market. Third, the Republicans are calling for a reduction of the tax rate on corporations and the wealthy in order to stimulate the economy (long term investment in domestic businesses). This reform has not yet taken place so it is still an open question as to whether or not this approach would in fact stimulate the economy and produce good permanent jobs. It is debated both pro and con but the long term would seem to indicate that there will be no advantage to lowering corporate and top end individual tax rates as long as there are no investment opportunities available in the domestic market. It will simply produce more funds to be invested in the international market where there is a chance of greater returns or increased investment in short term profit makers, such as the stock and commodity markets. Lastly, all of these above projections are intended to reduce the size of the federal government by returning some of the duties that have been given, or assumed, by the federal government back to the state and local governments. Regulations should be made and enforced at the local and state level where what is regulated is known and viewed on a daily basis. The investment market should be controlled by the local and state governments through the use of tax advantages, infrastructure perks, and other benefits given directly to businesses willing to open or expand in these areas.

The main area in which the Republicans are calling for a reduction in the size of the federal government, however, is in the area of welfare spending. Here again they would like to see the functions of the welfare system transferred downward to the local governments or the individual. Retirement, disability, chronic illness, school lunches, food stamps, etc., etc. should be handled on the basis of local governmental assistance, or by individual effort. Historically this has never proven to be particularly effective, that is, private charity and the local governments have never been capable of providing for all those in need of help. With a population of 350 million this capability is even smaller today than it has been traditionally. It is also true that the Republicans have not yet come up with plans that accomplish this goal. There is in fact no painless way to cut the benefits that are already in existence; and for that reason no one is suggesting that these programs should be tampered with even in the short term (next ten years or so after final passage of the reform legislation). The local governments, or individuals, are not in a position to handle even the true entitlement programs, such as food stamps, which today are providing benefits for 48 million Americans. The cost and the logistics are well beyond the ability of individual organizations and probably also that of the local and state governments. In this situation the US has created, or found, itself in a true catch 22 position.

In simplified form this is the basic dichotomy faced by the US political system today. The Democrats control both the Senate and the Executive branch of government and have done so since 2008. In 2010 the Democrats lost control of the House of Representatives largely through the efforts of the Tea Party movement within the Republican Party. The one major piece of legislation that passed before the House was taken over by the Republicans was the Affordable Care Act. Since 2010 there has been gridlock in Washington which borders on dysfunction. The Supreme Court, although not as conservative as the Tea Party faction, is conservative. The only other legislation passed between 2008 and 2010 of note was a sizable tax reduction for the middle class, that is, the indirect effect of not repealing the Bush Era Tax Cuts. Since 2010 the republicans have been able to block every attempt by the democrats to expand this earlier legislation, or to institute new legislation. On the other hand, the democrats have also consistently blocked every legislative initiative offered by the republicans. As a result nothing new of any import has hit the books and several very negative results have obtained instead. The fight to repeal or defund the Affordable Care Act has led to one government shutdown, and two near defaults on already incurred debt. The latter resulted in the downgrading of the American credit rating and thereby an automatic increase in the expense of maintaining the national debt. The emphasis in Washington has shifted from attempts to legislate solutions for the problems facing the US; to a focus on placing the blame for not resolving the problems on one or another of the two political parties. Sometimes this takes the form of blaming the executive branch for a failure to lead and a failure to initiate solutions; and at other times, blaming the two political parties for obstructionism. The two political parties have essentially through the gridlock taken themselves out of power. They are not obtaining solutions to the problems; providing leadership for obtaining these solutions; or even listening to the demands and requirements of the American public. There can be little doubt that the Chamber of Commerce; big business; and financial lobbies have stepped in to fill the void. The regulations that were put in place to prevent a reoccurrence of the practices that led to the 2008 recession are being ignored due to lack of enforcement and a return to these practices by the financial community is very evident. This may in time lead to another housing bubble, a stock evaluation bubble or some other failure of the economic system and a return to recessionary times.

The failure of the political system is temporarily on hold as a budget deal was passed on the Eve of the Congressional 2013 holiday break. It will become obvious quickly whether or not this latest "deal" translates into a long term ability to compromise. Lastly, the 2014 mid-term election gave control of congress to the Republicans. This represents a clear chance for the Republicans to attempt to institute their programs. The next couple of years should provide a real test of Republican ability to get things done. The result is likely to strongly affect the results of the 2016 election.

Politics in the US has traditionally been more or less fixated on ideological standards. Ideology, however, in the past has tended to be positive in effect, that is to say, that ideological positions were capable of pointing to policies, attitudes, myths, and other aspects of social ideals that acted as cement that bound the society together. Although ideology has traditionally marked the points at which issues tended to become gridlocked; it also pointed out the areas where possible compromise could be obtained. In short, although ideological positions have always been a part of US politics, sometimes even creating deadlock on issues, it has not under normal circumstances prevented the solutions to problems from being formulated and instituted. Over the last two decades this appears to have changed; at least in terms of the ability to find solutions to problems. The ideological positions assumed by the two political parties, and to some degree by the American public, have assumed a frozen aspect. There appears to be no room for either side to accept even the slightest compromise with the positions of the other side. This became painfully obvious when neither side was willing to compromise and forced the government into a shutdown and into a near default on debt. Little if any respect was paid to the possible consequences of these actions; nor to the demands of the public, which were put forth loudly and clearly. When looked at closely it is very difficult to determine just what has changed in the ideological positions of the two parties since the end of World War II. The Democratic Party is still the liberal party advocating big government, and the Republican Party is still the conservative party advocating limited government. The Democratic position has consistently been based upon the expansion and continuation of the various welfare programs to bring about an equitable standard of living for all citizens; a regulatory system that makes it possible to control the behavior of both businesses and individuals; and a strong military. The Republicans have based their ideology on the maintenance of a limited government, a strong military, and a free market economy. These ideological positions, at least on the surface, do not appear to have been altered much over time. What appears to have changed over time is the environment in which the ideological debate between the party positions has taken place.

The federal government, in particular, has become much, much larger in terms of its role in society than it was even after the Great Depression and World War II. The federal government has entered into a much more interventionist position in regard to the individual lives of its citizens than ever before in its history. The federal government has become the sole superpower economically, politically and militarily in the international arena and has been having some difficulty in adjusting policy to account for that new position. All of these changes have been brought about by the events which have occurred during this time period, that is, the Marshall Plan, The United Nations debate, the Korean War, The Great Society debate, the Vietnam conflict, the debate over individual rights (racial, women, gay's among others), etc. All of these issues, and many others, tended to polarize the two political parties, as well as the American public generally. The resolution of these events has consistently promoted the enlargement of the federal government and its ability to intervene in the general society. All that was needed was a seed that would grow into a reason to resist a continuance of this trend. That seed was provided by a grass roots movement that has become known as the Tea Party movement. A large block of the American public, made up largely of the middle and lower classes who have taken the pain in relation to the problems now facing the nation, are the basis of this movement. They seek, on one hand, solutions to the sluggish economy, high unemployment, and illegal immigration; while on the other hand, they seek protection from unemployment (unemployment benefits), foreclosure on their homes, etc. They do, however, represent a large voting bloc (a majority voting bloc in some areas) regardless of their inconsistency. The Tea Party wing of the Republican Party came into being to capture the votes of this grass roots movement during the 2010 mid-term election. They were successful in doing so and as a result were able to capture control of the House of Representatives in 2010. They have since that time pushed what they believe to be the demands of their voting bloc without compromise. This position they believe to be a return to fundamental religious beliefs, a limited government of the type advocated by Thomas Jefferson, a regulatory system controlled entirely by the local and state governments, a strong military (used to police the world), and a return to individual freedom and responsibility, and a return to the free market economy.

What the Tea Party wing of the Republican Party came up against when they gained power was the following: first, a big government that was solidly entrenched in the society and which was responsible for a vast array of vested interests, such as welfare benefits, tax credits and loopholes, business subsidies and other perks, and a large permanent unelected bureaucracy (a sort of fourth branch of government). Second, a regulatory system that had evolved over nearly two centuries and which encompassed nearly every aspect of daily life. Third, an American public that was much diversified in relation to the positions taken by the Tea Party segment of the public. Many areas of the nation were not interested in smaller or more limited government on the federal level; some segments of the population were not interested in less regulation, but in fact, were in favor of increased amounts of federal regulation; much of the public was not interested in a return to a more fundamental Protestant religious viewpoint. They found that limited government, at least of the type advocated by Thomas Jefferson, is a government that is no longer possible. They found that the economy as it exists today has nearly eliminated the historical concept of a free market. They also found that the American public has over time readily given up freedom and personal responsibility in return for someone else taking the responsibilities that go with them. In this case that responsibility was given to the federal government in terms of the welfare system and the use of regulations to control behavior. The Republicans are now pushing a more moderate agenda and were successful in capturing the Senate in the mid-term election of 2014. It appears however that the excitement generated by the Tea Party in the past has not waned with the results of adhering to the positions taken without compromise (as evidenced by a rather poor showing in 2012). In relation to the negative events that have arisen during the last three years the Republican Party, and in particular its Tea Party wing, have gotten the most negative ratings from the American Public. This did not keep the Republicans from control of the legislative branch. It is now the Democrats that must be prepared to respond to the new conditions that prevail in Washington.

One response that has been taken to this situation of frozen ideological positions deals with how this situation can be overturned. This response is based upon a clear sighted recognition that the current status quo, both politically and economically, is not going to change voluntarily. This response also takes the position that over the mid or long term that the current political and economic positions are unsustainable. The timing of the expected collapse, or the expected recovery, of the current political and economic malaise is undetermined. Some holding this position think it could occur at any time, or is already underway, for a number of reasons. Those who hold that the collapse is near, or already under way, cite the near default of the Euro Zone, the growing use of derivative swaps, the gridlock in congress, among others. Those expecting the early return of normal economic and political conditions cite the erosion of the influence of the Tea Party, the decrease in unemployment numbers, the slow, but increasing, rate of growth in the US economy, and the lessening of crisis conditions on the international scene. There are very few, however, that expect the total collapse of the US either politically or economically. What all agree upon in addition to the belief that the US will not completely collapse is the belief that the current conditions are not sustainable for the long term, that is to say, that at some point the US will need to act to correct the current conditions. It must be pointed out, as a word of caution, however, that even though no one foresees the onset of a new "dark age" now, no one living at the time of the collapse of the Roman Empire foresaw the onset of the first Dark Age. It is reasonable to expect, however, that a serious collapse of the US political and economic status quo would result in equally serious changes. For example, it would be very reasonable to predict a serious deflation of the value of the dollar, accompanied automatically by rapidly rising inflation; a substantial increase in the rate of unemployment (maybe 25% overall and with rates as high as 50 to 75% in some areas); and a serious increase in the number of people living at or below the poverty level. Lastly, it would be reasonable to expect that a relatively long period of time would be needed to recover from a collapse of this magnitude. In the past serious dislocations of the economic system took seven to twelve years to reach a noticeable point of recovery. During the time of greatest depression the society saw a dramatic increase in crime, hopelessness, drug usage and other anti-social behavior. In many cases relief came only in the form of mass migrations (the movement of the Okies from the mid-west to the west); or the initiation of massive warfare (the onset of World War II). The former may not be an option in today's world due to already massive migrations of people; but the latter is certainly not a possible source of relief.

At the very least it would be reasonable to expect a decrease overall in the standard of living existing today. This decrease in the standard of living would affect 80% of the people living in the US with the most powerful effects being on those at the lower level of the middle class and those currently in the lower class. At the latter level it would be expected that the reaction would include political activism, if not civil disobedience, especially at the local and state level. This was certainly the expectation during the Great Depression of the 1930s although it rarely happened. It is also to be expected that if a serious recession were to take place that little, if any, relief could be expected from any government level. The real difference between the Great Depression of the 1930s and today is not the economic conditions but rather the condition of the governments themselves. In the 1930s no level of government was overextended, that is, carrying large loads of long term debt. The collapse of the economy found the governments still healthy in terms of their ability to react to the conditions that came into effect. Today, however, the governments are a part of the problem as they were part of the cause of the collapse in the first place. The long term debt structure of these governments, when coupled to their need to run budget deficits, puts them in the position that makes them incapable of reacting to the problems they helped create. They will not be in a position to pull off another New Deal type response; nor will they be in a position to institute even "safety net" type programs for handling the suffering that will arise. This may extend the period of time that is needed to bring about a full recovery from any such collapse. It is also, under existing conditions, difficult to imagine a general war such as that of World War II coming to the rescue. The US is the sole superpower and militarily capable of defending itself against, or even annihilating, any number of nations at will. It is questionable if even a combination of Russia and China could defeat the US in such a war without completely destroying themselves. It is not likely, therefore, that a worldwide war will result from a global economic collapse. This again may result in a longer period of time to bring about a full recovery. This, of course, is not a question for those who believe that no collapse will take place and that we are merely experiencing the recovery time needed, under existing conditions, for recover from the great recession of 2008. Should this position prove correct then none of the ill effects set forth above would come into play. As time goes on this latter position appears more and more likely to be what will play out.

Regardless therefore of the timing; the direct causes; or the actual results both positions posit that existing conditions will in fact need to be changed. This is to say, there are those who posit that even though the status quo is not sustainable for the long term a solution is at hand. Some who hold this position seem to feel confident that the economy will head into a period of robust growth within the short term. Here also there is no agreement as to how the economy will reach and maintain this robust growth. Some predict the creation of yet undiscovered industries that will bring manufacturing back into its traditional place in the economy. These industries, they think, are most likely to be created by the ongoing uses to which new technologies are put. This position accepts the view that the US has now again become competitive in the international market in terms of labor costs and material costs. As a result the new industries that will arise from the forward movement of science and technology will find their home in the US domestic market. This, of course, will automatically lead to the creation of good paying, permanent jobs in the manufacturing sector; and vast sources of new revenue for the various governments. This is essentially a viewpoint which posits the rebuilding of the American middle class. The drawbacks put forward by this group, or viewpoint, include both the need to refurbish the infrastructure and the reform of the education system needed to prepare young people for these new high skill jobs. The new revenue created by these industries will over time produce not only reductions in the current budget deficits and reduction of the national debt; but also provide the funding necessary to fix both the infrastructure failures and the deficit in educational standards. Over the mid and long term such a result would also produce the time needed to reform the tax codes, reform the welfare systems and rejuvenate the American Publics belief in the federal government. All of this would be accomplished under this projection without the need for increased tax rates or new taxes.

There is, however, an old saying that essentially says, "If it is too good to be true, then it is probably not true." Over historical time new industries have appeared on the scene, e.g., the automobile industry, the airplane industry, the telephone industry, the computer industry, etc., and each has contributed its share to American wealth. Also over time, each has found ways to operate at greater efficiency, with fewer employees, in an effort to reduce costs and increase profits. Robotics has even at this point reduced both the automobile manufacturing and airplane manufacturing industries to a shadow of their former employment capabilities. Those industries that were still labor intensive by the early 1980s moved overseas where the needed labor could be obtained much more economically. It is the growing demand for higher wages and benefits by the workers in these nations that has led to the belief that the US has again become competitive in the manufacturing segment of the economy. This, however, is not true. Most of the new manufacturing facilities that have sprung up in the domestic market of the US are plants built by companies based overseas, such as Toyota, Volkswagen and others. Many of the employees, at least at the management level, are also employees of the parent country and not US citizens. It must, of course, also be remembered that not a single industry of this type has yet arrived on the horizon, let alone been instituted. At the very least a new industry, if one arrived today, would not be in a position to make a major contribution to the economic health of the US for at least a decade or more. This is wishful thinking at its best, but wishful thinking nonetheless.

On the other hand there are those who claim the status quo must change simply because it is not sustainable over the mid or long term. Under this position, action must be taken in the short term to produce the needed results in the long term. This position also accepts the concept that there is enough time to make the changes that need to be made. They call for the immediate reduction of spending, especially in the area of welfare programs, to insure that enough time is available. They would not change the existing benefits under Social Security, Medicare or Medicaid, but they would significantly reduce, if not eliminate, programs such as food stamps, the school lunch programs, and many subsidies both individual and corporate.

In addition, they would call for the immediate beginning to the reform of the tax code, the welfare system (Social Security, Medicare and Medicaid), the health care system (already begun under the Affordable Care Act), the educational system (even more emphasis on job training, research and development vs. the educated man), and the reform of the regulatory system (less involvement of the federal government). The aim of the tax code reform, under this position, is both to create increased revenue by eliminating tax credits and loopholes and to create an environment that makes it comfortable for businesses to make long term productive investments. This would be done without necessarily producing a need for the increase of existing tax rates on the individual or businesses. This would rejuvenate the industry that still exists within the US domestic market. In accordance with the reform of the tax code for the reasons stated this position also calls for the concurrent reform of the regulatory system. The aim here is again to promote healthy industrial investment due to a reduction of costs represented by the burden of government regulations and requirements.

Within this position the biggest rub currently is just coming into view. Initially this position was calling for the reform of the health care system without reference to federal legislation. The intent was to reform the existing system completely within the free market system, that is, through the private market. The passage of the Affordable Care Act has altered the terms of this debate. The health care system can no longer be reformed without reference to the federal legislation now on the books. As a result the debate has shifted to this legislation. The new law has begun its process of implementation and has been plagued with ongoing problems massive in scope. At this point it is too early to estimate the overall effect of the federal legislation on the health care system. It looks as if the new policies that are replacing the old policies under the law are much more expensive and include coverage that is either not needed or not wanted. The jury is still out on whether or not the new insurance policies available for those 40 million previously uninsured individuals will be affordable or not. Lastly, the jury is also still out as to what the enrollment rate will be for the young healthy members of society. The latter, of course, are needed to make the operation of a national risk pool possible. At this point in time the party backing this position has adopted as its program the repeal of the law. At any rate, neither reform nor repeal will happen before the expiration of several years. It seems reasonable to conclude that this stance is being taken as a result of the Republicans gaining control of the Senate. The law is also under piecemeal review by the Supreme Court which may rule portions of it unconstitutional. If so, if there is a court ruling defining constitutionality, the conversation concerning reform of the existing health care system can reopen.

A third position holds that little or nothing needs to be done. This position accepts that the current situation may be unsustainable over the long term; but it will not in fact need to be sustained. The economy is currently sluggish, but is recovering from the recession, despite the interference from all levels of government. This position holds that the economy has not yet fully recovered because of the intervention of the federal government in particular. The economic stimulus programs, such as the TARP funds, and the QE programs, not only have not been successful, but have actually put a drag on what would have been a natural recovery. The basic philosophy here is that under a free market system any interference in its operation automatically creates problems needlessly. As stated earlier, the normal recovery time from a serious recession is five to seven years. Five years passed at the end of 2014 and seven years will have passed at the end of 2016. Thus, if tradition holds, the end of the recovery period for the great recession would come about after the 2016 Presidential election. In this case the recovery may be delayed for an indefinite period of time due to the interference of the federal government. Those who hold this position are calling for the immediate cessation of the QE programs (this actually took place in Oct. 2014); as well as any further attempts to stimulate the economy by federal spending programs. The claim is being put forward that such action would allow the relatively rapid adjustment of values to take place in reaction to the recession just completed. These devaluations have traditionally taken place and have been the signal that the economy was beginning to return to a healthy growth rate (3.5% in third quarter of 2014). This position is supported by the current factual situation, that is, there is no real proof that either stimulus spending or the QE programs have had any significant effect on the economy; but still the economy has been slowly growing. Indeed, the proof, as it exists, seems to confirm that what growth has occurred, and what improvement has been seen, has come about in spite of the federal government interference.

This position, however, is not very popular with the political elite. It requires them to *choose* to do nothing — instead of just doing nothing, which makes them seem unnecessary. The call from all quarters is for the government to do something to heal the unemployment rate, the sluggish rate of growth in the economy, the decline of the middle class and many other things. This might be the case even if it were proven to the American public that the best choice would be to do nothing.

The desired creations of good-paying permanent jobs, a rejuvenated industrial base, etc., under the claims of this position are mere pipe dreams. What is needed is for the work force, the investment community and the business community to accept the new conditions and begin operating within the parameters of those conditions by beginning again to save money, to participate in long term productive projects, etc. The real importance of this position is that the economy will recover whether or not anything is done, however, it may take longer if the federal government continues to interfere. In short, this viewpoint holds that both sides (Republicans and Democrats) are wrong and should merely back off any programs they currently would like to see inaugurated.

The question for us, i.e., those without wealth, without power, without a voice, and essentially without hope, is whether any of the three positions set forth presents a valid picture of the future. The answer must begin with an honest assessment of the motivation for the predictions offered. First, economists, economic pundits, financial experts and investment wizards all have one common source of motivation, i.e., they are in it for the money and the prestige of being right. Second, the political parties and the entrenched bureaucracy all have a vested interest in the status quo; that is, their major concern is keeping their jobs and their power. It may be just this factor alone that creates the environment which makes compromise impossible in terms of ideological positions. On the other hand, the motivation that one finds in the banking, investment and business communities is somewhat different although it also is based upon money and power. These communities are not interested in ideological debate but rather are interested in concrete processes that will allow them to maximize their profit and power within the society. Without a doubt, therefore, everyone that is likely to have an idea for a solution to what they see as a problem; or for that matter a real solution — coupled with the ability to disseminate such ideas, or solutions, into the broader society — will have ulterior motives for doing so. It is truly naïve to believe any of these programs would be offered to the public simply because someone wishes to help you through trying times. On the other hand, it is equally likely that the ideas presented, or the solutions presented, have a basis in credibility even when the motivation is taken into consideration. There can be no doubt, for example, that constantly growing budget deficits and long term national debt will eventually hit a point where they become truly unsustainable. This has been already shown to be true in the case of Greece, Ireland, Spain and others. It should be of interest, even if it turns out to be unprofitable, to look deeply into the various claims being set forth.

A good a place to start would be the claim that the economy of the US is in a period of stagnant growth, if not a period of actual negative growth (that is, decline). It is clear that the method of measuring the economic status of the US is fraught with a large number of problems and is subject to many different interpretations. The difficulty arises from both the massive amount of data that is available and in need of interpretation; and the vast size of the American economy itself. This necessarily requires a distillation of the data into some compact form based upon the data actually included in the information. The various indexes for measuring the extent of economic activity are numerous, complex, and arbitrary. The results obtained from the use of these indexes are also complex and many times contradictory. As a result one can claim that all official ratings of the health of the economy are nothing more than educated guesses. If the actual state of the economy is not truly known in any accurate manner then any predictions as to what direction the economy may take are equally uncertain. What appears to be certain from all the predictions being made is the following: first, they are influenced greatly by the bias of those making the prediction. For example, the various investment experts are making their predictions based on what they believe are the most important factors for those relying on them for advice on investments. This is a tautology of the first order. The indexes used by these experts are geared to determine the risk involved in the investment policy recommended rather than the overall health or activity of the economy, although this may be taken into consideration also. Second, on a broader level the point being made may become clearer when we take into consideration the broadest indexes of economic health. This would include the determination of the real unemployment rate, the real measurement of GDP, the current evaluation of the value of the dollar, among others. The measurement of these factors are composed of so many interacting factors that accuracy is anything but assured. It is clearly understood that many factors are overlooked in reaching a final figure for any of them, and that all of them are commonly manipulated to show what is desired by those presenting them. The most common example is that of the unemployment rate. This figure, whatever it is, does not take into consideration those who are still unemployed but no longer drawing unemployment insurance benefits; or those who have completely dropped out of the labor market. A 5.8% rate of unemployment, therefore, translates into the percentage of working people who are currently unemployed and still drawing unemployment benefits. If one were to include all those still seeking employment, but not drawing benefits; and those who have stopped looking for work completely the real unemployment rate would be significantly higher nationwide. In some areas this real rate of unemployment might reach as high as 50 or 60% of the working population. Therefore, in relation to the economy what can be predicted (by educated guess) is simply that the economy is not growing at a robust rate, that it is growing slower than at other times in the history of the US, and that it may in fact be currently growing slowly, or actually contracting. What can't be predicted are the long term effects of whatever status the current economy is projected to be in. It is fair therefore to say that it is not possible to project how the economy will react in the future to any programs initiated to interfere with its natural progression, or its natural progression with no interference. In short, the search for solutions to what is seen as a problem is a chimera in two ways; first, the claim that a problem actually exists; and second, that solutions can be found for this non-existent problem.

It is clear that the economy historically has gone through periods in which growth was clearly seen to be robust and through periods in which growth was seen as sluggish or non-existent. The former is called a boom period, the latter a recessionary period (bust period). The exact moment (bang moment) at which the economy will enter into one or the other is not possible to accurately predict or control. Anyone's guess is as good as anyone else's. The real problem, and this problem truly exists, is the suffering, stress and deprivation of those who are unemployed or otherwise negatively affected by the current state of the economy. Under this analysis the Republicans are to be seen as demanding that those so suffering take personal responsibility for their own problems and do what they can, while the Democrats are demanding that the federal government tide these people over until good times return. Do we want to do either one, or maybe choose some middle course between the two? Probably the least likely solution, at least in terms of success, would be to place the responsibility with the state and federal governments. This has been the trend in the last few decades and, in the opinion of many, is the major reason that the US has found itself in its current condition both politically and economically. However, this being a democracy, not only the power rests with the people but also the responsibility for mistakes. Thus it will be profitable to look at the responsibility from both the point of view of the effects of government intervention and the lack of personal responsibility on the part of individual citizens. The next chapter will make an attempt to frame the debate in just such a manner.

Chapter 10. Government Intervention and Lack of Individual Responsibility

We can begin the discussion by taking note of a bestselling book by Mark Steyn titled *After America*. It is without a doubt one of the clearest examples of the extreme conservative viewpoint in relation to the positions set forth above. In this book Mr. Steyn, who styles himself as a perpetual doom and gloom monger, rakes America over the coals. The main contention of the book is that America is on the very edge of a total collapse, both economically and politically. This collapse is being brought about by the misuse of money, as was the case with the earlier Roman and British empires, according to Steyn. He uses an impressive number of factual quotes and anecdotes to prove his point. In a nutshell, however, his argument boils down to his claim that our debt — federal, state, and local governmental debt, as well as debt in the private sector — is unsustainable even in the short term. Although this claim can be, and is, debated, he claims that no question can be legitimately raised about this debt's sustainability. This is the position most often given by the far right wing of the Republican Party (conservatism generally).

The whole structure of debt at all levels of government, according to Mr. Steyn, has evolved from the development of the "nanny" state, or welfare state. The explosion of the welfare state, along with the massive bureaucracy needed to institute and enforce it, is in Mr. Steyn's view important for two main reasons: first, the massive debt encouraged by the increasing need for welfare benefits has over the last seven or eight decades produced a permanently moribund economy. This type of economy features high rates of unemployment, massive immigration of cheap labor (much of which is immigrating illegally), the flight of manufacturing concerns overseas to even cheaper labor markets, and lastly, the rapid growth of welfare programs to fill the gap. It is in his opinion a self-feeding phenomenon. It begins, therefore, with the money but the money is only half of the problem. Second, the moribund economy and the welfare state clearly are altering human nature in the US as seen by Steyn. This is a result of the growing number of people who have become either wholly, or at least mainly, dependent upon the government for their standard of living. Once again he uses a massive number of factual quotes to support this contention. The quotes used show a rapid increase in those unemployed; a rapid growth in those who are now qualified to draw disability benefits; the growing number of students requiring aid in obtaining their education; the recent extension of the period of adolescence to accommodate the long periods necessary to obtain an education; the massive loss of manufacturing jobs; the rapid increase in the number of people directly employed by the various levels of government; among other trends. What all of this boils down to, in Mr. Steyn's opinion, is a change from the traditional American principles of self-reliance, honesty, innovation and work ethic into a modern environment based on dependency and denoted by dishonesty, lack of innovation and motivation, and slothfulness. The facts that he quotes clearly show, although they are often debated in terms of their significance and true meaning, that human nature (or, if one prefers, American values) have indeed changed in a negative manner.

In short, Mr. Steyn reaches three very distinct conclusions. First is that the welfare system has caused an irreversible growth of dependency on the part of a very large segment of the American population. Second, that following the money shows clearly how this was brought about; and third, that this environment cannot now be corrected and that America will fall, and very soon, just as Great Britain and Rome fell before her. It should be pointed out for the sake of clarity that this prediction includes all of what is commonly known as "Western Civilization." This civilization became and has remained dominant on a global scale for about 500 years. Mr. Steyn also predicts that when she falls America's place will be taken by China and the Muslim nations. Again all of Mr. Steyn's conclusions and predictions can be debated on the basis of their substance and significance; but they are not beyond the realm of possibility. Anyone studying the problems facing the US, and the industrialized world generally, cannot deny that the possibility that some form of collapse or severe adjustment will take place is real. Some see the collapse mainly as a fiscal problem; some see it as mainly a political problem; and yet others see it as a problem of adjustment after the failure of the free market system. Whatever the cause, whatever the depth or scope of the collapse, and regardless of the form that it takes, one cannot deny that some type of collapse seems to be possible under the conditions that exist today. At the very least, Mr. Steyn's book has struck a familiar cord in the minds of many of his readers. As stated earlier the book is a good example of what can be obtained by applying a readily available mass of data.

The argument has been made in this essay that just those factors, that is, a moribund economy, political gridlock and incompetence, fiscal irresponsibility, loss of manufacturing capacity, the growth of the low paying temporary jobs associated with the service industry, the slow erosion of the infrastructure and the educational system has brought the US to the point where the system is unsustainable. The conclusions drawn by Mr. Steyn, however, appear to be more dramatic in effect than can be expected from the data. Although it is possible that the US as a society might collapse, it is unlikely that it will happen within the next two decades or so. The US appears to have a solid series of buffers in place to buy itself time should a serious crisis arise, that is, probably 20 to 25 years.

Let's see why Mr. Steyn's conclusions, although based on large amounts of data, are not realistic. First, we must determine just where the US (Western civilization) stands on the scale of sustainability. Is the current system now beyond being sustained, and if so, has it already begun to collapse? Is there anything that can be done, if it is determined that the system really is not sustainable, to put it back on the track of sustainability? If the point of not being sustainable has not yet been reached, is there anything that can be done to reverse the trend towards it being unsustainable? Mr. Steyn in his book *After America* accepted as a given that the point of unsustainability has already been reached, and that this fact of unsustainability is essentially irreversible. Have those who hold this point of view taken into account the opposite position, at full value?

First, it may be necessary to accept as a given that the American way of life, although not what it was even 70 or 80 years ago, is both sustainable and healthy. Second, assuming that the system is currently sustainable, although some aspects of the system are not sustainable over the long term, this trend can be seen as both reversible and capable of being eliminated. Third, there are several methods, to be explored as we move forward, that may be capable of reversing the trends that most see as current problems within the US system. A start can be made by recognizing that the vast majority of US citizens understand the basics underlying the current economic problems but do not have the technical knowledge that would allow them to offer real solutions. Their focus is much more limited, that is to say, they are fully focused on their jobs (or lack thereof) and the purchasing power of their dollars. Most people do not care to enter into an analysis of what is wrong in the system and what might be done to fix it. Therefore, books such as Mr.

Steyn's sell a lot of copies and draw people into a false sense of impending doom, or euphoria, depending on the point of view presented.

The real problem is that those who are in a position to know the scale of the problems involved, and are charged with the duty to find solutions to those problems, are also refusing to do what is necessary. On the other hand, most people clearly recognize that their lives have become more difficult. It is claimed to be harder to get a good job and harder to keep it. It is harder and more time consuming to obtain a solid education. It is more difficult to make ends meet, even to cover the major expenses for the necessities of life. It is more difficult to raise a family and maintain relationships over time. Any number of reasons are given. Communication, for example, is much easier and more widespread through the social media than ever before; on the other hand, the depth of the relationships established is much more superficial than in the past. One may brag of having fifty or a hundred friends on a Facebook page, without having a single friend to talk with face to face, sharing common experiences.

This aura of difficulty permeates all levels of society, with the possible exception of the very top level of the upper class. It is this sense of overall increased difficulty in accomplishing tasks that drives the generalized call for something to be done. Business leaders want a more comfortable and favorable environment for the startup or expansion of enterprises, that is, an environment similar to the prevailing environment between the end of World War II and 1970. Investors want the freedom to speculate in any manner that fits the need of the hour, again much in the same manner that was available to them from 1945 to 1970. The working population wants to be able to obtain good paying, low skill, and permanent jobs as easily as they could during the robust growth period of American manufacturing (1940–1970). That is what is being demanded. What is slowly becoming evident is that these demands cannot be fulfilled in the manner in which they are being demanded. Business in America is no longer unregulated or free to ignore the broader problems of society, that is, water and air pollution, a competition-free domestic market for manufactured products, a work force that can be manipulated to fulfill cost requirements, in short, a comfortable and favorable environment for the startup and expansion of businesses, especially manufacturing businesses. The investment and banking industries have shown themselves untrustworthy when left to themselves in regard to the regulation of ethical practices and procedures; as well as to the caution needed to maintain stability during periods of high speculation. As a result, they now find themselves highly regulated and prone to the same shaky procedures that got them in trouble in the first place, such as the use of derivative swaps and other devices to produce sub-prime loans. It is far more difficult for them to make money — they have to take greater risks — as evidenced by the increasing risk involved in sovereign bond investment.

A second position holds that the working population is becoming aware of the fact that easy-to-obtain good paying, low skill, permanent jobs are no longer to be found. Such jobs now require long periods of education to obtain the necessary skill sets. The awareness is also slowly beginning to dawn on the working population that the traditional middle class jobs are never going to return. Those who do attempt to research the problems that face the US society, and who attempt to bring about workable solutions to those problems, normally also reject Mr. Steyn's scenario. They seek solutions that can be instituted without increasing budget deficits, long term national debt, and political gridlock. These, of course, include the upgrading of education in a way that will make access to that education available to all who can benefit by it; and the upgrading of the infrastructure to at least the standard of the international community. These basic solutions are not simple as they also incorporate methods that could be used to maintain balanced budgets at every level of government and the slow the growth of the national debt, if not its complete elimination. The latter usually rely on two major contentions in the general support of their conclusions: first, that throughout history there have been economic, social, and political adjustments during periods of crisis. Such adjustments have meant traditionally that a period of hardship (personal responsibility) must be faced to reach the final establishment of the new order. What they contend is different about the current situation is the level of government intervention at all levels of the society. Traditionally the crisis was met by all levels of society voluntarily instituting the necessary austerity to meet the demands brought about by the adjustment. Businesses temporarily contracted their labor force, their production and their long term investment policies. Investment and banking institutions withdrew from policies of easy credit, high risk speculation and emphasized caution. The working population cut down on expenses, particularly in the area of necessities, while eliminating luxury purchases altogether, and they depended more widely on the extended family while growing gardens and using other cost saving methods. This austerity was voluntarily carried out for whatever period was necessary to reach the point at which the new environment became established and known. All levels of society, without actually attempting to do so, had already seemingly adjusted to the new environment and entered into it seamlessly when it finally came into place. This was true even during the Great Depression.

Today businesses have reduced their labor costs, but they have not reduced their production capability or their long term investment projects. They have removed them from the domestic market and put them overseas.

The banking and investment community has withdrawn its funds from domestic lending; and also have gone overseas for much of its short term profit making ventures. The only exception being the continued practice of investing in the domestic home market and maintaining the shaky derivative swap practices that got them in trouble in 2008. The working population has opted for demanding extended dependence on government benefits (unemployment insurance benefits, disability benefits, food stamps, etc.) to maintain their standard of living without austerity. The extended family is largely a thing of the past and the ability to grow gardens, repair your own appliances, machinery, etc. is also a thing of the past. Where such things are possible and being used, such as some areas of the South and Northwest, long term unemployment has been eased, but those doing so have slipped into the category of living at or below the poverty level.

Traditionally the adjustments required, and the price paid, during periods of change were relatively small under normal conditions. That is to say, the austerity needed was instituted voluntarily, and caused very little civil unrest, economic dislocation or political structural change. Even the Great Depression of the 1930s saw very little civil violence; yet a great deal of eagerness to take part in the government sponsored jobs programs was observed, that is, the CCC, the WPA and the TVA. Although the Great Depression did see large scale experimentation with socialist type plans or projects (TVA); these large scale spending projects were not truly welfare programs. This included the new Social Security program, which was set up as a self-funding program. Without a doubt the Great Depression was the greatest economic, political and social crisis to ever face the US and could easily have resulted in civil disobedience bordering on civil war. There was a great deal of suffering involved in the Great Depression with mass migrations from the Mid-West to the West, soup kitchens, starvation and homelessness, but everyone met the obligations put on them voluntarily. Some help was offered on a cash basis; but that was a minimal amount compared to what was needed. One can only guess at what would have been the result had the depression continued for another decade; which in fact might have been the case had not World War II begun when it did. As it was the Great Depression lasted for a decade with only a short reprieve in 1932 and 1933. By 1938 the New Deal had begun to fall apart for lack of support, especially from the Supreme Court; that is, most of the New Deal legislation had been ruled unconstitutional by 1938 and several aspects of the New Deal still faced Court decisions including the Social Security Act. The economy had again turned south in 1938.

It was at this point that the policies of Germany and Japan made it necessary for the US to shift its emphasis to the international arena. The

US instituted the lend lease programs to aid the allies in their fight with Germany, in particular. This put the manufacturing might of the US back into operation and began almost immediately to relieve the pressure of the depression, at least, in terms of the unemployment problem. What is usually overlooked is the fact that long term investment was again being made, especially in terms of wages and benefits, which in turn increased consumer spending and government revenues. The Supreme Court followed suit and allowed the remaining legislation of the New Deal to stand including the Social Security Act. This may turn out to be the single most important decision made by the Supreme Court in the 20th century, at least from an economic point of view. World War II acted on the US society in several different ways. First, and maybe foremost, it stabilized the social discontent within the society and acted as powerful cement binding the society together in a common cause. Second, the war slowly brought the depression to an end and ushered in a period of robust economic growth. Third, it brought the US to the point that it was the undoubted leader economically, politically and militarily in the international arena. Lastly, it gave the American society the belief that it was the last great hope of mankind in regard to the establishment and spread of individual liberty, justice and happiness (democracy in the American form). As a result the end of the war saw the US undamaged and capable of vast fiscal investment. The Marshall plan rebuilt the European nations from virtual devastation to economic health, while at the same time removing the need for them to provide their own defense. The same was accomplished for Japan and most of SE Asia through the support of the remaining colonial system in that area. The only stumbling block to the all out right of the US to have its way was the establishment of the Soviet Union and its bloc of allies in Eastern Europe.

The real story of the cold war, however, is not the antagonism between the Soviet Union and the United States but rather the consequences of that competition. The major consequence for the US was a shift from manufacturing solely for domestic and foreign consumption to manufacturing for military consumption. The arms race, the space race, and the race to obtain clients in the United Nations (foreign aid) quickly diverted huge sums of money from investment in research and development, education, and infrastructure for domestic products to research and development for military armaments, space vehicles and technology, and specialized education in science and mathematics.

Over time this was to have a dramatic impact on the manufacturing basis of the US economy. By 1980 the US had lost a substantial share of its preeminent position internationally in the economic realm in relation to providing quality products to the domestic and international markets. It now shared its economic preeminence with Japan, Germany, the Pacific Rim nations and S. Korea. It also shared its political preeminence with the EU, The Soviet Union and Japan. The loss of a significant share of domestic economic preeminence was mainly attributed to the non-competitiveness of American manufacturing in terms of costs of doing business. This lack of competiveness was evident in two main areas, e.g., labor costs, and efficiency of production. During the ascendency of American manufacturing the business community had failed to make the investments necessary to update both its physical manufacturing facilities and its equipment; allowing Germany and Japan, among others, to surpass the US in those categories. This also allowed our competitors to become much more efficient at producing products that were superior to ours at a lower cost. By the time that American business realized the changes that had taken place the cost of rebuilding manufacturing facilities and installing updated equipment far exceeded the cost of moving the whole operation overseas. What happened next is common knowledge. This is only one aspect of the many changes that occurred during the period from 1945 to 1990 which were either ignored or handled in the easiest least costly manner. In the end, the accumulation of consequences resulted in the 2008 recession and the awakening of the US to the fact that the world had changed and a need for serious adjustment had set in. Even in the worst case scenario, however, the US will undergo a crisis proportional to that suffered by Great Britain at the end of World War II; that is, the US may lose another degree of the dominance it has maintained since World War II in the economic and political realm; but for the foreseeable future the US will retain its dominance in the military and technological fields. Even the former, however, may be a temporary setback as the US continues to adjust to the new conditions. In this respect it is important to remember that all of the highly industrialized world face the same problems as the US; and in most cases are feeling the consequences much more deeply than the US. It is possible that the US currently, regardless of the gloom and doom scenarios that keep popping up, is nowhere near the economic, social, and political malaise that was evident at the fall of the Roman Empire, or even the demise of the British imperial system. As a result the conditions, in the opinion of those who hold this position, for a new dark age do not exist. It appears likely that the US has already faced and essentially overcome the changes required to adapt to the new environment that has been evolving since about 1990. Although problems still exist in the way that the problems are approached by the government, business and investment communities all have accepted the challenges faced and are adjusting to the new environment (with the sole exception of the federal government). The working population, however, has not yet had enough time to adjust to the new conditions and is still struggling to find a way to cope.

It is in this area that the most attention is needed to determine just what the new environment requires and how to get the working population prepared for handling these changes. It is in the latter case that government interference with the natural operation of the market system has had its greatest impact. The extension of unemployment benefits, and the lessening of the qualifications for disability benefits, has also lessened the need for the working population to cope with the changed environment. It is in this area that the most obvious consequence of dependency can be identified, that is, the growing complacency in the areas of work ethic and personal responsibility. The liberal position attempts to see that everyone is made equal in all ways, that is, the extreme left of the liberal spectrum, is where the derogatory term "nanny state" seems to be most often aimed.

The massive amount of information available, the complexity of this information, and the limited capacity of mankind to incorporate and interpret it is by far the greatest problem in reaching an understanding of the problems set forth above. As can be seen from the above two completely opposed positions (that is Mr. Steyn's and the so-called status quo argument) can be argued from the use of essentially the same data; sorting out reality from illusion is difficult to say the least. Add to this the literally hundreds of positions that can be adopted from the study of the same data; and which represent a middle stance between the above two positions, it can be of little wonder that confusion reigns. What is obvious is that beginning with the money, as Mr. Steyn suggests, leads automatically to stalemate. Only time will tell whether the money trail will lead to a total collapse of the US system; but it seems unlikely to a very high degree. It is more likely that if any further consequences are to be faced by the US as it adjusts to the new environment that the consequences will be much less severe than a total collapse. It is, of course, possible that the US has already faced the consequences of the new environment and has made the necessary adjustments, or, at least, is well on its way to making these adjustments; and is currently entering into a new robust period of growth.

There is one part of Mr. Steyn's analysis that demands further study, however, in relation to individual freedom. This is the statement made by Mr. Steyn that the worse effect of the current environment in the US is the change being wrought to human nature. A position can be taken here that human nature is not the most accurate way of describing what is meant by Mr. Steyn. Indeed, the position taken here is that Mr. Steyn is actually talking about the changing of the traditional American value system, rather than the actual human nature of its citizens. In this sense, we can limit human nature to such things as instinct, the fear reflex and other biological traits. Human principles, or values, however, are not given to the individual by nature but evolve from human thought and conscious practice. If the traditional principles that support the US system are assumed to be what is being changed by the current conditions in the US it remains to determine what principles we are taking about and how they are being changed. Once this is accomplished it should be possible to state what the new conditions are and how they can be met with success.

Let us assume for the sake of argument that the current economic conditions have been overcome by some means, and that the social and political fabric of the society have remained unchanged. From a sociological point of view what Mr. Steyn posits is that Americans have changed from individuals who were essentially self-reliant in most aspects of their lives to individuals who are dependent upon government in most aspects of their lives. In order to service this growing dependency it has become necessary for the various governments to increase the number of employees they have to service and enforce this dependency. As support for this argument Mr. Steyn quotes factual material showing that roughly 33% of the current US population is receiving governmental support of some type. He shows that roughly 60% of the employed population is hired in some capacity by the various governments. That over half of every dollar taken in by the various governments is paid out in some type of welfare benefit. In addition, he shows quotations that support the concept that when any problem arises within the society the most common approach by the individual is to demand that the government handle it rather than doing so themselves. For example, he quotes a letter written by a young girl requesting that the federal government paint the school, rather than the townsfolk doing it themselves, as Mr. Steyn claims they would have automatically done in the past. This example is probably true, and others like it can more than likely be found throughout the society without much effort. This is the basis of Mr. Steyn's claim that the whole system is a self-feeding organism. The more the people demand that the various governments intervene in their everyday problems the more inclusive the governments becomes. Each time such a request is made the people making the request trade the freedom they have to handle the problem themselves for the convenience of allowing someone, or something else to do it. The end result, in Mr. Steyn's opinion, is that the US will be converted from a democracy into some form of non-democratic government. The growing size of the federal and state governments in the area of welfare (the transfer of wealth from the productive aspects of the society to the non-productive aspects) is being matched by the shrinking of the productive elements that produce wealth. What is of interest is that this growing dependence is coupled to a demographic element that compounds the effects. The progressive aging of our society (and that of all highly industrialized nations) is reducing the number of workers eligible to enter the labor market, while at the same time the number of people qualified for receiving welfare benefits is expanding. This imbalance in the production of wealth and the overall need for wealth if maintained over long periods will result in the bankruptcy posited throughout Mr. Steyn's book. This has always been the case in history and there does not appear to be any reason to think that it has changed. Very seldom, however, has the imbalance continued long enough to result in the demise of the society it supports. This may, however, have been the case with the Athenian Empire, the Roman Empire, the Persian Empire and the Ottoman Empire. It does not appear, however, that this has been the case with the nations that have been formed since the late 12th century A.D. When one looks closely at the current economic conditions facing the highly industrialized nations, however, it is possible, on the other hand, to see that such a fate may yet overtake the western nations. In a realistic sense the Western European civilization has been operating for less than 600 years. The former empires spoken of above lasted up to a millennia or more; but the more rapid pace of technology and science may be responsible for the shortening of the period of time from youth to old age. Even in the earlier cases, the empires that existed were technologically and scientifically much more advanced than those that surrounded them; and they only lost their dominance when they had also lost their technological and scientific edge. Today the European system of nationalism has apparently not yet lost its edge in both the technological and scientific realms and may also not be in a position to lose its economic and political dominance. Either technology and science within European civilization has not yet been surpassed, or that has not yet been recognized. Technology and science may yet, it is claimed, provide the answers that will allow European civilization to remain dominant.

On the other side, it can be held that no change has taken place in relation to either human nature or the traditional principles of the US. This position might grant that the traditional principles remain intact in substance while in fact they have evolved over time and have taken on new aspects. For example, the American traditional principle of holding the family in high esteem may still remain the same; but the legal definition of what constitutes a family has changed. Traditionally, of course, the nuclear family was defined in relation to the dictates of Christianity. This definition limited the immediate, or nuclear, family to husband and wife and their children. Today a family can be defined as a husband and wife, a single adult with children, or two same-sex adults with or without children. Although the basic family principle still exists in much the same manner, it has changed in other ways. At the same time the traditional adherence to the concept of extended family, i.e., a community consisting of the nuclear family surrounded by uncles, aunts, cousins, and in-laws, among others, has changed both in substance and aspect. Traditionally, American society was not very mobile and most people remained within the community they were born in, or very close by. Today mobility is greater and more often taken advantage of, and very seldom do even the members of the nuclear family reside in close enough proximity to encourage intimate contact. The concept of extended family, although still capable of being identified, is in practice much less important and much less acted upon than in the past. These issues will again be visited later in the book. For now it is important to finish our determination of the actual status of the US in terms of its economic, political and social environment.

We have set forth two scenarios describing the data available to anyone curious enough to delve into it. We have rejected Mr. Steyn's analysis as overemphasized or exaggerated. This conclusion, however, does not leave us with the right to contend that the current problems facing the US do not rate consideration as a real crisis in regard to the system as a whole. The data used to support the position that a crisis does not exist is found in the slowly improving business activity, including long term investment in productive projects; the slowly improving job market, although those jobs are not necessarily the type of jobs that were expected; and the slowly improving level of confidence in the economy on the part of the general American public. This position, however, must face the negative factors to be found in the continued gridlock on the part of the two political parties; and the incompetence of the government in terms of controlling spending and the ever present extension of the welfare system. The business community seems to have accepted the fact that continued regulation of their activities is here to stay. They have adapted to the regulations, or have found themselves powerful enough to sidestep the most costly of the regulations. For example, business interests have through their lobbying activities been able to bypass the sections of the Affordable Care Act that they saw as most onerous simply by pressuring the executive branch into allowing their exclusion. The investment and banking communities have also found it within their power to sidestep the regulations intended to limit their activities in relation to products and policies that led to the 2008 recession. Again this power has been exercised behind the scenes and through the use of paid Washington lobbyists. The expectation is that the currently improving conditions will accumulate into a robust economic growth rate over the next few years. The result, from this point of view, will be the increase of good paying permanent jobs (the reconstitution of the American middle class); a decrease in the number of people benefiting from both unemployment insurance and the disability provisions of Social Security (as people voluntarily return to work). In addition, the other entitlement programs such as food stamps, school lunch programs, and rent subsidies, among others, will shrink significantly. The latter will result in significant reductions in budget deficits, assuming that the money saved is not spent on new or expanded benefits in other areas. The same effect will be felt in the private sector as people accumulate larger amounts of discretionary cash. Historically, increased income not only means more consumer spending but also increased debt reduction and increased saving on the part of the public. The biggest benefit, however, will be in the time that a robust economic recovery will provide for the restructuring of the most important economic maladies, that is to say, the reform of the tax code; a final adjustment of the health care system; a reform of the regulatory system and many others. This restructuring, if carried out with purpose, could lead to the reduction of the size of both the federal and state governmental systems. The fact that the public does not seem to be demanding the reduction of government intervention in their lives; but rather the exact opposite, seems to cast the purpose of regulatory reform in a different light. This would seem to indicate that the public not only wants regulatory legislation to control what they feel needs controlling, but that the public wants such legislation strictly enforced. In the long run, the holders of this position hope that it will strengthen what they see as the real traditional American principles, that is, independence (liberty), self-reliance, personal responsibility, honesty and civic pride (patriotism). There are some trends that seem to support this position. However, more trends tend to support a less opportunistic appraisal of this viewpoint.

Under this position the economy will remain in a position of slow growth for at least another two years and will only slowly obtain to robust growth over the next decade. Once obtained, however, the results will be the same, that is, the rather natural disappearance of the problems that are prevalent today. This position claims that the major problem facing the US today is political incompetence. This incompetence is usually presented as an extreme environment of stalemate brought about by an irrational attachment to a set ideological philosophy; or on the other hand, as a lack luster attention being paid to the business of government and too much attention being diverted to election concerns. Either way the political elite, that acts and reacts, without regard for the wants or needs of the American public in regard to the problems faced are seen as incompetent. As a result the people do not truly have a say in the governing of the nation and one can conclude that democracy no longer operates in the US, at least, as expected under the constitution. In the case of the US political elite the ideological battle has been almost exclusively over the concept of big government versus small or limited government. This battle, of course, has been going on since the beginnings of the nation. The initial battle between the federalists and the anti-federalists was one over whether the federal government should be independent of the states or whether it should get its power as a delegation from the states. The federalists had won this battle by 1820 and the state rights issue was put on the back burner. From that time until today the advocates of big government have essentially held the stage over those advocating limited government. Indeed, until recently the battle was not even joined under normal conditions with both the conservative and liberal factions advocating big government, with the only difference being the absolute size of the big government. During the last decade the grass-roots movement known as the Tea-Party movement has again brought this issue of big versus limited government to the forefront. It has done this in such a manner as to bring to the front a great deal of passion on both sides of the debate. As a result of the passionate positions taken the two sides have become locked into positions that are incapable of compromise; hence the situation in which severe gridlock has reduced political action to near nonexistence. On the one hand, it is argued that there is only one solution to the problems that face the US today, i.e., the federal government must become even more active and intervene strongly in every case in which a problem is perceived no matter how large or small (argument for big government). On the other hand, it is argued that the big government that exists today; including all of its intrusions into the daily lives of the people is the problem not the solution (argument for limited government). They, therefore, see the solution as a drastic reduction of the size of the federal government, in particular, the bureaucracy and its regulatory powers. They are calling for many, if not most, of the duties that now lie in the hands of the federal government to be delegated back to the state and local governments or to the people. The only true functions of the federal government under this view are national defense, the promotion of democracy within the US (and possibly elsewhere), and the protection of the general welfare of the society. These positions, especially since 2010, can fairly be said to have become frozen in place.

In relation to the extremes of these two positions no compromise has been capable of being obtained regardless of the issued approached by the middle, or moderate, branches of the two parties. A position that represents a viewpoint less extreme than the other two has been proven to be incapable of breaking the stalemate or of reaching any type of useful compromise on the issues. The result has been what one acute observer labeled as "kicking the can a little further down the road." This summary statement applies to the hard decisions affecting budget deficits, the national debt, tax reform, health care, immigration reform, financial reform (fiscal policy generally), among many others. In short, no decision, including a compromise, can be reached on any issue of even slight significance. The US in adjusting to the new conditions has administered some pretty serious self-inflicted wounds in the heat of the ideological debate. For example, it is still unsettled as to what adjustment the US will be forced to make due to the downgrading of its credit standing due to the inflexible stands taken on the debt ceiling issues. It seems as if the only result from the stalemate has been the increased emphasis of both sides on upcoming elections. This is to say, it appears that nearly 100% of the political elites time is spent in obtaining reelection even though the elections may be two, or even four years, in the future. Again it must be noted that US elections and politics in general have always been contentious and even at times vicious and nasty. The main difference as pointed out earlier is that today the process is continuous and without compromise. This appears to have become a part of the political scene mainly because there are only a few truly contested seats in congress and those seats control the majorities in both houses of the legislature. They are, therefore, more hotly contested than in the past and each seat carries a greater weight than ever before. The uncontested seats, on the other hand, provide the strength in numbers that allows each side to feel justified in approaching all problems with an inflexible ideological mind set. This could change, of course, but until it does the American public should expect more of the same. What would change the current political environment? One change would be a shift in the voting patterns of the public, i.e., a determined effort on the part of voters to manage the issues discussed by candidates, a demand for definite positions to be taken by candidates, an overall vote in elections that reflected these demands, and the ability to follow up on the promises and demands agreed to by office holders. This would mean a reinvigoration of democracy at the federal level and a focus from the public that doesn't seem to exist today. Politicians do not follow through on promises; they do not respect their constituency; but on the other hand, the public in general doesn't seem to care; or are not motivated to change things. In short, the public votes party rather than candidate and that means voting for the demands of special interests who pay the campaign tabs.

One of the consequences of the current political environment in the US, according to Mr. Steyn, is the wasting of human capital. His view is that America is rapidly becoming a country run exclusively by a bureaucratic elite. This elite wants only one thing: all the power they need to administer the life of every individual from birth to the grave. This will be accomplished through the establishment of all power in the federal government (the end game for big government), and in particular in the executive branch of the federal government. Big government will reach this stage of being all powerful when a complete dependency of the individual on the federal government for all the necessities of life has been accomplished. The recognition of this stage will become apparent when one realizes that they can do nothing that does not require a license, or is not specifically mandated by the federal government. The current number of people, at least on the road to this stage of power in the federal government is rather impressive as we have seen. About one half of the current population of the US is receiving some sort of benefit from federal welfare programs. It is not known what percentage of the population cannot act without a license of some type but the number can be guessed to be very large indeed. There also can be no doubt that the overall trend in the US is that individuals normally seek solutions to their problems from governments rather than solving them on their own. Under this view the American public has already shown an overwhelming capability, or willingness, to trade their liberty, personal responsibility, and civic duties, among others for a dependency on government benefits. This extends to even the responsibility of providing the means by which one obtains their own personal standard of living. It is claimed that under this type of environment the citizens quickly become soft, effeminate, lazy, and complacent to the point that the society cannot be maintained. Under Mr. Steyn's view the world after the demise of America will belong to the Chinese and the Muslims. The US, on the other hand, will have been completely mexicanized, that is, the majority of the population will be of recent Latin American origin. Granting that such a picture is grim it must be determined whether more realistic scenarios can be found.

Let us begin with the idea that the status quo cannot be considered as the solution to the existing problems. This is no doubt an accurate statement if for no other reason than kicking the can a little further down the road is no solution at all. Let us also begin with the contention that the gloom and doom conclusions of those like Mr. Steyn's are offered in only a half serious manner even by those making them. What remains is the conclusion that action, real action, must be taken to avert even a significantly milder result than the picture offered by Mr. Steyn; but less rosy than that offered by those who call for no action at all. Having set forth the parameters of the alternative solution we must decide where to start our inquiry. A good place to start might be to determine whether or not there is any one point at which all aspects of society come together to begin their interaction with each other. The next chapter will concentrate on this question.

CHAPTER 11. COMMON RELIGIOUS, ECONOMIC AND POLITICAL PRINCIPLES

Up to this point, several conclusions have been reached. First, it has been determined that the traditional political principles of democracy and federalism are still alive and well in the US social structure. They may operate differently than they did for the first 100 years but they still remain the foundation of the political structure of the United States. Second, the same conclusion has been reached concerning the traditional economic principles, that is, the sanctity of the concept of private property and the importance of the free market system. Again, they operate in a fashion different from that of even 50 years ago, but they are still the foundation of the American economic system. Third, it has been determined that the status quo must be changed by some type of action, real action, being taken to meet the problems currently facing American society. It has also in this regard been determined that such action can only be taken in response to demands from the American people. The remaining question is whether or not the American people will in fact stand up and make the demands that need to be made. In the view of the doom and gloom crowd, the traditional principles that once made the American people capable of this focus are lost and have been replaced with a complacency that will not allow them to make such demands. In short, that the traditional social principles that were the foundation of the nation have become a thing of the past. The remainder of this work will attempt to determine whether this is accurate.

Before looking at this issue in depth, it will be necessary to clear up a type of confusion concerning the concept of traditional American values. The two political parties have for some time been debating whether or not traditional American values have been lost. One of the problems presented by this debate is the subject matter included within the catch phrase. Some people mean the loss of traditional religious values. For others, it is the economic or political principles traditionally held by Americans that have been diluted or lost. Yet others are disturbed by a rather vague list of secular social values or principles that are difficult to articulate but easy to subsume in a catch-all phrase. Because of the confusion the term "traditional American values" carries with it, that term will not be used. Instead, for our discussion we will rely on the use of the word "principle" applied separately to the three major pillars of American society, that is, the economic, the political and the social. This will help to keep the religious element within context and also help to maintain a greater level of specificity.

All of the principles that will be discussed had their origin during the colonial period (1620–1770) or prior to the colonies being formulated. They were, however, brought into a unique perspective by the foundation of the United States as a sovereign nation. As a result they will deserve the classification as traditional American principles. Many of them had already become a rather unconscious, or visceral, part of the fabric of American society by the time that independence was attained. This was true of all the principles to be mentioned, by no later than 1800. On the other hand, they have all continued to evolve as part of the American culture over the last 200+ years. An attempt will be made to show that many of them have evolved to the point that they would not be clearly recognized by someone living in 1790. Others would be clearly recognizable but would show a considerable change in the content of what is meant in relation to the modern environment. None of them has escaped this process and it remains an open question whether they could be recreated, if lost; or revitalized, if they are merely being ignored. This is, however, the basis of the current debate over traditional American values between the two political parties.

Now, let's look at the two questions: whether the traditional principles that were the original mainstay of American society have been lost, or are being ignored; and how likely it is that they could be recreated, if lost, or revitalized if they are being ignored. Lastly, we may consider whether they have already been replaced, or should be replaced, by new principles if the traditional principles are no longer viable in today's environment. In light of the third, an attempt will be made to determine how this would be accomplished as a natural process of evolution; while on the other hand, an attempt to determine what would need to be done to recreate or revitalize the traditional principles will be made. It appears that the best, and probably easiest, way to accomplish these goals is to separately approach the three major ways in which they have manifested themselves over time; that is, as economic principles, as political principles and as social principles. The third will again be divided into two sections, that is, a discussion of traditional religious principles and a discussion of traditional secular social principles.

The first to come under discussion will be the principles that underlie the fabric of American social structure.

A. Religious Principles

Beginning with a discussion of the religious principles underlying American society, it can be without a doubt stated that these were all found within Christianity. It must be noted that in the case of the US these religious principles were not just those of Christianity generally, but rather were found mainly within the Protestant branch of Christianity. For the most part, religious principles came to America with the Northern and Western European Protestant sects that were being persecuted by the Catholic branch of Christianity, along with the original Protestant Lutheran sect. Of course, many of the principles found in the various Protestant sects were also a part of the Catholic and Orthodox faiths. Catholicism, however, had little impact on the evolution of the American society during the colonial period, or during the early decades of the new United States. As we all know, one of the major reasons behind immigration to North America from Northern and Western Europe was the above-mentioned persecution. Many people can clearly recall the names of the leading Protestant sects that came to North America, that is, Quakers, Baptists, Anglicans, Congregationalists, Methodists, Presbyterians, Lutherans, Huguenots, Calvinists, etc.

All of them had suffered through many years of severe persecution which had at least two major consequences. First, it made those who belonged to them more fundamental in their religious outlook than probably would have been the case had they been allowed to develop naturally. Second, they tended to expect a strict adherence to the principles developed within the sect. In most cases the principals were either written down in denominational study guides, or delivered orally with nearly every sermon. Over the colonial period, and early development of the United States, the fierce independence of the various sects led to a strong denominational movement within the American society. That is to say, each church, or sect, was tightly bound to its own denominational council in terms of the principles accepted by them as part of their "faith." Some of these principles were essentially the same in all sects, therefore, the general belief that the New Testament was the part of the Bible meant by God to be for the use of Protestants; and that each individual was capable of interpreting the New Testament for himself without guidance from an ordained Priesthood. Indeed, it was exactly the latter principle which made it possible for the Protestant branch of Christianity to splinter into a large number of sects. Again these principles had been a part of the evolving American society for a century or more prior to the creation of the United States. The list of principles that could be drawn up is long, and subject to debate; as many of them overlap some of the principles that many would be seen as secular social principles and not particularly related to any religion. From the modern debate concerning religion a list of the most prominent of the principles can be drawn. This list would include, but, of course, not be limited to the following: one, a firm belief in the redeeming power of Jesus Christ; two, a belief that the New Testament was the most important part of God's word that was intended for Protestants; three, that the Ten Commandments were the literal desire of God for the way in which mankind should conduct itself. Beyond these general principles each sect had its own list of principles that it held each member accountable for in everyday life. These were also said to have been sanctioned by God, for example, the Calvinistic principle of hard work (strict work ethic), or the Baptist principle that dancing and other frivolous pleasures were the work of the devil. The point is that all of these had become a rather unconscious, or visceral, part of the daily lives of the new citizens of the United States prior to independence.

One issue in the current debate is that these religious principles have been lost or replaced by other, nontraditional religious principles. Those that are still living according to the traditional religious principles have become so small in number as to represent essentially a social backwater. The blame for the loss is usually placed on either the decline of individual religious commitment or the growing dependence on the welfare system. In both cases it is claimed that the Protestant principles that traditionally underpinned American society have been lost or replaced by new non-Protestant, or secular, principles. It is in this part of the debate that much of the confusion mentioned earlier can be found. For example, the loss of faith on the part of the general American public is expressed by such things as the loss of a commitment to the traditional family, a lack of commitment to be honest, the loss of self-reliance, and a general lack of respect for authority (religious or secular), among many others. Many of these concepts were incorporated into the principles adopted by the various Protestant sects; however, they were also a part of what made up the secular standards for ethical or moral conduct. Therefore, for those who defined traditional American values from a religious viewpoint they were all seen as religious values; while on the other hand, those who were not attempting to define traditional American values from a religious point of view, but rather a secular point of view, considered the same concepts to be a part of the traditional standards for social conduct. Regardless, however, what is being attempted is to show that these principles, or values, have been lost or are being ignored and as a result the US is facing a series of problems. It is further being claimed that if these principles were reinstated or revitalized, the problems could, and would, be solved.

In discussing whether or not this is an accurate vision of the current environment in the US, and whether or not the conclusions drawn are correct, a start can be made by stating that every citizen in America in 1789 expected that all of these principles would be accepted by anyone joining the society. Such an expectation is basic to the peaceful operation of every society. Many historians claim that this expectation remained a reality as long as the immigration to the new world came from Northern or Western Europe. The same historians also claim that when immigration patterns centered on Southern and Eastern Europe, or Asia and Latin America, this expectation began to become more a hope than a reality. However, it can be seen that even with the changing patterns of immigration, assimilation to the dominant culture, although more difficult, was normally accomplished by the third generation. The majority of those new immigrants, especially those from Southern and Eastern Europe, were of some type of Christian heritage, generally the Catholic or Orthodox branches of the Christian faith. As a result they were familiar with the principles of the Protestant sects, although many had developed a large dose of antipathy to them. Asian immigrants may represent an exception to this rule, as their belief systems had different foundations. Many immigrants of course did not speak English, and this made assimilation to the existing American society difficult albeit doable.

There were also two populations of people that were intentionally segregated from the dominant society, that is, the Native Americans and the African Americans. It can be claimed with some justification that this remains the case today. Yet a third population, while coming to America voluntarily, also consciously remained outside the dominant social structure. This population is best represented by the Chinese Americans who established living arrangements separate from the predominant society, that is, China Towns. In some degree this also still remains the case today. In the latter case, however, there is little, if any, resistance on the part of the dominant society to prevent assimilation if such is chosen. The point is that even though the new immigrants had little reason to identify with the traditional Protestant principles, assimilation was accomplished by the third generation. Lastly, although little attention is paid to the historical circumstances set forth above, the people who take this position in the debate clearly recognize that major changes are occurring within what they define as the traditional American value system.

Today the focus is largely on the large number of immigrants who are entering the country (legally or illegally) from Latin America and the various Muslim nations. A claim has been made that a majority of these immigrants are not interested in becoming US citizens and therefore are not at all interested in adopting the dominant principles that underlie the society. In addition, a claim can be heard that a large segment, if not a majority, of the citizens of the US are voluntarily giving up any commitment to the traditional principles. Within this argument it is sometimes pointed out that not only are they willing to voluntarily drop their commitment to traditional principles but that they are also unable, or unwilling, to replace them with new principles. It can certainly be shown that this argument is backed up by the rapid growth of government issuance of standards of conduct, essentially principles, to fill the void. Under the government standards being issued the core Protestant principles are being replaced with a set of diversity rules which require that all religions, ethical codes, and moral standards be allowed an equal weight in determining conduct.

There can be little doubt that the US has become a much more diverse place than it was in 1789 in terms of the number of religions being practiced, the number of languages being spoken, the number of differing cultural backgrounds, and the number of differing historical circumstances that exist. It is likely that this has been true at least since 1900, so it is no wonder that the traditional Protestant principles are no longer adopted by the majority of citizens. In this sense, it can be concluded that the traditional Protestant principles have indeed lost their dominance within the social fabric of the United States. It also allows the conclusion that their reinstatement and/or revitalization is unlikely to solve any of the major problems facing the nation. However, we must take a look at the segment of the debate that holds that traditional secular social principles have replaced those of Protestantism in terms of our discussion. This will be done in another context as many of the same principles are involved.

B. What Constitutes Traditional American Principles?

Research indicates that it would be a very difficult task to come up with one list of principles that all Americans could agree upon. Indeed, it would even be difficult to come up with a definition of the word "traditional" in relation to the concept of principles. It does seem, however, that if pushed to make such a list, most Americans could come up with at least a few candidates they believe should be on the list. What is remarkable is that the various lists that appear on the Internet contain religious virtues, political principles, and economic principles as well as social beliefs. It would also seem fair to say that whether or not any particular item actually represents a principle or belief is irrelevant; what we are discussing is what Americans believe are principles or beliefs.

Many lists contain items such as democracy, equality before the law, and justice — which many people consider to be political principles. Other lists contain such items as free enterprise, capitalism, and other concepts that many would classify as economic principles. Again, some lists contain such items as a belief in one God, or a belief in Christianity, and the divinity of Jesus Christ, among others, that essentially are religious principles. One can find lists of principles covering nearly everything that one could wish to include.

Most Americans have not thought a great deal about what they would consider to be the principles that support the American social structure. Many would resist making a list for themselves if asked to do so. However, if a list were presented to them, they would be able to choose the items they felt belonged there relatively quickly. Indeed, they would rather quickly be capable of choosing those items they believed were "traditional" in the overall American culture.

It is, therefore, arbitrary to choose any one set of items for a short list of traditional American principles. Accepting that caveat, the following list represents a compilation of the principles that arguably could be found on most lists.

• Equality is one of the most basic principles held by the American culture. It is so deeply ingrained that it was included in the Declaration of Independence, e.g., 'that all men were created equal.' It is included in the United States Constitution, e.g., 'all citizens will be equal before the law.' This principle has been held since the founding of the United States.

• Individualism is another principle that, I believe, would be universally found on any list drawn up by Americans. The individual is valued as being unique and precious. This principle is seen as totally positive even though it leads to a diversity of opinions that are capable of being stated anywhere at any time.

• Privacy is a principle that most Americans would say that they believe to be important in their daily lives. This principle shows up in many ways but may be best expressed in the everyday statement made by many Americans 'that if I do not have at least a half hour a day to myself, I will go mad.'

• Self-help is another principle that would make nearly all American lists of principles. Americans deeply believe that one can only claim as accomplishments those things that they have done on their own. This concept of self-help is the basis of all rags-to-riches stories. It is also the basis of satisfaction that many CEOs and others of that ilk obtain from participating in physical labor from time to time. It is fair to conclude that most Americans believe that they are responsible for whatever success they have obtained in life.

•   Competition is so important in American life that it is inculcated in the individual almost from birth and continues until the individual is in his or her grave. Competition is not only a fact of life for Americans, competitiveness is also seen as a very positive trait that should be cultivated by everyone. It is seen as responsible to the success of both Americans and America in the last 200 or so years.

•   Change is seen as a positive principle by most Americans. They accept change, as well as accepting the speed at which things change. They see change as bringing better things into their lives and do not regret the falling away of traditions. People are meant to control their environment and handling change is one part of handling one's environment. Americans seek out change and are not content to sit and wait for fate to provide for them.

•   Americans have adopted as a principle a very specific work ethic. This principle is seen by the individual as the basis of whatever success he or she may achieve in this life. The work ethic is normally expressed as working hard, working efficiently, being innovative and honest. Following this work ethic leads to success and those who don't achieve success it is because they do not work hard enough, etc. This principle is seen as positive even though it might produce workaholics.

•   Informality is a principle that most Americans live on a daily basis but very seldom think about. The United States was specifically founded on the basis that it would not include royalty or even an aristocracy. Americans do not base their respect for individuals on wealth, social status or birth. Essentially everyone is seen to be equal and this equality is in the eyes of many across the world a sign of a lack of respect. It is fair to say that Americans are casual as can be seen in many employers refusing the honorific of "sir" in relations with their employees.

•   Americans maintain the principle of practicality and hold it dear. This shows in the fact that Americans are responsible for more patented inventions than any other people. It also shows in the American tendency to value the entrepreneur, manager, lawyer and doctor at a higher level than the philosopher or artist. Americans pride themselves on being objective, even scientific, as opposed to being subjective or idealistic.

•   Americans are generally highly materialistic. They hold that a focus on material goods goes hand-in-hand with the work ethic. If people work hard, the belief goes, they will have more money and be capable of buying more material things and leisure. (Although if they were asked, Americans would probably deny that they are crassly materialistic.) Indeed, anyone who does not succeed in obtaining material wealth is considered to be lazy. As a result of the principle of materialism, Americans also tend to discount the value of material things and are capable of easily exchanging them, for example, trading cars yearly.

This list of ten traits and their all too brief description is, again, arbitrary. Many other traits could be added and some could probably be subtracted. This list, however, can stand as well as any other as the basis of discussion revolving around the American system of principles. Most Americans believe that they form a basic part of life in the United States.

One aspect of the American system of principles is the current debate being held concerning whether or not the "traditional American principles" have been lost or eroded to the point that they no longer support the American social structure. In its most obvious sense any principle held by Americans is traditional if it has been around for a relatively long period of time. Some of the traits listed above have been a part of the American social structure since the foundation of the United States. Equality, individualism, the work ethic, and self-help would be among those included. Others have been a part of the social structure for a considerable period of time. Competition, informality, materialism and others would probably fit this category. They can all, therefore, be considered to be "traditional" principles. The debate as it is framed today boils down to whether or not these principles have been 'lost' or 'eroded'. We can look at our list and attempt to determine whether they have been lost or eroded to the point that they no longer support the social structure of the United States. This, indeed, is a procedure that could be followed with any list of traditional principles. Such being the case, an attempt will be made to set forth our list and to follow how each has evolved over time.

Equality at the foundation of the United States had a definite meaning. It was seen as a universal principle in that all men were created equal. There can be no doubt, however, that in practice all men were not seen as equal. Equality between individuals depended upon color, gender, race, religion and in many cases geographical origin. The equality of nations was dependent upon who controlled them, i.e., nations controlled by whites could be considered relatively equal; but this was not the case with nations ruled by blacks, browns or reds. The US Constitution and the Bill of Rights both incorporated this inequality into their basic structure.

Today it can be argued that a belief in equality is held more universally than ever before. Men today are seen not only as equal in the eyes of their creator or before the secular law, but rather as equal in every way, that is, in intelligence, physical attributes, opportunity and many others. Equality is the natural possession of all people regardless of color, race, religion, intelligence, physical capability or handicap, and opportunity. In the US, a belief in the principle of equality is almost universally recognized.

This is, of course, different from the "traditional" manner of seeing the principle of equality. The debate centers on whether or not the expansion of the principle of equality is a positive or negative trait. Many accept that the change is positive and seek to promote the concept of diversity and the responsibility to in fact treat everyone as equal. Others see the change as negative as it requires the government to make decisions concerning the equality of individuals before the law. This position would limit the principle of equality to being equal in terms of opportunity and not extend it to universal equality.

Individualism as practiced at the time of the birth of the United States was normally opposed to the membership or dependence on the group. Therefore, the individual was seen as unique and precious in opposition to the tribe, the state, the church and possibly the family. The individual was expected to be a member of various groups, that is, the state, the nation, the church, the family and others, but was seen as unique in terms of all other members of the group. In short, the individual was man qua man.

The principle of individualism has again evolved over time. If anything the individual is seen today as even more unique and precious than in the past. The individual trumps the state, the nation, the church, and the family. The individual is seen as having the right to obtain as much material wealth, leisure, etc. as is possible, by whatever means are necessary to get it. Public service, patriotism, sacrifice in general are seen as opposed to the rights of the individual. In short, no opinion, theory or whatever is to be held as more valuable than any other.

The principle of individualism is not what it was traditionally but may in fact be held more universally than in the past. This change is again debated as to whether it represents a positive or negative trend. The religious right (maybe religion in general) would undoubtedly come down on the side of this being a negative trend. In this case the individual is subordinated to the will of God, or at least, to the dictates of God. On the other hand, those who no longer find religion a force in the formation of their social views would probably hail this expansion of the principle of individualism as a very positive trait indeed.

Privacy was not a principle held in the early American social structure. The way of life of the majority of people at that time involved the practice of agriculture. This, as a natural part of the occupation, involved a great deal of isolation from everyone except the immediate family. As a result of this isolation it can fairly be judged that many, if not most, people were very lonely. Loneliness has always been seen as a negative in relation to the life of the normal human being. Privacy at this time was not sought after but rather avoided whenever possible.

Over time, however, Americans found themselves constantly in the presence of their workmates, their neighbors and outright strangers. The principle of privacy came into existence at this point as something positive and to be sought after. Again, if anything, although privacy was not a traditional principle Americans have been seeking it long enough for it to become seen as a traditional principle to be sought after. The debate over privacy is for all practical purposes limited to the effect of governmental policies. The intervention of government in the everyday affairs of Americans is described by many as an invasion of privacy. As this type of invasion has constantly been growing more prominent the claim is being advanced that the principle of privacy has been lost. However, in the case of the individual there is no doubt that privacy is as sought after as it always has been and is seen as a distinctly positive trait. It is fair to say, therefore, that the argument of invasion of privacy through governmental policy is a specialized limitation.

The principle of self-help was held in a very peculiar manner at the time of the foundation of the United States. Those involved in agriculture, or the general rural way of life, were self-reliant out of necessity, not by choice. In most cases if they needed something, they had to provide for themselves. This they did without any thought as to whether or not they were being self-reliant.

Later, however, when circumstances had changed, Americans looked back at their ancestors' ability to provide most of what they had as a positive principle in their lives. What had been a necessity came to be seen as a goal, a positive trait that should be sought. At this point Americans accepted that the only accomplishments they could take credit for were the ones they produced on their own.

This principle is still held by a majority of Americans, even those who in fact do not provide anything for themselves. The modern debate again centers on the effect of governmental policies in relation to self-help. It is claimed that the modern welfare state has grown to the point that it has eliminated the principle of self-help in those that receive the benefits. As the numbers of individuals who are depending to some degree upon government benefits continues to grow those holding this position claim that the principle of self-help will disappear. On the other hand, those who are in favor of continuing the welfare state see the benefits as a temporary safety net intended to provide help to those in need. They fully expect that at some point the majority of those now drawing benefits will stop doing so. At any rate, it is not important whether or not Americans are actually providing anything for themselves; but rather whether they believe that it is a positive trait to be as self-reliant as possible under the circumstances. This most Americans still believe to be true and still hold it as a positive principle in the American social structure.

It is very probable that competition was either not a principle held by the American public, or one that was of small importance, in everyday life in 1789. There was of course competition of many different kinds even at this time; but it can be argued that it had not yet gained the status of a principle. In reality it may have come upon the scene as a principle held by most Americans so recently as to not qualify as a traditional principle at all. Competition is if anything more universally accepted in the American social structure than ever before and is most definitely seen as a positive trait. As stated earlier it is inculcated into every individual from birth to death. It even is seen as the most valuable aspect of the economic principle of free enterprise.

The debate concerning competition is again centered on governmental activities related to the operation of the free enterprise system. Those who see the governmental regulations, taxes, and welfare as blocks to the operation of the free enterprise system normally couch their objections in terms of a limitation of competition. This, however, is not directly related to the principle of competition as a factor in the daily lives of individuals. In this latter sense competition is actively held as a positive principle as ever.

Change is another principle that can be argued to not have existed, or to have been held by Americans, at the time of the foundation of the United States. It may also be seen as one of the most recent principles to have developed within the American social structure. There is little doubt that change occurred at a much slower rate in 1789 than it has since 1950. Change was so slow that it can be held that most Americans did not notice it. In 1789 most Americans were as conscious of tradition as Europeans, and valued it nearly as much.

Today, however, there can be as little doubt that change is so rapid and so pervasive as to be impossible of escaping an individual's notice. Most Americans have accepted change as bringing better things than those available in the past; and they embrace the speed by which things change. As a result they see change as a positive principle that is to be sought for itself. Any debate that might be found centering on change is limited to concerns about whether it is coming to fast, in too many ways, and if it can be controlled. These concerns have nothing to do with change as a principle held by the American people as part of their social structure.

The work principle ethic, like all traditional principles, has become ingrained in the American's daily life. The work ethic from the beginning has consisted in the belief that hard work, innovation, discipline and efficiency result in good things happening. These good things include a belief in class mobility, higher wages, better jobs, higher standards of living, among others. Those who do not have these goods in their lives are seen to be lazy, indolent or loafers.

This principle does not seem to have changed much during American history and still remains one of the most prominent principles held by Americans. Whatever debate is being conducted is again centered on the effects of government policy. In short, the use of welfare, in the opinion of those who see government policies as a problem, has reduced, if not eliminated, the work ethic in those who receive such benefits. The recipients are seen as becoming lazy, unmotivated, and nonessential. However, it is at least possible to argue that those who are receiving the benefits spoken of still accept the work ethic as something positive and to be sought after even though they may not in practice be living that belief.

Americans in 1789 were undoubtedly less formal than their European ancestors. There was even some debate as to what title should be used to address the President of the United States. It was decided to simply call him the President of the United States rather than your majesty or some other veneration. This being said, it is also true that most Americans were more formal in 1789 than they are today. A quick look at the original source documents of the time, i.e., letters, newspapers, and magazines, will show the validity of this statement.

Today informality has come to be valued as a positive trait in American behavior. There is no deference normally given to, or in the minds of most Americans associated with, wealth, social status, etc. (or the lack of it), but rather it is seen as a right of individual expression and is valued as such. Informality is observed much more today than in the past, as is clear from the manner of dress associated with work, formal events, and other occasions, as well as in the manner in which people greet one another, among other things. If any debate is being conducted concerning this principle, it revolves around whether or not it has reached a point where it is no longer to be sought after but rather avoided. This stance is normally associated with claiming that this level of informality represents unfriendliness, disrespect and other negative traits. Regardless the American does hold the principle of informality and sees it as a positive trait to be sought after.

As stated earlier, practicality was a way of life forced upon the majority of individuals in 1789 as a result of their agricultural activities. Even in the early urban life, individuals were much more dependent upon their own ability to produce what was needed than at any other time in American history. America being free of any type of caste system, or a truly effective guild system, left individuals essentially free to work in whatever manner they saw fit. As a result they were very apt to seek ways of increasing their efficiency and reducing the amount of labor needed to do a job. As a result they created more inventions than any other people on earth and earned the resulting reputation of being an ultimately practical people. All of these were accepted as very positive traits and traits that should be sought after actively.

This principle has changed little since at least the industrial revolution and probably earlier. It is still deeply held by most Americans and is also one of the few principles that is not subject to some form of debate. Americans believe they are objective and realistic rather than subjective and idealistic although there may not be as much truth to this as Americans think.

Materialism is another of the American principles that seems to have had little social importance in 1789. There were few material things to be had at that time and most Americans did value the possession of material things in the same way as today. Even such items as beds, pots and pans were seen as items to be passed on from grandparents to parents and parents to children,.

Today materialism is an ingrained way of life. There can be little doubt that most Americans feel it is their right to have material possessions due to their hard work, innovative wealth accumulation and so forth. It is seen as a positive result of hard work and is seen as deserved and is to be sought after. Little or no debate surrounds this principle in terms of it having been lost or eroded. The debate is whether or not the principle has become a negative trait.

When seen in this way, the argument concerning traditional principles is essentially a battle against windmills. Many American principles are traditional and still held, or even enhanced, in today's world. There appear to be none, or few, that have either been completely lost or to have been severely eroded. At the very most what debate exists revolves around how widely the principles are held and whether or not they have changed substantially over time.

The real problem seems to arise when a limited group attempts to discuss principles in relation to whether or not the goals of that group have been lost or eroded. For example, the modern religious right expresses their feeling that many of the traditional American principles have been lost. They then proceed to set forth as a traditional American principle the biblical injunction that a family is to consist only of a man, woman, and their children. It is then pointed out that today's society has accepted the concept of family to include single parent, same sex parents, and other expansions of the religious family. What is missing in this debate is whether or not the change in the legal definition of a family has anything to do with whether Americans hold the family as a positive principle that is to be sought after. Again it is possible for a trait to be held as a basic American principle without anyone actually practicing it, at least, as long as Americans belief it is part of their principle system. The same would apply to most of the debates over whether or not governmental policies are responsible for the lost or erosion of American principles.

C. American Traditional Political and Economic Principles

The same approach as above can be duplicated concerning the traditional principles which underlay the American economic and political systems. That is to say, the traditional principles, or at least the most prominent of them, can be set forth; a determination can be made as to whether or not these principles still maintain their hold in today's environment; and if they don't whether it would be possible, desirable, and worthwhile to recreate them or revitalize them. In addition, in relation to the problems now facing the US whether or not these principles play any role in solving them.

In the political realm at the highest level of generalization it can be held that the US was created as a representative democracy. This meant, theoretically, that initially all sovereign power was held by the people. The constitution was drawn up to allow the people to delegate whatever powers and duties they saw fit to the various levels of government. Essentially, the constitution was a contract drawn up by the people to designate and control who would represent them in the exercise of sovereign power. It is why the US is deemed to be a representative democracy. The constitution also laid out the principle by which the people desired the various governments to operate within. They created three levels of government, that is, the local, state and federal governments and deemed them all to be sovereign in their own right. In short, the constitution created a government that was to operate as a federal system. The local governments, of course, were brought forward from colonial times and did not receive direct notice in the constitution; but it can be assumed that it was the local governments that intended to retain the powers of the people. The national government (the federal), and the state governments both were delegated a series of powers and duties by the people, as well as, being denied specific powers and duties. Therefore, there would be initially a national government and thirteen state governments all too some degree sovereign in relationship to one another. Although this type of arrangement had never been adopted before it was a relatively natural development from the colonial experience. The 150 years of colonial status had been experienced in relative freedom from direct control by Great Britain. The thirteen colonies were essentially allowed to govern themselves for the most part, and the local governments were not even within the intent of Great Britain to control. The local governments, therefore, literally represented the powers and duties held by the people. The states were seen as the governmental level that was most in touch with the people both in terms of wants and needs and in terms of the loyalty of the people themselves. The national government was created as a sort of general overseer of the rights and duties of the other two. The constitution, through the representatives of the people, delegated what was intended to be the duties and powers to be held by the federal government. It also prohibited both the states and the federal government from the exercise of specific duties and powers. All duties not delegated to the state or federal governments, and those denied both of them, were to be retained by the people (to be exercised by the local governments). This literally is the definition of a federal system of government, that is, the principle of federalism. The constitution did not, however, stick strictly to the principle of federalism as it did delegate some powers that were to be exercised solely by the federal government, such as the power to declare war and peace. The use of exclusive power in the national government comes under the principles underlying the concept of nationalism, that is, a system in which exclusive power is held at the national level and all lower levels of government receive their duties and powers by delegation from the national government. In a very limited sense the US was created as a mixture of federalism and nationalism with the balance heavily weighted in favor of federalism. Therefore, the two traditional principles that underlie the American political system are democracy and federalism.

One of the issues being debated in today's environment is whether or not the United States is still operating under the principles of democracy and federalism; or is in the process of becoming something other than a democracy or federal system. It has been clearly established earlier that the two main traditional political principles that are the foundation of the US system have not been lost nor are they being ignored. However, it was also concluded that both have undergone a series of attacks brought on by a changing environment. These attacks are seen as serious and over time capable of destroying democracy and the system of federalism as the foundation of the American political system. As a result a call was made that suggested that the only process whereby these trends could be reversed was through action on the part of the American people. One aspect of this call is whether or not under current conditions the public has it within their power to actually accomplish this goal. It appears that the answer to this question lies in whether or not the American public has become so diverse as to make it impossible to act in concert. This aspect of the problem will be addressed at the end of the work, but it appears that even though diverse there are still enough commonalities to make action effective. There are many who are claiming that the American public is not only unable to do this but also unmotivated to do so.

Initially individual life in the US was based largely upon associations that existed as socializing factors that intermediated between the nuclear family and the state. This included the associations with the church, various professional societies, local businesses, the Chamber of Commerce, etc. There was little contact between the individual and the larger social organizations, such as the state governments, the federal government, and the national political parties. Even in the case of infrastructure, local roads, bridges, schools, little contact was needed between the local governments and the higher levels of government. In this sense the people (local governing bodies) were essentially self-reliant and responsible for providing what the people needed, if they did not do it themselves. At this time the only portion of the federal government that was directly elected by the people was the members of the House of Representatives. The members of the Senate were appointed through the actions of the various state legislatures, and the executive branch, that is, President and Vice-President, were nominated by the federal legislature through the electoral system. As a result the people were involved, even at this early date, through people they knew personally for the appointment of the main offices of the federal and state governments. In turn the loyalty of the people tended to be located in the local and state governments rather than in the federal government. For example, the sense of commitment people felt for principles such as the duty to pay taxes, obedience to the law, and patriotism were directed towards the local and state governments rather than the nation itself. As with the traditional social principles, this remained largely true until around 1900.

In relation to the two major traditional political principles, it is important that an understanding be developed as to how they have evolved over time. After 1900 several major factors came into play that are claimed to have brought on the loss, or ignoring, of the traditional political principles. First, the US society was initially based on the agricultural industry. The vast majority of citizens then existing in the US were involved in one manner, or another, with agriculture. They were either actually farmers, members of the farmer's family, or involved in providing the services needed by the farming community. This environment was marked by a low rate of mobility, that is, most people tended to remain in the area in which they were born. As a result they tended to have strong commitments to the nuclear family, the extended family, close neighbors, and those who provided the local services they needed. This in turn is claimed to have fostered a strong feeling for self-reliance, honesty, friendship. This type of feeling is clearly emphasized by the old saw that only a handshake was needed to be assured that one's word would be kept. In short, the agricultural environment is claimed to have resulted in what is today being called traditional American principles.

These can be set forth as follows, but this does not, of course, represent an exclusive list of the principals involved: a strong commitment to the nuclear family (which at the time was defined as a husband and wife and their children); a strong commitment to the extended family (uncles, aunts, cousins, grandparents); commitment to a rather close knit circle of friends (this usually included those with whom one attended church, did business with and neighbors). There also developed during the colonial period a strong attachment to the colony rather than to the British government. This commitment was carried over when independence came to a loyalty to the state rather than the federal government. Generally speaking the public had little knowledge concerning what the federal government was doing and were therefore little influenced by it. There were exceptions, however, such as the federal plan to tax the production of alcohol. This direct effort to produce revenue ended with the people rising in revolt under what came to be known as Shay's rebellion. Again this state of affairs remained essentially in place until about 1860. As a reference point to the demographic state of the Union prior to 1860 it is noted that the census data counted any collection of people amounting to more than 8000 citizens as a city. There were a few large cities but they were the exception rather than the rule. At this point the whole life of the individual was local in nature and the principles by which one lived were common to everyone that surrounded the individual. Second, after 1860, or thereabout, the industrial revolution began to come into its own in the US. The industrial revolution had two major effects upon American society at the time. One, it slowly began to change the US society from one based upon the practice of agriculture, to one based upon the manufacturing industry. Two, the industrial revolution began to change the demographics of American society. The placement of factories around the larger cities, and the areas where resources could be obtained, for example, water sources, meant that those who wanted employment in them had to travel to them. Even at the early stages of the industrial revolution the various industrial organizations had no trouble inducing people to come to them. In short, they were largely responsible for an increasing rate of mobility among the public. Initially this mobility affected a large number of young females, and young males who wanted off the farm for one reason or another. This increase in mobility resulted in the slow drift of society from rural life to a live based upon urbanization. This process had also become noticeable by no later than 1900, although urbanization would continue for some time after that date.

As a result of these two effects of the industrial revolution other changes began to become noticeable. Some of these changes are as follows: one, those who were employed by the businesses (factories) were slowly becoming less self-reliant, at least, in terms of providing most of their own wants and needs; two, the rather open reliance on honesty and trust began to weaken as individuals were forced to deal with an ever growing number of people they did not know or understand; three, the need for a close knit nuclear family, an extended family, and lifelong friendships also began to weaken and was replaced by individual association with the work place, the urban neighborhood and the denominational church. However, as we shall see, some of the traditional principles were much slower to change, that is, the commitment to religion, the commitment to the traditional definition of the nuclear family, and attachment to the local government. The latter now being the city, or portion of the city, in which one lived rather than to the village or town where one was born. At any rate, by 1920 the agricultural base of society had essentially finished its conversion to one based upon manufacturing. As has been shown the manufacturing base included principles that were different from those of the agricultural base, although not necessarily antagonistic to them. Some of the changes that were beginning to become noticeable among the public, but not necessarily discussed, included the following in relation to our discussion: for example , the slow migration of sovereign power and duties from the local governments to the urban and state governments, and a little later from the urban and state governments to the federal government. This issue will be revisited in the context of our discussion of the current societal environment in the US, that is, whether or not the US is still operating under the traditional political principles of democracy and federalism.

Returning to the contention that two traditional political principles supported the American political system, it becomes necessary to inquire whether these principles still operate in today's political environment and at what degree of importance. As we have seen one side of this issue claims that they are not, or at least, that they are not operating as they should. This side tends to call for the revitalization, if not recreation, of these traditional principles. The other side of the issue claims that both federalism and democracy are alive and well and operating pretty much as they were intended too under the constitution. This debate is carried on under the conditions that prevail today and ignores the fact that three significant segments of the general population were denied representation in the government throughout American history. That is to say, the Native Americans (at independence numbering about 200,000), the African-American population (at independence numbering about 500,000), and women (assumed to be something on the order of one-half of the total population of 3.5 million). The first two were intentionally segregated from the society that was formed in 1789 and in many ways remain segregated from that society today. The latter over the intervening years were able to get themselves into a position where they could participate in the representative democracy, but not until 1920. In short, one half of the total population of the US was essentially denied participation in the democratic political system operating in the US until well into the 20th century. As a result, it can be justifiably claimed that the commitment by this population to the traditional political principles was not the same as those who had been participating since 1789. At any rate, the current debate so far has failed to take into consideration that these populations may be operating under a different set of principles, or have very little faith in the traditional principles, to solve the problems facing them. It can be of no wonder that such phrases as life, liberty and the pursuit of happiness meant little to these populations. Regardless of the plight of these three groups the traditional political principles did exist and were at least accepted, if not truly believed in, by nearly all people living in the US until about 1920.

The last stage was accompanied by the growth of the duties and powers of the federal government. This process, of course, had an effect on all three major segments of the American society; and these effects in many cases overlapped from one segment to the others. In relation to the traditional political principles the debate has focused upon the following aspects of growth in the federal power: First, the settling of the majority of sovereign power in the federal government has forced a major chance in the manner the public sees its loyalties. The public, for the most part, has very little connection with the local and state governments. While it is true that the local and state governments still have a rather long list of duties and responsibilities, such as manning and operating prisons, K–12 school systems, and insane asylums, they do so under a large amount of financing and regulation by the federal government. The same is true of their duties in regard to the infrastructure and other large scale needs of the people. As a result the people have less regard for the local and state governments.

One aspect of the current environment clearly points to this conclusion. The public, or those who are eligible to vote and who do vote, don't bother to vote in most local and state elections. As a result, even in very small villages, most people do not know who represents them and what issues they feel are important to the people. Indeed, there are very few organizations located within the community, such as churches, businesses, professional organizations and the like, that are truly focused on local issues of importance to all the residents. These duties and responsibilities tend to be handled by up and coming professional politicians attempting to work their way to national power through service in the local and state governments. This road to national power is controlled by the two political parties and the interest groups that support them. The interest groups that finance these local political campaigns are the same as those that finance the federal campaigns. The politicians, therefore, tend to be more concerned with national issues than local or state issues. In turn the people are subjected to national issues even at the local and state level and only a few, or minority, of people are truly concerned with local and state issues. It seems somewhat incredible but even local issues that are of major importance to individuals, such as property taxes, school issues, and infrastructure issues, for example, generate very little general discussion within the whole public, although they might generate considerable passion in those directly affected. This may be a result of the fact that people, even in small villages, tend to no longer be surrounded by family, close friends and well known neighbors. The traditional attachment to individualism also seems to be giving way to the concern for group rights, that is, women's rights, gay rights, Hispanic rights, among others.

The question in this case focuses on how the public views the two traditional political principles in the current environment. It appears to be true that most people are focused on the issues, that is, jobs, economic growth, gridlock, and so forth, rather than on democracy and federalism. This is, of course, to be expected as the issues directly affect the quality of the life style lived by the individual. Once again the public's focus on the larger issues also seems to be driven by groups (interest groups). Tax reform, reform of the immigration system, reform of the health care system are all framed by the political parties and the interest groups affected by the various policies. Most American, it can be argued, are well aware of the issues, but unless directly affected by them do not care much about them. If directly affected the opinion driving the individual is less based on his or her own research and conclusions, than that of the group with which she or he identifies. Only a small minority of the American public can be truly classified as truly active in the political realm. This has probably been true throughout American history, especially at the federal level. However, now it is much more true at the local and state level than in the past. This seems to be the result of the loss of relevance of these levels of government in the daily lives of the people, at least, as the people perceive it.

The problem posed by this is how to shift the public back from indifference to active participation in the democratic system. One answer might lie in the answer furnished by the so-called "Arab Spring." In this case an organized group in several different nations began a social media campaign to protest the policies of the current regime in power. The campaign was effective enough to draw tens of thousands of people into the streets to protest. It was also effective enough to force the ruling regime to negotiate and in a few cases to resign their control of power. This method, however, can also be used to produce very negative results as is shown by the ability of the Islamic State to use it to recruit "lone wolf" terrorists. Another approach that has been used effectively in the past is grassroots movements such as the recent Tea Party movement. These types of reactions on the part of the people historically have been most effective when focused on the local and state level of government and while they remained outside the established political system. As both the Tea Party and Progressive Movements show once incorporated into one of the major political parties independent action becomes very difficult.

D. Economic Principles

In regard to the traditional economic principles it was again decided earlier that both the concept or principle of private property and the free market system are still accepted as the foundation of the American economic system. As with the traditional political principles it has also been decided that a real attack on the traditional economic principles has occurred and is still underway. The end result is the same in this case also, that is, that the trend in current times is to forego the operation of these to principles as the means by which the society will get the fairest distribution of the good things in life. The goal has always been a just distribution of both the social rights accorded to the citizens (essentially an equal opportunity to compete) and a fair distribution of the material wealth of the society. Initially this was seen as best accomplished by holding private property to be nearly sacrosanct and allowing the economy to operate within the free market system. The question, of course, is whether or not the same remains true today.

It would seem true that both are under attack largely as a result of the weakening of the public's commitment to a solid work ethic, individualism and self-reliance. The trend clearly seems to be in favor of allowing the state and federal governments to decide how the social benefits and material wealth of the society are to be distributed. Hayak in his book "Road to Serfdom" clearly put an appeal for the acceptance of the individual's duty to make these decisions for him or herself. Karl Marx, on the other hand, clearly put out the plea that these decisions could best be made by the state rather than by the individual. This is, of course, the basis of the debate that is going on today. Most Americans, it can be argued, still believe that the majority of social benefits and material wealth should be earned by the individual through hard work, genius, innovation and creativity. The problem is that a large segment of the population is not living these beliefs even though they might hold them. At the base of this belief lies the trust in the rule of law to provide equal opportunity for the individual to act, and the ability to use private property to advance ones chances of success without undue influence on the part of society or the government. One of the major questions in the current environment is whether or not the welfare system as it exists restricts the rule of law in providing an equal opportunity; and whether or not it restricts the free use of private property, innovation and creativity. Many are of the opinion that it is in fact the result found in the welfare system. If this is true then again the question will be how to draw the public's focus back to the traditional economic principles.

It can be stated from the beginning that very few Americans are concerned about the operation of the free market system. They are focused, instead, on their job, or lack thereof, the state of the economy, and gridlock among others. However, more Americans are becoming concerned about private property, especially in relation to the reasons that their assets, such as homes, businesses and retirement funds are losing real value. This was brought to the attention of the American people by the practices of the financial community, the effect of budget deficits and national debt and the part they might play in their perceived ability to enjoy the good things in life. At the same time, they seem to be capable of ignoring the signs of continuing risk acceptance on the part of the financial community and the growing possibility of a stock market bubble. Indeed, mobilizing action on these issues on the part of the general public is paramount not only to the salvation of the American economic system but also the American political system. At present the confusion on the part of the public is only increased by the rhetoric of the political parties and biased news media. The political parties, the interest groups, and the media are all pushing for solutions that fit their narrow view rather than solutions that are truly to benefit society as whole. The solution is again to find a way to bring the public into an attempt to force the application of the free market system and the concept of private property as solutions to the economic problems facing the nation.

As a preparation for deciding what might be done to revitalize, or recreate, the public expression of what should be done to solve the problems facing the American system another look will be taken at how we got to the point we're at today.

CHAPTER 12. THE INTERPLAY OF THE MARKET SYSTEM AND DEMOCRACY

So the first step is to determine how the problems interact with one another. It is not very difficult to identify the major economic problems: unemployment in all its forms; a stagnant or negative growth economy; the decline of the real value of income and assets of the middle class; a lack of long term, good paying, low skill jobs; the devaluation of the dollar; the lack of opportunity for long term investment in the productive sector of the economy; the lack of a solid educational base for those seeking employment; budget deficit financing; exploding levels of national debt; the creation of investment bubbles such as the Hi-Tech, housing, and stock market sectors; the increasing artificial transfer of wealth associated with the growing welfare state and the unlimited printing of money.

There is also no real difficulty in understanding that all of these factors interplay with one another as the economy continues to operate. They interact in both known and unknown ways, producing both intended and unintended consequences. The question asked earlier had to do with whether or not any one factor was more important than the others in the sense of being the one factor that drove all the others. The evidence would seem to clearly indicate that all of the above factors are in reality symptoms of an underlying problem, or problems that are rarely contemplated. When one draws their focus away from the symptoms the underlying problem becomes clear at least in broad outline. The problem is that the environment in which all of the symptoms operate has changed over the last few decades; while the manner in which we look at them has not. The claim is made that the time tested remedies have not worked in the past, except to relieve the pressure of the symptoms, but is ignored by the catch phrase "this time will be different." In fact, treating the symptoms and ignoring the underlying problem didn't work in the past; and will not work in the present or the future. The underlying problem is, of course, structural in nature. Until a solution to the underlying problem is found treating the symptoms will only bring temporary relief. Then the symptoms will again return with renewed strength. If there are any lessons to be learned from economic history this is the most important of them.

Now that we have a general understanding of the underlying problems and the fact that they are structural in nature, we must identify the structures involved. In the US economy, at least roughly speaking, there are two structural elements first, the free market system or capitalism. Simply put the free market system allowed for the natural interplay of economic market forces free from undue governmental interference. In the same manner the free market, or capitalism, allowed for the free investment of capital, labor, and materials with the expectation that a return in the form of profit would result, again without undue influence on the part of government. The interplay of the free market system was believed to result in the maximization of profit, and or wages, which encouraged the investment of funds in productive activities, creativity, innovation, equipment, inventory, and labor. As stated above it is understood that no economy has ever existed within this system and operated at maximum efficiency. In return this means that the maximum of profit and wages has also never been obtained under natural conditions. It may be claimed, however, that the economy of the United States between 1820 and 1920 operated at as near maximum efficiency in relation to the free market system as ever in history.

The free market system, under existing conditions, operated in a relatively free manner, in particular, in regard to undue governmental influence; even though it did suffer from artificial restrictions put in place by the private sector, such as monopolies, interlocking directorates, etc. As a result of this relatively free interplay during this period both profits and wages tended continuously to grow larger free of government influence. Our task, therefore, is to try and determine whether the free market system still operates in a relatively free manner; or if not what effect this has had in relation to producing the symptoms that today we treat as the problems. If the free market system no longer supports the US economy we must determine if possible what has replaced it. In addition, it must be determined if the symptoms can be removed by reinvigorating the free market system; or whether it is only possible to remove the symptoms by inaugurating a new treatment based on the new principles. The second structural factor is the concept of private property. Under this concept ownership of real and personal property has slowly come to be the right of private individuals, as we saw above. The individual is seen to have an almost sovereign right to use the property in any manner he or she sees fit. There are some restrictions on the use of property, such as zoning laws, environmental mandates; and restrictions of a strictly political nature, such as taxation policies and regulations. However, for all practical purpose no one in the current debate is questioning the status of the concept of private property. It is apparently seen to be operating in what is believed to be the traditional manner. As a result the concept of private property comes under little discussion other than in relation to the transfer of wealth from the productive sector to the non-productive sector; and in relation to the shrinking of the real value of private property, such as the value of homes. These aspects have either already been covered or will be covered in a later context.

In the free market system several factors seem to support the contention that the market does not, in fact, operate as freely as one would expect under the theory. First, the vast amount of regulation of business activities at all levels of government has placed a great deal of restriction on the operation of the market system. Indeed, these regulations are claimed to have reached the stage where it is impossible for a business to determine what the cost of doing business will be; and therefore, what rate of return (profit) can be expected from any given level of investment. As an example of the level being discussed it has recently been noted that some 1500, or more, new regulations were offered at the federal level since the beginning of 2014 alone.

There can be no question that the various levels of government are interfering with the free interplay of market forces. Many, maybe most, experts claim that it has now reached the level where that interference is undue in relation to the free market system. In the case of private property the same can be said of government interference, that is, policies which save inefficient, or defunct businesses, from going bankrupt or covering incompetence and fraud in business actions has weakened the concept of private property and its interplay within the free market system. The use of subsidies to bolster profit margins, such as farm subsidies, or oil drilling subsidies, coupled with active tariff and export policies also artificially restricts private property from free interplay with the market generally.

The biggest restriction, however, at the government level appears to be the artificial transfer of wealth from the productive forces of the economy to those who produce no value within the system (unproductive forces), e.g., the welfare state. What seems to be apparent is that the US economy is no longer based upon the free market system as it was understood at the time the US was created. However, neither is the US economy based upon a truly closed system such as those that were developed under Nazi Germany or the Soviet Union. The US economy is not truly free, nor truly closed, but rather is a hybrid. It is fair to say that the trend is toward an ever greater degree of control over the economy. As such it would be accurate to label the

US economy as a relatively controlled economy in comparison to what most would consider a free market. It is likely, however, that a name has not yet been selected for the economy as it exists today in that the structural nature of the changing economy has largely remained out of the discussion. At some point as the new structural nature of the economy comes into focus a name will be applied.

The current economy is based to a large degree upon the choices that are being made by the bureaucracy in the implementation and enforcement of the laws, edicts and orders issued by all levels of government. These regulations, edicts, and orders are intended to directly affect the manner in which businesses are created, operate and go out of business. The bureaucracy, at least in part, was created to implement and enforce these rules. In this task the bureaucracy was intentionally given as much flexibility in carrying out their orders as was possible. This has essentially resulted in the creation of a fourth branch of government. The elected portion of the various governments were expected to oversee the operation of the bureaucracy. Initially this system seemed to work efficiently enough, that is, the legislative and executive branch were responsible for initiating most of the regulations, edicts and orders and in overseeing the implementation and enforcement of them. Under normal conditions, for example, the executive department was capable of determining whether conditions demanded a strict or lax enforcement of the rules and how they were to be implemented. Over the last few decades, however, the rules have proliferated to the extent that the executive branch no longer can keep track of the implementation and enforcement procedures. The bureaucracy, at the same time, has grown so large and cumbersome that it cannot see the consequences of its own departments upon one another. Regulations are strictly enforced, or not, as the various departments or agencies see fit without necessarily any connection with the conditions that surround the activity being regulated. In many cases it seems as if no one truly understands the regulation in question, at least in whole, or the consequences intended by its implementation and enforcement; therefore the bureaucracy acts in what it believes to be the intent of its employer (normally the executive department).

This is most certainly the case with the Affordable Care Act. No one had read, nor did anyone completely understand, the whole of the 2300-page document, that is, the legislation, before it was passed. No single department or agency is responsible for the implementation and enforcement of this bill; but rather, the implementation and enforcement are spread out over nearly the whole gamut of departments and agencies in the federal bureaucracy as well as being divided between the state and federal governments. In short, it appears that the act was created in such a way as to insure that the right hand does not know what the left hand is doing.

Indeed, the right hand does not even have a way to determine what the left hand may be doing. The intention was to resolve the most glaring, if not all, existing abuses in the private health care system. The fact that the various elements of the existing system, that is, doctors, hospitals, insurance companies, and the drug industry are all in favor of the act would clearly indicate that the bill does not accomplish its intended task. This would indicate that the act limits the private market in terms of free interaction of market forces rather than promoting them. It may, however, over time relieve some of the symptoms found in the existing system, such as preexisting conditions clauses, the large segment of uninsured within the general population (40 million) and the rising cost of medical services. The botched roll out of the program should be a clear indication that the right hand not knowing what the left hand is doing is a fatal flaw within the system. In the meantime the interplay of existing market forces within the health care industry of the economy are substantially restricted. The best that can be expected in regard to the end results may prove to be worse than if the existing system had been left alone to solve these issues through the operation of a free market at the private level. The Affordable Care Act regardless of its failure, or success, will stand as an example of the results to be expected from attempts to institute national planning policies as reforms within the US economy. This type of controlled planning not only effects the traditional economic principles but all others as well.

One of the most glaring examples is in the area of civil rights. The federal government, as well as most of the state governments, were forced to act on behalf of the various interest groups involved. The individual citizen had very little, if any, choice in how the civil rights issues would be viewed or how they would be handled. The actions, for example, that had earlier been taken by some states to put restrictions on the right to vote were not subject to debate. The states involved claimed that it was within their constitutional rights to set qualifications for voting and that as long as they were applied to every citizen equally they were legal. Due to pressure applied by the civil rights movement the federal government determined that the state actions were unconstitutional and forced the states to scrap them and replace them with the voting standards of the federal government. The states involved, and therefore their citizens, were not given the chance to correct the policies they had in place; or to choose an alternative method to remove the restrictions. The point being not whether the actions taken by the states were right or wrong, but rather, that the solution was removed from the people.

The second major pillar was the relatively unrestricted operation of democracy as a political form. In this case the founders, through the creation of the Constitution, formed a democracy that is a hybrid system which incorporated both the concept of federalism and nationalism. The system formed was federalist in nature based upon the creation of three distinct levels of sovereign government, that is, the local, state and federal governments. Each level was to be independently sovereign of the others with its own distinct duties and powers. The base level of all power was meant to reside with the people and be delegated by contract (Constitution) to the various levels of government. It was also meant to contain some elements of nationalism in the sense that the federal government would be more powerful than the lower levels of government in specified areas. These areas included the sole power to declare peace and war, the sole power to create and maintain a national currency, the sole power to oversee the operation of international and interstate commerce, and that the federal laws would be the supreme law of the land.

Over the last 100 plus years, as we have seen, the power and scope of the federal level of government has been vastly increased at the cost of the duties and powers of the local and state governments. This was the unintended consequence of many different factors; the most important of which were the voluntary delegations of state and local duties to the federal level; and the fact that the federal government stepped into each area where the state and local governments failed to act on their own. Regardless of the source of the duties and powers obtained, today the federal government clearly controls and uses the vast majority of the sovereign power to be found in the US society as a whole. Some claim as a result of this process that the US is no longer a democracy of any form. This, however, does not seem to truly register the facts as they currently exist. It may be true that federalism has to a large degree morphed into a state of nationalism, that is, that the federal government now holds power and delegates downward to the local and state levels. It is also true that the large professional bureaucracy is not directly responsible for its power to the people, that is, operates outside the normal governmental pattern. As a result of these two factors a very large degree of the power is held at the federal level and is also implemented and enforced at the federal level.

It is also true, however, that the various levels of government are still elected by the people and must remain responsive to the demands of the people to a significant degree. The US, therefore, is in fact still operating under a democratic form of government. Federalism is also still active within the system, but it may be accurate to say that the amount of power exercised at the local and state level is much reduced from what it was when the constitution was created. In this sense the US democracy is displaying a larger compatibility with nationalism than federalism. As with the European Union (EU) the bureaucracy has assumed more and more power in the form of the power to implement and enforce laws than was true at the time of the founding of the US.

This has led to the twin complaints that the US is tending to become a technocracy and is suffering a democratic deficit. It is certainly true that even the duties and powers that are still exercised by the local and state governments are beset by the fact that they to a large degree depend upon federal regulation and financing to complete their tasks. One needs not look deeply to determine that the majority of people who serve at any level of government are no longer directly elected by the people but are in fact nominated, or hired, to the positions that they hold. The state and federal bureaucracies are both professionally trained for their offices and unelected to their positions. It is here that both the EU and the US are accused of having a democratic deficit. This, of course, has always been true in the US, that is, elected officials have always relied upon appointed, or hired staff, to carry out the duties of their office. Up until relatively recently, however, the elected officials were capable of exercising an efficient oversight and control over the operations of their unelected staff and employees. At both levels, but especially at the federal level, the bureaucracy has grown so large that effective oversight and control appears to have slipped beyond the ability of elected officials to exercise. The recent activities, if official statements are to be believed, of the IRS and NSA are good examples of this lack of effective oversight and control. It would appear that the bureaucracy in many cases is not only capable of independent action, but in fact, takes independent action based on its perception of the needs of its employer.

There are three branches of government and in only one branch are the majority of officeholders elected by the people. The House of Representatives and the Senate make up the two houses of the legislative branch and all their members are elected by the people directly. Each member, however, has a relatively large number of staff and employees who act on their behalf. In this branch of government, however, the elected members seem to have sufficient oversight and control when they choose to exercise it. In the Judicial branch, the majority of the main offices are appointed by the President and confirmed and approved by the Senate, but none are elected directly by the people. They also have relatively large staffs but again they also seem to have sufficient oversight and control of the staff. In the executive branch the majority of the officeholders are not directly elected by the people. In this case only the President and Vice-President are elected by the people through the electoral system. The other major officeholders, such as department heads and the heads of the major agencies are all appointed by the President and approved and confirmed by the Senate. In this sense the original plan initiated by the Constitution has changed very little over the years; indeed, it has become more democratic with the addition of direct election of the Senate. It is to be noted as stated above the bureaucracy is largely a creature of the executive branch and is not elected or even under the direct supervision of the people. There is no doubt that this branch of government is also the least democratic.

The Constitution provided not only for three branches of government to share the power of the society; but also provided a system of checks and balances that were intended to prevent one branch of government from tyrannizing over the other two branches. Over the years that have intervened since the drafting of the constitution, however, the power of the checks and balances system seems to have eroded to a significant degree. The executive branch, largely through the power of the bureaucracy to implement and enforce the laws of the US, has usurped a good share of the powers and duties delegated to the federal government. The executive branch has also been the main beneficiary of the voluntary delegation, as well as default loss, of state powers and duties to the federal government. This again represents a weakening of the system of government intended under the original Constitution.

Lastly, the people themselves, as we have seen earlier, have willingly transferred power from the local and state governments to the federal level for one reason or another (usually financial or compatibility of enforcement). The trend has existed for a relatively long period of time but under the current atmosphere seems to have accelerated to a large degree. The level of gridlock that now exists within the legislative branch of government is without historical precedent. Since 2010, in particular, the ideological stalemate between the two political parties has inflicted several serious wounds to the US political system. The economy, and therefore the people have been negatively impacted by the 16 day shutdown of the federal government imposed by congress solely to gain leverage on unrelated issues; and the credit worthiness of the US credit standing has been lowered simply because the credit of the US was used as a bargaining chip in relation to other issues. The failure to keep the government open for business and the intentional flirtation with credit default is clearly a result of political infighting on the part of the members of congress. These two issues are of particular importance, but the failure to be able to compromise on any significant issue has had further impact. As of the beginning of 2014 one poll found that 70% of those surveyed believed that the federal government (congress in this poll) was incapable of solving the problems that faced the nation. From such a survey it is easy to conclude that people have not only given up on democracy but have given up hope. There can be no doubt that the incompetence and ideological inflexibility are in utter disregard for what the people need or demand. It will be important to see whether or not this general loss of hope, or faith in the current political system, translates into affirmative action on the part of the people. It is fair to say that the people are acting as if they have abandoned the traditional belief in democracy. The very low voter turnout, especially when compared to other industrialized nations, would indicate that Americans no longer believe that voting is important or effective in resolving their needs. This is certainly the case at the local and state levels where voter turnout is abysmal.

The fact that the people tend to demand solutions to all their problems by the various governments rather than tending to them themselves clearly indicates that the American people have given up dependence on self-reliance. The fact that a growing number of Americans appear willing to give up the effort to find suitable employment and are falling back on the welfare system clearly shows that the traditional work ethic has been abandoned for the acceptance of a lower standard of living provided with no effort required. As was pointed out earlier this is rapidly becoming a generational dependency rather than just an individual dependency. As a result, the governments (at all levels) are being asked to do more and more of the duties that traditionally were considered to be the duty of the individual. This, of course, does not mean that the US is not still operating as a democracy because it is still doing so. However, it does seem to indicate that the trend is in favor of a substantial weakening of the traditional belief in the democratic way of life, that is, individualism, self-reliance, a healthy work ethic, and acceptance of change. It appears that the people are drifting towards a complacency that is sapping their ability to earn their freedom in return for an idealistic belief in the government's ability to legislate freedom.

A conclusion drawn by those holding these views is that a return to the traditional political and economic principles must occur and is obviously based on a belief that they have been lost or are being ignored today. They further conclude that the economy of the US is operating in a manner that barely reflects a reliance on the free market system and private property; or it operates outside the boundaries of the concepts as originally developed. The political system of the US is equally operating outside the original concepts of federalism and representative democracy as evidenced by the administrative overrule of the Constitution. The political system is only superficially democratic and federalized; or it is operating outside the recognized parameters of either concept. The question arises, in fact, whether the above is an accurate description of the current US environment, and if so what has replaced these two concepts as the pillars of the American system? As we have seen the claim is that federalism has been replaced by a reliance on the concept of nationalism where power and duties are delegated from the top to the lower levels rather than vice versa. The free market system is claimed to have been replaced by a controlled economy which is a hybrid of national planning and federal regulation. It is, therefore, concluded by those of this view that the two have combined to severely limit the operation of both the free market system and democracy in the US. The result is most clearly emphasized in the power of the bureaucracy to implement and enforce the laws of the US beyond the control, or even the knowledge of the people. It is further claimed that the most glaring results of this conversion of the American system include the following: First, the inability of the elected representatives of the people to provide effective oversight and control of the bureaucracy. Second, the loss of the free interplay of market forces due to the negative influence of governmental regulation and mandate. Third, the conversion of profit and wages from return on investments in productive forces and labor to investment in "paper wealth" such as stocks, commodities and other short term investments and/ or reliance on government welfare benefits. Fourth, the loss of credibility on the part of the public in the governmental system to address their needs; as reflected by the low rates of voter turnout and lack of value placed on public service which has led to the loss of democratic traditions. Currently the US political system seems largely dysfunctional either because the older traditions have not yet fully been replaced by the new; or because the new traditions are changing the structural nature of the system. The debate, therefore, continues to determine what the current status of the traditional principles might be.

Any solutions that are to be offered must take into consideration the new environment that is currently in place. Any solution that does not address US problems in terms of the probability of loss of traditional economic and political standards will be doomed to failure. Accepting the fact that nationalism and bureaucracy have replaced federalism will give any solutions to the current political dysfunction a certain character that could not be made without those assumptions. The solution must be constructed in such a manner that it can be effectively implemented and enforced from the top down to the local level. There are at least two methods which could accomplish this goal. The first, of course, is for the federal government to continue to gather all power unto itself and then delegate whatever duties it wishes to the local governments, including duties of implementation and enforcement (reliance on the concept nationalism). The second is one that would reinvigorate the federalist system under a modified conceptual base. Under this system the federal government would retain the power and duty to provide the solutions to problems; and to pass the laws necessary to implement and enforce the solutions chosen; but would place the duty and power to actually implement and enforce the laws in the hands of the local and state governments. This would provide the uniformity of solution needed in today's world, while at the same time placing the actual solution in the hands of those best qualified to solve the problem. Input would, of course, still be sought by the federal government from the appropriate experts in the private sector; but the implementation and enforcement duty would be taken out of the hands of the federal bureaucracy. This would have the positive side effect of reducing the need for vast amounts of federal regulations and mandates in many areas. In short, such a solution would entail a delegation of power back to the local and state governments from the federal level.

Under the first option, for example, the function of the free interplay of market forces, such as the cost of labor, supply and demand, and prices would now be found in the hands of the bureaucracy. Through the use of regulations and mandates these functions would be arbitrarily and artificially controlled. Wages, for example, could be mandated to fall within a scale beginning with the minimum wage set by the federal government (this is already being attempted); supply and demand could be controlled by both regulations and licensing functions (some claim this is already the case in many areas); while prices could be controlled through the use of pricing caps and subsidies (again some claim this is already taking place). All of these functions, plus the other normal functions of a market place, would be determined in advance and passed down to the private actors. This is, of course, exactly the approach that has been taken with the Affordable Care Act; for example, although this act includes implementation by the health care industry itself. This may, in fact, be one of the major flaws in the act and one of the major reasons for its possible failure. This solution is in essence the system used under all truly national planning schemes, which as was said earlier have all been failures. Whether or not the hybrid system found currently in the US could overcome the stigma of failure remains a matter of debate.

Under the second option a modified federalism would evolve in which the duties would be divided between the federal and local governments. The federal bureaucracy would not be called upon to implement and enforce the regulations and mandates produced at the federal level; but rather these functions would be delegated to the lower levels of government. This type of federalism, although not a formal governmental system, has developed over the years within the EU, that is, the European level agencies produce the laws, regulations, edicts and mandates but rely on the member national governments for their implementation and enforcement. In the US the federal bureaucracy has shown itself in many cases to be grossly inefficient at implementing and enforcing complicated regulations and mandates; the current roll out of the Affordable Care Act being only the latest example of this type of inefficiency.

A strong argument can be made for placing the duty for solution to nationwide problems at the federal level. It can be argued that federal solutions would be capable of drawing on the largest data base and expertise for solutions; that the solutions would tend to be uniform across the nation and that the federal solution would tend to direct focus towards the same issues. However, an equally strong argument can be made for the implementation and enforcement being placed at the appropriate local level. This would allow the solutions to be activated by those who had the best knowledge of the local intricacies of the problem. It would also promote, or allow, for small on site corrections to be made to account for small local variations in the way that the problem is manifested. It would also produce a rather large increase in the amount of local jobs needed to actually implement and enforce the solutions offered. Most important it would bring the solutions closer to the people, if not actually involve them, allowing them the ability to contribute to and control the actions taken. It can also be expected that local implementation and enforcement will result in very substantial cost savings at the federal level in terms of the number of employees needed and reductions in the number of departments and agencies needed; not to mention the cost savings in reduction of fraud and abuse. This approach has not yet been truly tested in the modern conditions that prevail in the US; therefore it is impossible to predict with accuracy whether or not it would be successful.

In terms of the loss of the free market system a new system is evolving on its own; that is, a hybrid form of controlled economy. The new system has been clearly marked by the federal reaction to perceived problems in a somewhat arbitrary manner. By arbitrary is meant that the reaction is targeted specifically at one aspect of the problem rather than the whole problem. For example, the Fed (Federal Reserve System, or central bank) has reacted to the sluggish economy by instituting the Quantitative Easing (QE) programs in which the federal government bought $85 billion of its own bonds each month. The intent was to keep interest rates artificially low; to stimulate investment in the economy; and to reinvigorate the housing market. These are, of course, only three factors within the total picture resulting in a sluggish economy. In fact, many believe that the QE programs, although effective in keeping interest rates artificially low, have resulted in negative effects on other factors within the economy resulting in a still sluggish economy. For example, the QE programs are claimed to also stimulate the growth of inflation and is at least partially responsible for the rapid increase in costs found in the food, fuel and health industries. In short, the QE programs seemed to have failed to stimulate investment in the productive forces of the economy and were ended as of Oct. 2014. Inflation has not developed as was expected although no real explanations of why it hasn't has yet been given. Indeed, it seems that a good share of the QE money was directly invested in the stock market and other short term profit vehicles (maybe due to a lack of long term productive investment opportunities). At any rate, the QE programs represent one way in which the free interplay of market forces can be artificially restricted, that is, the naturally occurring rate of interest produced by the free interplay of market forces was being controlled by the QE programs.

There are many other examples but the most recent being the attempt to control the free interplay of forces in the health market by controlling them through the implementation of the Affordable Care Act. The main difference here is that the latter represents an attempt to control one whole segment of the economy rather than just a portion of that segment. The act, therefore, represents a pure case of national planning in its most negative sense. Under current conditions many expect that the trend towards a controlled economy will continue. The question is partly whether or not this trend will be altered should the economy enter into a period of robust growth, that is, should the current symptoms for whatever reason disappear. On the surface it would appear that it is likely that the new conditions have not reached a point of final stability and that a resurgence of the economy could reinvigorate the free play of market forces. It is more likely that the trend towards a controlled economy will only end when the people demand an end to it, that is to say, until the actions taken by the people reinstate the traditional principles in the modern environment. It is likely, in the predictions made by many experts, that high levels of unemployment, the lack of permanent high paying low skill jobs, the increase in part-time and temporary employment and the increase in need for welfare benefits will become the new normal, at least, until the conversion to a new service base is complete. Thus the structural change may have already progressed to the point that it cannot be reversed. If all of this turns out to an accurate portrayal of modern conditions then it can be concluded that if the free market system still exists it will operate with a much reduced economic role in the future, or at least, a much different role will be played.

As a final conclusion on the economic and political fronts, as regards the current environment within the US, the complete loss of the free market system, the concept of private property as understood in the past, as well as federalism and representative democracy is a distinct possibility; but it may even be more likely that they will continue to play a role but in a much less prominent manner. A large group of people claim that these pillars of the American system have already been lost and that they are not capable of being recovered. In short, they are predicting the imminent demise of the American system. Many others, probably the majority, offer a somewhat different opinion. They accept that the US system is undergoing profound economic and political changes, but refuse to accept that the free market system and democracy have been lost or will be lost in the foreseeable future. They claim that the two pillars could easily be reinvigorated by the creation of new industries in the US once again producing permanent well paid low skill employment (the rebirth of the American middle class). At the most, they are willing to accept that both pillars may operate in the future with a role that is reduced in comparison to the past, but still remain of vital importance to the American system. This is, of course, the basis of the current debate between the political parties over a bigger federal government versus a more limited federal government. The American public has not yet effectively weighed in on this debate. It is doubtful, in the opinion of many futurist types that a new industrial base will become established within the US system, at least robustly enough to reestablish the manufacturing dominance that it once held in the economy; and that the free market system will not be reinvigorated. It is more likely that any new industries that come on the scene will be rather high tech orientated businesses requiring low levels of human employment. This type of employment requires highly skilled workers and requires long terms of education to become qualified. The likelihood of the rebirth of the middle class without the projected industrial rebirth seems moot.

In relation to the role of democracy in the US system it again appears unlikely that the system will become more; but rather, less democratic in nature. The large numbers of people within the US who are to varying degrees dependent upon government benefits for their standard of living, or their jobs, is unlikely to change rapidly in the future. These people, if history is accurate, will be very resistant to any attempt to alter their ability to maintain their government benefits and jobs (golden handcuffs); and the current transfer of wealth from the productive to the non-productive sectors will continue unabated. As a result the system will likely continue to be weighted in favor of power and duties being located in the federal government. In all likelihood federalism will continue to play a smaller role within the system; and the bureaucracy will continue to play an ever larger role. As a result democracy, at least in the sense, of power being located in the people, will play an increasing smaller role. Democracy will undoubtedly continue to play the theoretical role it has always played in the American system with the main difference being that the role played will now largely remain in the realm of theory.

Chapter 13. Public Reaction to Change

We have looked at the results of the changes on the public level in both the economic and political arenas; and it would be worthwhile now to attempt to put forth what results are evident with the American public, that is, on the private front. Persistent high rates of unemployment have affected not only those who are actually unemployed, but also those who still retain jobs. The latter live, to some degree, in fear that they may lose their jobs or that their jobs may disappear. Some jobs may become automated (the use of robots), or they may be lost because the business to which it is attached fails. In addition, the public is very much aware of the shrinking value of both their real income and the real value of their major assets. A part of this awareness is the knowledge that they will more than likely be very restricted in their ability to obtain a new job should they lose their old job. It is evident that the best paying, most permanent jobs in modern times require very highly skilled employees; and that obtaining these skills is very expensive and time consuming with no guarantee that a job will be found after expending the funds and time. This is particularly true of those who have not yet entered the labor market but are still in the process of trying to obtain the needed skills. A very large number of college graduates are finding it very difficult to obtain a job in the field that they have trained in and are being relegated to low paying service jobs while they seek other employment. In addition, the amount of time between becoming unemployed and the finding of adequate replacement employment is becoming ever more difficult and time consuming. All of this tends to make those suffering under these conditions likely to lose hope in their future prospects.

Those who are actually without employment are beginning to clearly realize that even if successful in getting back to work the job obtained will probably not replace the wages and benefits of their former employment. Those in this condition normally have about two years of government benefits to help them survive until they can replace their former employment. This benefit currently averages about $1350.00 per month. By the time they have exhausted this benefit, they have normally already been forced to reduce their standard of living.

There have recently been rather routine extensions of the unemployment benefits in recognition of the fact that two years is an inadequate time for job replacement in many cases. The latest extension of unemployment benefits was allowed to expire on Jan. 1, 2014, so that 1.3 million people were left with no income to count upon. This extension may be reinstated but the fear has already been made real that at some point the benefits will disappear. One does not have to guess at what this has done to the attitude of the people affected. The alternative for most of the 1.3 million involved is to take temporary or part-time jobs that are low skill and low paying; or attempt to qualify for permanent disability under Social Security, which would provide a benefit essentially equal to the unemployment benefit. This route has been made easier in the past few years by lowering the qualifications for disability to include stress from long term unemployment.

Some 1.8 million people are now qualified for the disability program with many of them entering the program over the last six years. At any rate, it is likely that the attitude of these people is even more negative than those who are still actively expecting to return to work. The attitude of the chronically unemployed, technically disabled, and those suffering other disabilities are not just that of being negative but hopeless. All in all if one takes into consideration the total work force of about 135 million people and compare it to the number of people who are drawing some level of government benefits it will be found that nearly half are involved in gathering some type of benefit. This includes the 2.6 million that are still classified as unemployed, the 48 million people who are using the food stamp program, the 14 million people who are drawing disability benefits (this number includes children drawing benefits on the basis of their own disabilities), and the estimated four or five million people who are unemployed but no longer officially in the job market. The total for just these four categories is roughly 70 million people. An even larger percentage would be found if one was to include those who are officially employed but who are chronically underemployed or holding temporary jobs. This is, of course, out of a total population of approximately 315 million. The other 160 million people are made up mainly of children, those who are incarcerated for one reason or another, and retirees. If one finds that 49 million people are retired then about 110 million of them would be children of various ages. This is not essentially important to the argument being made but does give a certain perspective to what is being argued. In addition there are also about 14 million illegal immigrants in the country who do not figure in the numbers set forth above. It is, however, necessary to take them into consideration as a significant number of them have been qualified to draw various forms of benefits from the federal and state governments; mainly in the areas of health care and schooling (including the free meal programs). One also must take into consideration those who are working full time at the minimum wage level ($7.75 per hour) and who still do not earn enough to lift them out of the official poverty level. At any rate, all of this clearly points to solid reasons why the American public seems to be slowly losing hope for the future and show even less hope in the traditional principles being able to solve the problems facing them.

It is also apparent why the task of reducing the size of government, especially at the federal level, seems to be impossible. The future appears especially bleak for people who are drawing benefits from the government as their income is fixed and the real value of that income is constantly shrinking. The only segment of the population that has essentially escaped this growing pessimism are those who earn over $150,000 or have a joint family income of $250,000 or more per year. This segment of the population represents approximately 5% of the working population, or nearly 7.5 million people. Those in this segment are generally to be found in large corporations working high skilled jobs in information technology or management; or at the professional levels of government employment. The rest are those who have been able to obtain the long educational background and licenses needed to practice the various professions; or are operating small to medium sized business operations. The top 1% of this group are made up of the most highly paid executives and big business owners, sports figures and those in the entertainment field. Essentially the wealthy, and the bureaucratically entrenched, are the only safe havens remaining in the modern economic environment.

One point of interest is the claim being made that the US is rapidly becoming a two class society, that is, a lower class and an upper class; and that the gap between the two classes is steadily becoming wider. This not only reflects the loss of the middle class by movement into the lower class at one end and movement into the upper class at the other end; but the natural result of the shift away from manufacturing. It would only make sense that if the middle class was to totally disappear that the gap between the two remaining classes would be greater than if the middle class continued to exist. This is not what is meant when talk turns to the gap between the classes. The debate is meant to reflect the claim that the wealth differential between the classes is getting wider, that is to say, the rich are getting richer and the poor are getting poorer. It also reflects the fact that the claim is being made in terms of pure numbers, that is, the lower class is steadily getting larger while the upper class is steadily getting smaller. In some cases the figures given are that the top 5% of the population, in terms of income, now control approximately 70% of the total wealth of the society. The upper class in total is believed to contain about 15% of the total population in regard to income and to control roughly 80% of the total wealth of the nation. This would mean that the remaining 85% of the working population controls only roughly 20% of the total national wealth. One point becomes crystal clear. The vast amount of wealth that is represented by the 20% controlled by 85% of the population.

The US has, as a nation, very little actual starvation and even very few people who are truly living at the subsistence level. A much larger number are living at the official poverty level; but in comparison to many places on earth, this level does not truly represent poverty. Nonetheless, when our focus is limited just to the US, it is no wonder that the attitude of hopelessness is so wide spread today. This negative thought is related not only to their own lives but also to the lives of their children. For example, one does not have to look far to find someone who believes that their children will be denied even the opportunity to live the American dream of homeownership. Under current conditions the bottom 85% have very little to look forward to in the future outside of government benefits. The result, of course, has been a very rapid and very massive increase in the payment of these benefits. One result of the growing pessimism at this level is the growing loss of belief that working hard, and being practical, self-reliant and honest will result in securing the good things in life. These are in fact, as we have seen, the very beliefs that are credited with the US being a representative democracy operating under a free market system. Many of these people are not living these beliefs even though they may in some degree hold them.

In addition to the economic reaction of negativity it must be added that the American public is faced with a government that appears to be dysfunctional. This is not only true of the federal government but also of many of the state governments. It is clear beyond any doubt that many local and state governments are operating without proper fiscal restraint. The pension plans of these governments are woefully underfunded in many cases and it appears that without breaking many of the promises made by them they cannot be repaired. Indeed, many of these same governments have acted in a fiscally negligent manner in relation to their spending and credit policies resulting in their being technically bankrupt. The same picture, written much larger, can be found at the federal level. The federal government is currently running budget deficits that exceed $750 billion per year and is carrying a national debt in excess of $17 trillion. Other examples of fiscal incompetence can be found with the failure of the federal government to prevent the near failure of the congress to raise the debt ceiling to pay for the debts already contracted for by the congress; and the shutdown of the federal government for a period of 16 days. In addition, new welfare benefits are steadily being approved without any concern with how they are going to be paid for; all the while the infrastructure and educational systems continue to decay. The cost of these practices is so large that they cannot even be accurately calculated. As seen earlier the practice of democracy has also fallen into decay. This is most evident on the federal and state level in the operation of election campaigns. These campaigns have reached the point in terms of cost that only those who are independently wealthy; or capable of garnering huge sums of funding from special interest groups, and others, can run a campaign. This fact clearly points out why there are complaints of ever increasing gaps between those who serve in government and those who elect them. Added to this is the spectacle of the two political parties having adopted such frozen ideological positions that they find it impossible to even speak the same language when debating issues. As a result the executive and legislative branches of government have been unwilling, or unable, to conduct the everyday business of the nation leaving the nation to be run by default through the administration. This has sparked a debate over the constitutional limits of the president's power to act without congress, that is, through executive order. The polls clearly indicate that the public is dissatisfied with the current state of the political environment, especially in Washington. The polls also clearly indicate that the public is ready for rather radical changes in the political arena, as is evidenced by the popularity of the Tea Party Movement in 2010 and since. What the public would actually choose to reform, or change if it was possible, is open to anyone's guess. Obviously, since the public believes that the American system is a democracy, the willingness to change could include a form of government that is not democratic in nature.

In the end this is what many experts would call the real problem rather than the symptoms. It is also what they are claiming needs to be focused upon rather than the symptoms that are getting all the attention today. If this is an accurate evaluation then the first step would be to determine whether the democratic nature of the US government can be restored, or revitalized. One call that is heard on the Republican side of the issue is for a return to the limited government concept as expressed by the early republicans under Thomas Jefferson. Initially, as we all know, the founders intended to set forth the powers that were specifically to be delegated to the federal government. They were, in fact, few in number. There were only eight articles in the constitution with the first three devoted to establishing the three branches of government. At any rate, the main powers that were delegated to the federal government can be set forth as follows:

a. The power to declare war and to make peace.

b. The power to supervise the value of currency.

c. The power and duty to create and operate a national postal service.

d. The power to implement and enforce all laws duly passed by congress.

e. The power to pass laws at the national level.

f. The power to establish and collect all tariffs and customs duties.

g. The power to oversee all interstate and international commerce.

h. The power to provide for the general welfare of the nation, including the right to put down internal insurrections if requested to do so.

i. The power to make and enforce treaties with foreign nations.

j. The power to send and accept foreign ambassadors and representatives.

k. In addition there were several powers or duties that were specially denied to the federal government:

l. The power of direct taxation, such as property taxes, sales taxes, and income taxes.

m. The power to quarter soldiers in the homes of private citizens.

n. The power to establish a state religion, including the power to require a religious oath to obtain public office.

o. The power to deny equal rights under the law, including the power to pass ex post facto laws and laws of attainder.

It can reasonably be expected that the Republican call is actually a call for a return to the limited government called for in the Constitution; or at least, some form of government that comes as close to the original intent as possible. Starting with the fact that the reach and scope of the federal government today touches in some degree every aspect of life in the US this would be a monumental task. In order to even partially dismantle big government it would need to be determined what could be eliminated from the duties and powers now held by the federal government. The actual plan as set forth by the Republicans seems to focus on several major points. The first is the reduction of the power of the federal government to issue regulations and mandates controlling the operation of the private sector economy. This is normally interpreted as regulations and mandates effecting the operation of businesses and investment practices within a free market system. The second area involves the power of the federal government to tax, both individuals and corporations (businesses in general). This area is normally interpreted to mean that the taxing power should be reformed to provide for a larger share of funds to be devoted to investment in the productive forces of the economy. This would not necessarily reduce or limit the power of the federal government to create and enforce taxes. The third area would involve reduction of the number of departments and agencies that make up the federal bureaucracy. This would be accomplished by delegating the duties now handled by the federal bureaucracy back to the state and local governments, including the problems involved with illegal immigration. Lastly, it would include the elimination or repeal of the Affordable Care Act and all other national planning schemes. This would include the return of these powers to the private sector and the free market system.

The reduction of the power of the federal regulatory system and the reform of the taxation system are relatively straight forward propositions; but might need some additional clarification. The public understands the call for a reduction of federal regulations and mandates to mean both a reduction of those that currently exist, as well as a reduction of the power to create new regulations and mandates. The first can be accomplished at the federal level simply by the passage of laws making the existing regulations and mandates unenforceable. The limitation of the power to regulate and issue mandates in the executive branch of the federal government would also require the passage of laws delegating these duties back to the local governments and prohibiting action by the executive branch. The latter might in fact require the passage of a Constitutional Amendment; or at the very least a positive ruling by the Supreme Court that the issuing of such regulations and mandates are unconstitutional. Neither of these alternatives seems very likely under the conditions that prevail today. Even the use of congressional laws to limit the federal power to issue regulations and mandates seems unlikely in light of the gridlocked state of affairs within congress. It is, therefore, unlikely that any real power now held by the federal government will be curtailed to any significant degree, or returned to the local and state governments voluntarily. As was stated earlier in a different context the most plausible way of limiting the federal powers in these areas is to require the power of regulation and taxation to remain intact at the federal level; but to allow the implementation and enforcement of them to be delegated to the state and local governments. This would at least have the effect of reducing the size and scope of the federal bureaucracy and reestablishing to some degree the system of federalism. It would over time also reduce substantially the cost of operating the federal government.

Outside of these reductions in the bureaucracy there also appear to be a serious overlap of powers and duties within the various departments and agencies of the bureaucracy. For example, it is claimed that the law enforcement departments and agencies, such as the FBI, the NSA, and the Homeland Security agency are all duplicating services and could easily be combined for efficiency and cost savings. Whether this is accurate, or not, it would be worthwhile to take a hard look at this claim and adjust the bureaucracy according to what was found. In the case of the Affordable Care Act the law has already begun to be implemented and has also been confirmed as to its constitutionality by the Supreme Court. The only remedies left in this case are not to enforce the law, or to repeal it. At this point in time it appears that repeal is out of the question as several attempts have been made to pass such a bill but all have failed. The fact that the implementation has been incompetent, to say the least, may change the environment over time allowing for the law to be repealed at a later date. At the moment, however, the only alternative appears to be not to enforce the bill. As long as the Democratic Party maintains control of the executive branch, and therefore the bureaucracy, this option will not be exercised. The Republicans having gained control of congress will undoubtedly attempt to repeal the law and such legislation will be vetoed by the President if passed. If the Republicans win the 2016 election repeal may be possible at that time. Meanwhile, the Supreme Court may rule portions of the law unconstitutional. There appears to be only one area in which there is a reasonable expectation that the size and scope of the federal government can be limited and that is in the reduction of the duties and powers of the bureaucracy. This one area, however, if the reduction is made in an efficient and practical manner could reduce the cost of the federal government by as much as 15% to 20%.

There is one area, however, that seems to be consistently off the radar in the call for a more limited federal government, that is, the military. In today's world no one would expect that the military of the US would be completely dismantled. The federal government has the constitutional duty to protect the nation from external invasion or threat and there is no way to do so in today's world without a professional standing military. The question, therefore, reduces itself to the type and size of the professional military needed. For example, it can be questioned whether or not there is any longer a need to maintain a full scale arsenal of weapons of mass destruction. In many ways it could be assumed that such weapons were never needed, but that is truly a case of hindsight. If such weapons are truly no longer needed then continued efforts should be made to eliminate them on a global scale. It may, however, for one reason or another be determined that although not really needed precaution would warrant keeping a reduced stock pile of such weapons. The same procedure could be applied to the conventional arsenal of the military. It can be asked how many planes, tanks, ships, small arms, and so forth are needed to provide effective protection from external invasion. Again precaution might suggest that a larger conventional readiness be maintained than what is actually needed; but it is surely legitimate to ask if the US should continue to spend more on its military than the rest of the world combined. The answer would appear to lie in the answer given to the question of how much is needed. If only the capacity to fight off an actual invasion of the nation is involved the answer would be presented one way; however, if the answer is that the US must maintain its dominance of the world's oceans and seas; as well as, acting as the world's policeman the answer will be presented another way. In the former the size and scope of the military would likely be greatly reduced from what it is today even if a small nuclear capability was maintained. If the latter answer is given the size and scope of the military is likely to remain much as it is today, if not actually increased. Whatever the answer given, the fact remains that the military budget represents about 25% of the current spending of the federal government.

A second focus is often offered by the Republicans to effect a reduction of size and scope in both the state and federal governments. This call is for the reform of the current welfare system. Here again the call represents a mixture of eliminating some programs and reforming others. There appears to be little question that neither party is willing to offer reforms that will affect the existing benefits being paid out under Social Security, Medicare, and Medicaid. This decision would affect some 63 million people overall. What is called for is a reform that alters both the qualifications for drawing benefits from these programs; and some reduction in the benefits to be drawn in the future. The reforms would not affect those who would be eligible to qualify for benefits within the next ten years, but would affect all those who became qualified after that date. One suggestion currently on the table is that people not be eligible to draw retirement benefits from Social Security until they reach the age of 67. The current age of eligibility is 62. The same would apply to the eligibly standards for both Medicare and Medicaid. On the side of program elimination the Republicans are targeting what most people consider to be the true entitlement programs, that is, programs in which the beneficiary has not made any direct contributions to the fund out of which the benefits are paid as is the case with Social Security and Medicare. These programs include such things as the food stamp program, housing subsidies of several types, farm subsidies, oil company subsidies, the free school meals programs, and student loans. In many cases the Republicans are calling for the full elimination of these programs over time. Recently the congress passed a bill that cut the food stamp program by 1%, but continued the farm subsidy programs. There is no question that this bill represents a token attempt to placate Republican voters while at the same time salving the Democratic Parties call for increased welfare spending. Clearly the bill is another example of the congress attending to the demands made by special interest groups, paying service to the ideological position of the political parties, while ignoring the needs and demands of the American public altogether. With attempts such as the recent farm bill it is fair to conclude that the congress appears not to have the stomach to reform or eliminate any of the current governmental benefit programs.

In short, the only actual place where the goal of creating a more limited government appears possible is in the reduction of the size and scope of the bureaucracy. So far even in this area no plans have been submitted as to how this would be accomplished as the bureaucracy is a very powerful interest group itself.

The next step is to understand how the free market system might operate under modern conditions. As stated earlier it seems that the economy is no longer operating under the tenets of the free market system, at least as they were understood in the time of Adam Smith and Karl Marx. The tenets of the free market system are largely locked into a society that was undergoing the industrial revolution and adapting itself from an agricultural base to a manufacturing base. The tenets of the free market system were essentially the rules under which this conversion proceeded. Labor, for example, was to be left unregulated so that the free interplay of market forces could determine the natural wage to be paid. Under the concept of supply and demand wages would be higher or lower based upon the supply of labor and the demand for that labor. If the supply of labor was low but the demand was high wages would tend to be high and vice versa. The natural interplay of market forces were from the beginning manipulated in one way or another. For example, the natural supply of labor was increased artificially by including the labor of children and women; while the absolute demand for labor remained the same. This lowered the wage that could be obtained for labor by adult males. Later, laws were passed preventing the use of child labor and limiting the number of hours that could be worked. This artificially reduced the supply of labor, while again the demand essentially remained the same, and the level of wages rose. These two examples are to be seen in comparison to what wages would have been had the free interplay of market forces taken place. Supposedly under this latter case the level of wages would have been substantially midway between the two extremes. Even later business began to collect itself into larger and larger organizations and through the use of monopolies and other market limiting techniques was able to reduce competition and the free interplay of market forces artificially affecting the cost of labor, the cost of materials, the quality of products produced and the prices obtained for inferior products. Labor reacted by forming itself into larger and larger organizations, or unions, for bargaining power equal to that of big business. Eventually they became powerful enough to demand wages and benefits beyond the level of businesses to sustain in an internationally competitive market. In addition, big government got involved and at first backed the policies of big business and later the policies of labor unions again affecting the natural interplay of market forces in both cases negatively. In the end this artificial interference with the free market system led to the conversion of the US economy from a manufacturing base to one based upon services. As a result the free market system, at least as it was formed under the earlier conditions, was forced to adapt once again.

It is apparent from the experience of the last few decades that this conversion has reduced the need, or at least the practical application, of the free market system to the new economy. The jobs in the new economy tend to be less stable, require less skill, and are lower paying than the jobs found in the former manufacturing economy. Even the absolute number of jobs needed to fill the needs of the economy is much lower than in the past resulting in a relatively high level of permanently unemployed people. Those who are now permanently unemployed have two choices, that is, they can enter into the temporary and part-time jobs field found largely in the service arena; or they can attempt to qualify for disability under the Social Security system. Most have opted for the former; but several million have taken advantage of the recent simplifications of the rules for qualifying for disability and have successfully signed up (1.8 million). Another significant number of people are working at jobs, either full time or part-time, that pay only the minimum wage mandated by the federal government, that is, $7.75 an hour. None of these people whether full time, or not, are capable of earning a wage that puts them above the official poverty level. Another significant group of people refuses to take temporary or part-time work at wages that are substantially below the wages and benefits that they received in the lost manufacturing jobs. This makes the hiring of American employees even more difficult for the businesses attempting to do so. Because the businesses cannot, or will not, pay wages high enough to attract American workers this need is being filled by cheaper labor provided by illegal immigrants (approximately 14 million). The above has put, at least, thirty million working people beyond the reach of the free market system. Immigrant wages are artificially kept lower than would be the case in a free labor market; and those on disability are completely removed from the labor market. An even larger class of workers qualify for the classification of underemployed. The question is whether or not the wages, working conditions and other benefits are being artificially repressed by the monopolistic consolidation of the service industry giants, such as Wal-Mart and McDonalds. This may also be affected by the federally mandated minimum wage. It would appear also to be the effect of illegal immigration.

There is no doubt that the service industry has undergone specular levels of consolidation over the last few decades. One merely needs to look at the food delivery industry, the fuel delivery industry, clothing outlets, and financial industry to confirm this suggestion. It can be claimed that these consolidations border on monopolistic control of the market, and may be restricting the free play of market forces. Most services, at least in the US domestic market, are provided by very large corporations, or holding companies, which directly own or control a vast number of individual outlets or franchises. Very insignificant amounts of the service industry is provided by the "mom and pop" businesses of earlier times, that is, what represented a good number of those classified as middle class in the 50s and 60s. Once again due to the relatively low rate of return on investment in any one unit, and the brutal competition between the various businesses providing the same services, any limitation that is placed upon the free interplay of market forces, such as regulations and mandates will be very significant. The regulations, such as environmental compliance regulations, mandates such as minimum wage standards, and taxation policies are so significant that they can easily determine which businesses will fail and which will succeed. The reaction as in the past is to control the business factors either through virtual monopoly; or equally effective lobbying techniques. This explains the Republican call for deregulation and tax reductions for small to medium size businesses that cannot rely on scale to stay in business.

As a result, the adaption of the free market system to this conversion also has not yet been completed. Because of the state of flux produced by this adaption to a still evolving market system a debate has been ignited concerning whether the free market system has been lost in the shuffle. While many believe that it has not been lost it is very possible that it will evolve into a system that is not recognizable in terms of the old manufacturing system. Both democracy and the free market system are likely to survive the traumas being experienced as the economy converts from a manufacturing base to a service base; but both will be transformed in how they operate and possibly in the level of importance of the role they will play in the new environment or "new normal".

Overall it is likely that the welfare state will remain essentially as it is today; although there may be rather dramatic shifts in the types and size of benefits received and in the manner and ease by which one can qualify for them. This will be one significant factor that continues to limit the effectiveness of both democracy and the free market system in the future. It is also to be expected that the completion of the conversion of the economy to a service base will continue and that it will take a relatively long period of time to reach completion. During this period, and possibly afterwards, unemployment is likely to remain relatively high, the economy will remain relatively sluggish, and the opportunities for long term investment in the productive forces of the economy will remain low. This latter process will have its most devastating effect on both representative democracy and the free market by way of the loss of faith by the public in these two traditional principles. It is also likely that the governmental dysfunction will continue to plague the public at least until the next presidential election in 2016.

The beginning of a solution to the problems facing the nation is for the people to take back the power now residing in the two political parties. This can be done most effectively through legislation reforming the manner in which campaigns are conducted. The legislation must give the public real opportunities to select the candidates, especially at the local and state level; to select the issues on which they want the candidates to take a stand; and to reduce or strictly limit the amount of money that can be spent on any election or campaign. Whether or not this legislation is best passed at the federal level or the local level is a matter for debate. In the end the symptoms which in today's environment are being treated as problems will slowly disappear as the structural changes are completed. Whether or not the free market system and democracy continue to be the two main pillars of US society will depend on how the structural changes are accomplished. If the symptoms continue to be treated in the manner they are today, that is, through the governmental control of the economy it is likely that they will not survive; or will survive with a much less vital role to play within the society. If the emphasis is shifted away from treating the symptoms and reducing the governmental role in the completion of the structural changes underway it is likely that both will not only survive but be revitalized. In the latter case both may be altered in some manner as regards the manner in which they operate but their role and importance will be as great as ever. At the moment the momentum seems to be in favor of continuing the governmental interference through tinkering with the symptoms and ignoring the structural changes that are taking place.

CONCLUSION

Now that it has been determined that the major traditional principles underlying the American system have not been lost, or are not being ignored; but rather are currently operating outside their traditional meaning; and further that a new set of principles have arisen to fill the void left by the changing traditional principles; it remains to be seen how the problems facing the US can be resolved under these conditions. It must be noted here that the new principles that have arisen still contain the traditional principles of democracy, federalism, the free market system, private property and traditional social ethical and moral principles. It can also be noted that these changes are being claimed to have been made in relation to the structural change of the American society from one based on manufacturing to one based upon the new service industry. Lastly, it must be noted that in all likelihood both the principles in question and the structural components involved are still in a stage of transition from one form to the other. If this is truly the case then it should be possible to influence the manner in which this final transition takes place. Indeed, one of the central issues being discussed today is whether or not this influence will flow from the federal government or from the private sector, including the lower governments (local and state governments). Looked at in this light it may be fair to ask the question as to whether or not the people of the US deserve to maintain these freedoms.

The modern environment tends to show that the American public is largely apathetic to both the political and economic issues facing the nation. They have grown pessimistic concerning the economic future and express very little confidence that the political elite will be able, or willing, to face the problems. On the social front they have been persuaded in large numbers that relativism is the correct posture to assume in relation to secular ethical and moral principles.

From the rate of voting found over the last few decades within those eligible to vote the conclusion can be drawn that the public sees little value in their right to vote. Lastly, it appears that a growing segment of the population is willing to sell their economic freedom and accept a form of serfdom within the welfare system. They seem willing to accept a lower standard of living, along with a restriction on their ability to make economic choices; all for the ability to maintain life without expending much effort. All this would seem to indicate that the American public no longer deserves the freedoms that were intended for them under the original constitution. They seem willing to accept whatever definition the federal government wishes to give to the terms life, liberty and the pursuit of happiness.

The acceptance of the status quo, which is one option available within the above debate, will mean that the "new normal" will prevail with its high levels of unemployment, welfare benefits, budget deficits, large national debt, and political gridlock. Within a continuously sluggish economy there will also be a persistent decreasing of the overall standard of living in the US, and a growing wealth gap between those involved in the so-called "core jobs" and those on government benefits. There will also be a continued rise in the rate of drug abuse, crime and homelessness. Overall the trend seems to favor federal governmental intervention in every aspect of the individual's daily life. These effects will be most strongly felt by the lower class and the lower middle class, but will be felt in a lessening degree by the rest of the middle class and the upper class. Those still working for wages, or the profits of small to medium sized businesses, will continue to see the real value of their wages or profits shrink; as will the real value of their most important assets, that is, their homes, businesses, and retirement accounts. All levels of government will continue to indulge in their spending spree with budget deficits growing larger (the current Illinois budget being a case in point). They will only take notice when outside factors, such as bankruptcy, forces them into it. In short, accepting the status quo and waiting passively for things to get better appears to be the worst option available, at least, for the near and mid-term. This acceptance in the end may lead to the complete loss of democracy, federalism, the free market system, private property, and the traditional social standards of ethical and moral behavior as some have already claimed. Therefore, the conclusion can be drawn that some type of action must be taken if the current problems facing the US are to be resolved, especially in the short term.

Action, within the current environment, will only happen if it is forced upon the legislative and executive branches of all levels of government. As can easily be seen this action can only be forced by the public, the various interest groups, or by the bureaucracy within the current system. The bureaucracy can be seen as a vested interest in the status quo due to its relative acceptance of "golden handcuffs" and position of power. This in a general way puts the bureaucracy in the position of maintaining the status quo even with all the results listed above. It is unlikely that the motivation for change and/or reform is going to come from this sector. The interest groups, as was pointed out earlier, are a vested interest in that they have real power through their financing ability in relation to the political parties. It is not that they are wedded to the status quo or unable to force changes and/or reform; but rather they will only accomplish any desired change and/or reform to benefit a specific group rather the society as a whole. In the case of the interest groups they will, in fact, continue to force changes on the federal government, and thereby the society, but these changes will not necessarily be of any benefit to the society as a whole. This seems to leave only the people with the duty to force its government into the desired changes and/or reforms. Historically if the public yells long enough, loud enough and in great enough numbers, they will eventually be heard.

Up to this point apparently the public has not yelled long enough, loud enough, or in great enough numbers to force the changes and/or reforms they desire. The Tea Party movement within the Republican Party does clearly indicate that the American public has the power to force change; but also seems to indicate that it should not be directed from within the existing party system. One of the major issues is whether or not the current environment (existing economic and political problems) can be sustained long enough to allow the growth and success of a grass roots movement. The progressive movement mentioned earlier, for example, took nearly thirty years from its original organizing actions (1890s), until the height of their political agenda (1920 or so). If this type of time line holds true for any grass roots movement that comes into existence within the next couple of years the system will need to be maintained until at least 2044. It is possible, of course, with the advent of information technology that this time line could be substantially shorter. The current estimate is that the Social Security System, for example, will remain solvent only until around 2030. There does not seem to be a solid estimate as to how long the current budget deficits and national debt structure can be sustained. The point is, however, that many experts in the various fields do not hold out much hope that they can be sustained even as long as 2030. If they are correct then the effectiveness of a new grass roots movement appear to be somewhat limited. Indeed, there does not currently appear to be a traditional type of grass roots movement even on the horizon, or expected within the near term.

Under these conditions the most effective means of forcing the national government into the desired changes and /or reforms seems to be the organizing of peaceful protests (revolutions). If the American public is truly concerned about the loss of their freedoms they will have to earn them back. They will need to organize marches on Washington; large scale social media blitzes aimed at their congressional representatives; and the President, as well as forcing their state representatives to weigh in on their side of the issues. If successful in this attempt it will, of course, be necessary for the public to follow up on the success by keeping watch over the elected representatives to insure they follow through on their promises. In short, the American public will have to become passionately involved in forcing the desired changes and reforms upon their elected officials (direct democracy rather than representative democracy). As Thomas Jefferson once claimed, the revolution does not necessarily need to be violent; but if violence is the only recourse it should not be shirked. The earlier protests (social revolutions) against labor abuse (union organizing), racial discrimination (civil rights), and the war in Vietnam (social standards) all contained levels of violence on both sides. These violent events ironically were the events that brought the greatest attention of the greatest number of people to the demands being made by the causes represented. They were largely responsible for the changes made both publically and privately. This lesson should certainly be kept in mind in relation to any protest launched against the status quo.

The final conclusion, therefore, is that the American system, if it is truly under attack, will not be healed from within the existing system. If the American system is to be retained in any semblance of its traditional form it will have to be saved from outside the existing political arena. This, of course, is a rather classic portrayal of political revolt. It can be hoped that this revolt can be prosecuted without undue violence; but history seems to confirm that when large scale vested interests are involved they are not given up without a real fight. At this point in time it does not appear that conditions are ripe for such a revolt. Conditions have not yet reached a point where a large enough number of people are willing to yell loud and long enough to be heard. The collapse of the existing American economic system in the near term, as many experts claim it will, the conditions would change rapidly in favor of large scale protest. Without this protest it seems clear that some form of the status quo will remain in power, at least, until it collapses from its own weight. This would appear to be the worst of all possible worlds in the opinion of the gloom and doom group.

What follows is a pure fantasy aimed at showing one way in which the public can begin to make their voices heard; especially if the results of the mid-term election make no difference in the political environment.

An American Fantasy

The campaign was simple and only asked a series of questions which were to receive a direct answer. The questions and answers were those set forth below:

1. Are you better off now than you were in the year 2000? If you are, you are one of the lucky few.

2. Are you unemployed, or have you been unemployed since 2000? If so, join with 14 million of your brothers and sisters in the misery.

3. Are you drawing any type of welfare benefits due to your inability to find gainful employment? If so, join 48 million of your brothers and sisters in trying to make ends meet on these benefits.

4. Have you gone on permanent disability to avoid being permanently unemployed? If so, that is greatly to your benefit but costs us all one healthy worker.

5. Are you working a part-time or temporary job (or two or three of them) to try to make ends meet? If so, join with 30% of the work force that cannot find a full time job.

6. Have you lost your home since 2007? Join the millions of other homeowners who weren't saved so that your bank could be bailed out.

7. Do you live with monthly budget deficits and growing individual debt? If so, join with your local, state and federal government in the biggest debt binge in history.

8. Do you trust your representatives in the local, state or federal government? If not, join 75% of the population of the United States.

9. Do you believe that your vote counts? If so, try to explain in what way it counts.

10. Are you pleased that you are being forced to accept a deadlocked federal political system? If not, join the vast majority of your brothers and sisters in the United States.

11. Are you willing to do something about it? If so, then join our media campaign and stand up for what you believe.

The response to the call, in terms of number of hits and comments made, was most gratifying. The sponsors of the campaign knew that with a concerted effort they could truly have an effect on the 2016 presidential election. Even more important, both the media pundits and the elected political elite also knew it.

At first the reaction of those in elected office was shock. It had never once dawned on them that a social media campaign could organize opposition to them so effectively. No one seemed to have any real good ideas for handling the situation. This was not unexpected, since the same people had not been able to figure out how to conduct the day to day business of the government; or even their own representation of the public. Instead they had settled for years on the same old deadlock and blame game. The elected elite did feel uncomfortable with the situation and knew that they would face it again in spades in 2016. It was clear to even those in the so-called "safe" seats that they had only two years to do something, not only something, but something important enough to defuse the revolution underway. It was also unclear to the elected elite just what that important something might be that would satisfy the people that they were being truly represented.

These doubts were quickly resolved as a new media campaign swung into action. Several issues were made clear by the response of the public to the social media blitz.

First, the public made it clear beyond a doubt that they wanted something done to resolve the Middle East issue with ISIS-ISIL-ISLAMIC STATE. They wanted a clear policy to be instituted that would include the use of US ground troops to stop the Islamic State in its tracks. The demand was made in the following manner. The public demanded that the US make it known to all the nations of the Middle East that they were expected to join a coalition to disarm all terrorist groups. If they refused, it was made clear that the US would unilaterally, or with western allies, disarm them. The administration immediately instituted a demand through the United Nations calling for this coalition. The thorniest problem revolved around which organizations in the Middle East would be considered terrorist organizations and which would be classified as insurrectionist organizations. For example, there was some question as to whether the Syrian rebels would be considered a terrorist organization or not. The demand also called for a determined effort to be made to settle the underlying causes of terrorism, that is, the Palestinian issue, the Kurdish issue, the Syrian civil war, the Iraqi civil war and the Iranian nuclear problem. So far, as usual, there has been a lot more talk than action, but time will tell.

Shortly after the public submitted its demands in relation to the Middle East and the Islamic State, it submitted a demand for resolution of the domestic immigration problem. The public made it crystal clear that they wanted a resolution that dealt with the already existing population of illegal aliens; the growing problem of unescorted young people coming into the country; and the issue of continued illegal immigration. It was suggested that the public would accept a system whereby those illegal immigrants already here would be offered a fast track to citizenship. It was recognized that the problem of unescorted minors would be best resolved by the local governments involved rather than the federal government. The same was recognized in relation to the control of future illegal immigration. Legislation was immediately passed, and signed into law by the President, returning the control of illegal immigration to the states, including the problem of unescorted minors. Legislation was also passed which made it possible for those already in the country to take the citizenship test and apply for citizenship without a waiting period. If they could not, or did not want to apply for citizenship, a procedure was made available for them to quickly obtain a one-year work visa that could be renewed indefinitely with good behavior. Many states responded, especially those most affected by illegal immigration, by passing strict laws concerning immigration, work visas, deportation and criminal status. They also authorized the use of the National Guard, Border Patrol, and State Police to patrol the border within each state. Most importantly the legislation included provisions for the providing of negotiations between the federal government and the Mexican government to coordinate the resistance to illegal immigration. It has already become noticeable that both the federal government and the Mexican government are not particularly interested in ending immigration, whether legal or illegal. If nothing else the campaign did bring out in the open the real problems that make it nearly impossible to stop illegal immigration across the southern border. Some progress, however, has been made with a cooperative effort by the US and the Latin American nations to bring the drug cartels under control and to address the problem of poverty and violence in the Latin American community. The solution to these problems is the real answer to the problem. Solving these issues removes the reason for immigration whether legal or illegal.

The revolution then turned its attention to the government policies surrounding the budget deficit and national debt. The demand was made that a balanced budget be put in writing for the fiscal year 2017. This demand included the authorization to reduce the benefits paid under the welfare system, including future Social Security, Medicare and Medicaid benefits to help balance the budget. The public also called for a scrapping of the current federal tax code and its replacement with a flat rate tax code that would allow no deductions, exemptions or credits. The code was to be graduated as follows: All private individuals who made less than $17,500 per year were to be untaxed; all private individuals that earned between $17,500 and 125,000 per year would pay a flat 10% income tax; all private individuals who earned between $125,000 and $250,000 per year would pay a flat rate of 15%; all income over $250,000 per year would be taxed at a flat rate of 20%. All corporate income above $50,000 a year would be taxed at a flat rate of 18%, whether earned domestically or internationally. This was to begin with the tax year of 2017. Within the public's demand was also a call for the legislation to earmark all surpluses obtained on a yearly budgetary basis to be used to pay down the national debt. In short, the demand called for formal legislation requiring a balanced budget (rather than a constitutional amendment); a flat rate tax code; and legislation mandating national debt reduction. The legislation is currently being considered by congress and appears to be nearing completion. It will then have to be voted on by both houses of congress, but at least the legislation prohibits the addition of any new clauses (riders). This will mean that the vote will be a straight vote only on the proposals demanded by the public. If passed, and this seems very likely, it must go to the President to be signed, again this seems very likely to happen. It will be interesting to see if the public resolve continues to hold once the contemplated reduction of welfare benefits actually kick into place.

More recently the public brought forth, through the social media revolution, a demand that legislation be passed to cure the problems with the Affordable Care Act. The demand contained the authorization to scrap the Act if a reasonable reform of the act could not be obtained. The legislation is still in committee and has not yet been reported to the floor. Many states, due to public demand, have discarded any attempts to enroll their citizens in the program and have waived the collection of any penalties assessed. In many cases the states are attempting to heal the health system problems by focusing on the causes of high costs, gaps in availability, and health care facilities and providers through local action. So far this had led to efforts to cap the awards that can be given in mal-practice suits; caps on the advertisement and development of duplicate drugs; the elimination of pre-existing insurance clauses; basic coverage insurance policies for those who cannot afford full care coverage; and other cost cutting measures. There is, however, a lack of uniformity in the state efforts which over time may create problems, but overall the efforts have already been more successful than the Affordable Care Act in responding to the same problems.

The most recent effort of the social media revolution was a demand for the federal government to do what was necessary to prevent the

Iranians from producing a nuclear weapon technology. This demand also included the taking of a very tough line with the N. Koreans on the nuclear issue. The public appears to be aware that the use of force against N. Korea is not a viable option. The Chinese proved capable of stopping the invasion of N. Korea in the 1950s and probably could do the same today. It is likely, however, that through the cooperation of both The Russian Federation and the Republic of China that N. Korea can be completely controlled in regard to distribution of nuclear weapons.

The Iranian problem is of more direct interest of the United States. The Iranian support of jihadist terrorism will over time make it likely that nuclear weapon of some kind will be used in the area; or for acts of terrorism in other areas. In our hypothetical revolution, the earlier demand calling for a coalition of Middle East nations to disarm terrorist organizations might be extended to a further demand to address any aggressive expansionism on the part of The Russian Federation, into the Ukraine and/or the Baltic nations. This could include an authorization by the public to demand the use of force through the NATO organization should a member be attacked by Russia. The use of force in this area of the world is highly problematic as the US is the only member of NATO with the capability of facing the Russians on the field of battle. As a result it will again be interesting to see how long the public resolve in this area remains intact.

The public seems to instinctively understand that the federal government cannot be expected to produce any positive results in regard to the economic problems facing the nation. This understanding seems to carry over to the ability of the states to offer any effective remedies to these problems. In accordance with American principles, the unemployment problem, the sluggish economy, and the global economic slowdown will only be healed by the involvement of the free market system. There is no reliable gauge of how the economy is actually doing; but overall it seems that the business and financial communities have adjusted to the new conditions brought about by the shift from a manufacturing base to a service base; and to the conditions brought about by the great recession (collapse of the financial system). Both of these sectors of the economy appear to be poised to enter into robust activity to reestablish their position in the economic sector. The public also seems to have reined in its credit binge and has entered into the debt reduction mode which includes a drift back to a healthy savings rate. The problem seems to revolve around making sure that the various governments do nothing to prohibit the natural return of the economy to a state of health. The Federal Reserve System has dropped its QE programs and interest rates will be allowed to adjust under the free market. The federal government must be forced to stop intervening in the economy with useless and harmful regulations. The local and state governments must be forced to look at the education system from the point of view of preparing its students for the new so-called "core" jobs. Should these things take place it is likely that a plethora of new permanent, high paying, medium to high skilled jobs will become available over time. Once this happens it is likely that the middle class will be reinvigorated and resume its traditional position within the society.

One issue that has not gained the attention of the social media revolution is the problem of political gridlock. What has been accomplished, however, is a by-product of the demands and actions already taken along with the Republican victory in the mid-term elections. The demands listed earlier have forced the legislative and executive branches to work together to meet the demands of the public. The gridlock that existed through the mid-term election of 2014 has fallen by the wayside as a natural result of forced cooperation. Both political parties were given a serious wake up call, as was the political elite. It is also obvious that the force of the revolution has not yet been spent and will carry over into the Presidential election of 2016. This by itself will be enough to force the political parties to nominate candidates that will show concern for the public demands already made and for those that are expected to arise in the future. It is likely that the revolution will focus on the individual candidates and rate each of them on their desirability to carry out the public demands. In short, democracy will once again be more participatory rather than representative, and individual votes will count for more than they have in the recent past.

If nothing else, the revolution has sparked the political interest of the public and caused them to become directly involved in what is happening on the political front.

REFERENCE SOURCES

The sources listed below represent the major sources of the ideas contained in the book. Many newspaper op-ed articles, magazine articles and talk show editions are not specifically listed.

I. Background sources for American political principles:

The Constitution of the United States, Great Books of the Western World, Vol 43, Encyclopaedia Britannica, Inc. Chicago 1952

The Articles of Confederation of the United States of America, ibid.

The Federalist Papers, Alexander Hamilton, John Jay, and James Madison, ibid.

The Declaration of Independence, Thomas Jefferson, ibid.

America a Narrative History, George Brown Tindall, David E. Shi, Fourth Edition, W.W. Norton & Company, New York, 1996

II. Background sources for American economic principles:

The Road to Serfdom, F.A. Hayek, The University of Chicago Press, Chicago, 1944

Capital, Karl Marx, Great Books of the Western World, Vol. 50, Encyclopaedia Britannica, Chicago, 1952

The Wealth of Nations, Adam Smith, Bantam Books, New York, 2003

Endgame, The end of debt cycle and how it changes things, John Mauldin, John Tepper, Mauldin Economics, 2015

III. Background sources for American social principles:

Lectures on Ideology and Utopia, Paul Ricoeur, Columbia University Press, New Haven, 1986

Trust, the social virtues and the creation of prosperity, Francis Fukuyama, Simon & Schuster, New York, 1995

Principia Ethica, G.E. Moore, University of Cambridge, Cambridge 1991

IV. Background sources for modern discussion of American political, economic and social principles:

After America, get ready for Armageddon, Mark Steyn, Regnery Publishing, Inc. Washington D.C. 2012

The Progressive Era, Jamil S. Zainaldin, New Georgia Encyclopedia, 2014

The Tragedy of American Diplomacy, William Appleman Williams, W.W. Norton & Company, New York, 1972

Ideology and U.S. Foreign Policy, Michael H. Hunt, Yale University Press, New Haven 1979

The Next Decade where we've been and where we're going, George Friedman, Doubleday, New York, 2011

Living History, Hillary Rodham Clinton, Simon & Schuster, New York, 2003

Decision Points, George W. Bush, Crown Publishers, New York, 2010

The New Dealers, power politics in the age of Roosevelt, Jordan A. Schwarz, Alfred A. Knopf, New York, 1993

Printed in the United States
By Bookmasters